GOODRICH CASTLE

*To my wife, Jennifer,
who has kept me on the straight and narrow
throughout the production of this book*

GOODRICH CASTLE
ITS
HISTORY & BUILDINGS

edited by
Ron Shoesmith

with contributions from
Bruce Coplestone-Crow
Pat Hughes
Loretta Nikolič
P.J. Pikes
Thomas Richards

Logaston Press

LOGASTON PRESS
Little Logaston Woonton Almeley
Herefordshire HR3 6QH
logastonpress.co.uk

First published by Logaston Press 2014
Copyright © text of each chapter with its author 2014
Copyright © illustrations those as acknowledged,
with all reconstruction drawings, elevations and castle plans © English Heritage

All rights reserved. No part of this publication
may be reproduced, stored in a retrieval system,
or transmitted, in any form or by any means,
electronic, mechanical, photocopying, recording
or otherwise, without the prior permission,
in writing, of the publisher

ISBN 978 1 906663 83 4

Typeset by Logaston Press
and printed and bound in Poland
www.polskabook.pl

*Cover photograph of Goodrich Castle © Chris Musson and The Woolhope Naturalists' Field Club,
with thanks to both*

Contents

Acknowledgements *vi*
Introduction *vii*

Part 1 – The Goodrich Area
Chapter 1   Background   3
Chapter 2   Goodrich Village   13

Part 2 – The Historical Background
Chronological Table   22
Family tree   24
Chapter 3   After the Conquest (1066-1204)   25
Chapter 4   William Marshal, Earl of Pembroke & his Sons (1204-45)   33
Chapter 5   The Valences (1247-1324) & their Heirs (1324-27)   37
Chapter 6   The Talbots, Earls of Shrewsbury (1327-1590)   45
Colour Plate Section   57
Chapter 7   The Castle & its Tenants (1590-1645)   65
Chapter 8   The Civil War & Slighting of the Castle (1642-65)   71
Chapter 9   The Castle as Ruin & Tourist Attraction (1690-1915)   85
Chapter 10   The Ancient Monument   95

Part 3 – The Buildings
Chapter 11   Earthworks & the First Stone Castle   105
Chapter 12   The late 13th-century Castle – The Ditch, Curtain Walls & Corner Towers   117
Chapter 13   The late 13th-century Castle – The Gatehouse, North-east Tower & Chapel   131
Chapter 14   The late 13th-century Castle – The Internal Buildings   141
Chapter 15   The Barbican & Access to the Castle   147
Chapter 16   The 14th-century Alterations   155
Chapter 17   The 14th-century – The New Western Range & South-west Tower   165
Chapter 18   The Gradual Conversion to Houses, from the 15th to the early 17th century   179
Colour Plate Section   193

Part 4 – The Finds & Life at the Castle
Chapter 19   The Medieval Household at Goodrich   203
Chapter 20   The Detritus of War   211

References & Endnotes   217
Index   227

Acknowledgements

In the first instance I would like to thank Pat Hughes, P.J. Pikes and Bruce Coplestone-Crow for their patience with my continual requests for alterations and amendments, especially as the deadline for publication approached. The work involved by authors of shorter sections – Loretta Nikolič and Thomas Richards – is also gratefully appreciated.

Various people associated with English Heritage have been exceedingly helpful – especially Jeremy Ashbee (who read the draft text and came up with many useful suggestions), Helen Keeley (who was a great help with the general administration), and Mark Fenton (who re-jigged the coloured plan, originally used in the guidebook, to fit my interpretations). Many of the coloured artistic reconstructions that were produced for the castle guidebook and are used in this book were originally made by the late Terry Ball, a good friend and first-class illustrator. At the Castle, the staff, first at the hut in the barbican, and more recently at their much more palatial visitor centre in the car park, have always shown a friendly face and been of great help and assistance.

Survey and excavation work took place at Goodrich Castle from the early 1980s mainly under the auspices of the City of Hereford Archaeology Unit. The careful drawings by the many people who took part have meant that fine details of the castle have been properly recorded and analysed. Amongst those involved were David Beeley, Andy Boucher, Kath Crooks, Tim Hoverd, Martin Knight, Dale Rouse, Robert Williams and Bob Hook, together with many others.

Without the work of one individual, the analysis of the castle would be much less complete; this is Richard Morriss, to whom I will always be exceedingly grateful. In addition, Bryan Byron was responsible for enhancing many of the plans and elevations and producing reconstructions that are used in this book; again my many thanks.

The new publication project was set up with Dr Nigel Baker of Herefordshire Archaeology as project manager, and both he and Dr Keith Ray have been of great assistance. The Goodrich Archive was collected together by Headland Archaeology (in succession to Archaeological Investigations Ltd., and the City of Hereford Archaeology Unit) and was of considerable use throughout the project. My thanks go to all involved.

Many people have helped and encouraged me throughout the recent parts of the project including Frank Bennett and Roger Barrett, who both took much interest in the ownership of the castle, whilst Roger was of great help to me with my new laptop and general understanding of Microsoft Word. My thanks to them both. During 2013, John Stevenson took most of the photographs of the finds, the castle and the surrounding buildings that were needed for the book. Tragically he died suddenly whilst the book was going to the publisher. He was last at Goodrich with his camera only a fortnight before his death.

I very much appreciate the efforts of Andy and Karen Johnson of Logaston Press who have spent much time in sorting out the many typos that I continue to make, and have seen the book through all the publication stages, with thanks to English Heritage for funding the completion of this publication.

Ron Shoesmith, January 2014

Introduction

The first 'Feasibility Study' for a book on Goodrich Castle was prepared for English Heritage in July 1989.[1] The main part of the project took place between 1999 and 2002. At that time it was intended that this should be an academic publication, and almost 180,000 words were written with exhaustive details about every feature, large and small, that could be examined. It was overseen on behalf of English Heritage by Dr Glyn Coppack and Tony Fleming. Unfortunately, the programme was put on hold and went into abeyance in 2002.

With much help from Dr Nigel Baker of Herefordshire Archaeology it was rescued in 2012 and funding restored.[2] However, the revised project was to be a book of popular interest – all those long descriptions of mouldings, door fastenings, etc had to go, the text had to be reduced by half and many site drawings were replaced with photographs. With much effort and with many groans from the various contributors, this has been done.

Throughout the editing period many changes have been made to the original layout. The book is now in four distinct parts – The Goodrich Area; The Historical Background; The Buildings; and The Finds & Life at the Castle. The first part sets the scene and covers the background history and the main buildings associated with the castle and the village. The historical background deals with the people who built and lived in the castle, the destruction caused by the Civil War, and the gradual emergence of the building, first as a romantic ruin and then as an ancient monument.

As for the buildings themselves, originally it was intended to follow a system of considering each building element in turn and describing it through its many changes to the present day. When coming to write this reshaped volume, it was felt that it would make it easier to understand the changes to and general shape of the castle if it was considered as a whole; the description being by constructional period rather than individual building.

Throughout the book, the castle is described with approximate compass settings as shown on the plan (Plate 1, p.57). The book begins with the possible earthworks and the first stone castle; then the second section deals with the grand 13th-century Edwardian castle which included the addition of curtain walls, corner towers and some internal buildings. This is followed by chapters covering the alterations and additions of the 14th century, including the great hall and large south-west tower. The barbican is dealt with separately as it is, in effect, a separate small castle by itself. It is of at least two constructional periods which cannot be accurately phased within the main constructional events of the castle itself. The final chapter in this part describes the gradual conversion from a defended castle to a private house. The final two chapters deal with finds associated with the medieval household and the debris left and buried in the castle following the Civil War (Plates 2, 3 & 4, pp.58-9).

Part One

The Goodrich Area

Chapters 1 – 2

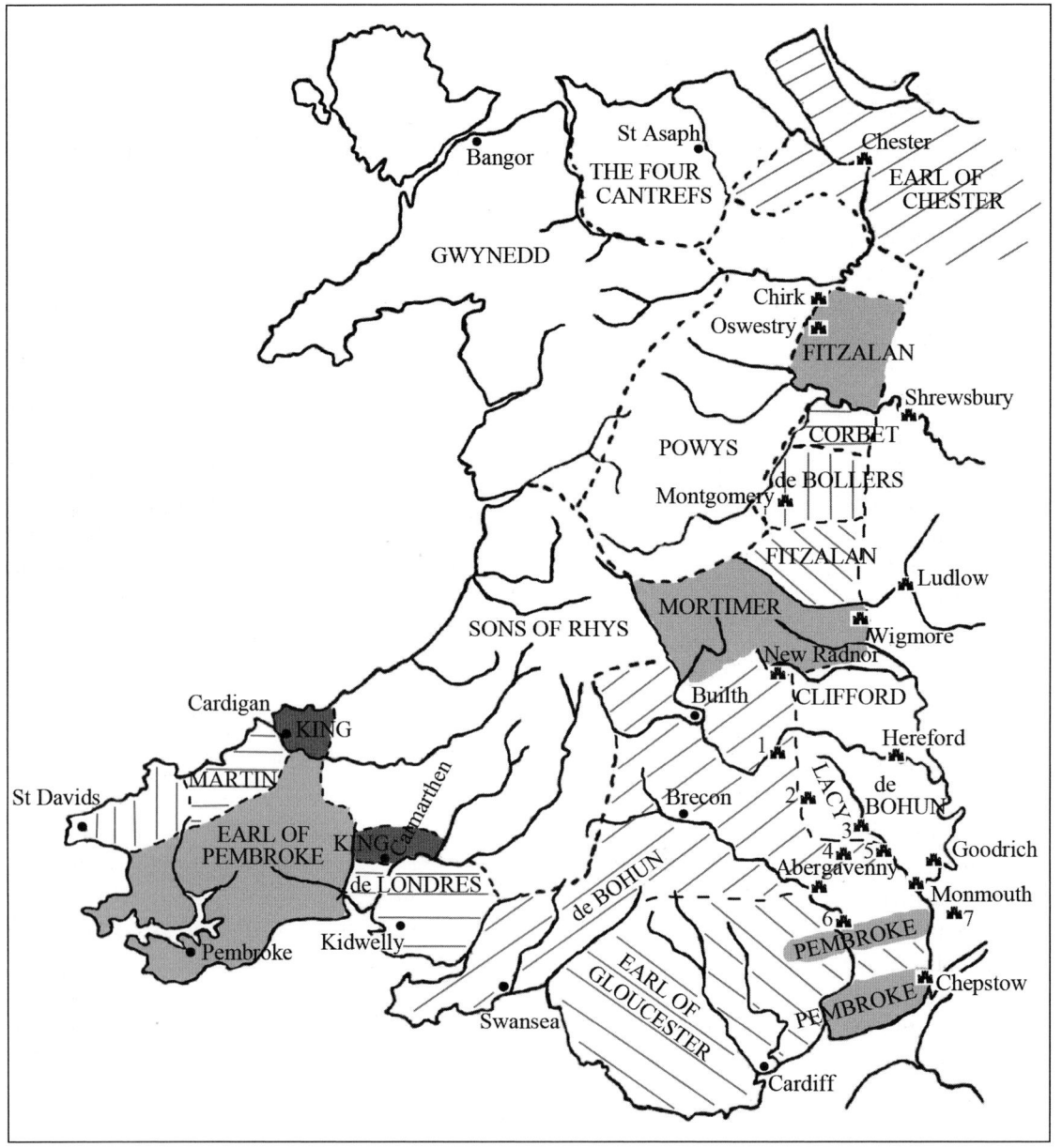

Fig. 1.1 The Marches, showing the various lordships in the early 1200s, and some of the other major castles in the vicinity of Goodrich:
1 Clifford; 2 Longtown; 3 Grosmont; 4 White; 5 Skenfrith; 6 Usk; 7 St Briavel's

1   Background

by Ron Shoesmith, Thomas Richards, Loretta Nikolič, & Bruce Coplestone-Crow

The Welsh Marches (*by* Ron Shoesmith)
The Welsh Marches, that borderland between England and Wales, stretching from Chester on the River Dee to Chepstow at the junction of the Rivers Wye and Severn, has more than its fair share of castles – some still inhabited, but many in ruins (Fig. 1.1). However, Goodrich Castle is only one feature in a landscape that is full of history. There are considerable indications of the importance of the whole area during the prehistoric and Roman periods, well before Goodrich became the site of a Norman castle.

The castle stands in splendid isolation on a promontory adjacent to one of the few fords across the River Wye that could be used most of the year round. It is on the right-hand bank of the river (looking downstream), roughly one third of the way between Ross-on-Wye and Monmouth (Fig. 1.2). In ruins since it was slighted in 1646 after the Civil War, the castle did not suffer from the depredations of stone robbers, as happened to many other castles in the Marches, probably due to its distance from the village and to the importance of its romantic setting as part of the Wye Tour (see Chapter 9).

Geology and Geomorphology (*by* Thomas Richards)
Like much of Herefordshire, the Goodrich area is underlain by Old Red Sandstone rocks, formed between 416 and 359 million years ago in a period of time known as the Devonian. During this time Britain was located about 15 degrees south of the equator, forming part of a newly-created landmass since called Laurussia. The environment was very hot and dry, with seasonal rivers crossing the landscape. The collision of ancient landmasses that formed Laurussia created a large mountain chain to the north-west of the area. The erosion of these mountains provided huge amounts of sediment to the surrounding lowland and coastal plain, slowly resulting in the formation of thick layers of rock.

Three distinctive Old Red Sandstone rock units outcrop in the area. The oldest and most widespread is called the Brownstones, formed during the Lower Devonian (416 to 398 million years ago). These rocks consist of pebbly, cross-bedded, red-brown (occasionally chocolate-brown and olive-green) sandstones. They are the bedrock of the low-lying ground in and around Goodrich village, and extends both north and west across much of central Herefordshire.

After the formation of the Brownstones, the surrounding land was subject to a period of uplift. During this time, no sediments were laid down, or any that were laid have been eroded.

This resulted in no rocks forming, and a subsequent gap in the geological history of the area, known as an unconformity.

Above the unconformity are rocks of Upper Devonian age (385–359 million years ago), with the oldest being the Quartz Conglomerate. It forms a very noticeable and easily traceable horizon right across the edge of the high ground flanking the Forest of Dean, forming resistant crags along Coppett Hill, as well as Huntsham Hill, Howle Hill and beyond. The rock consists

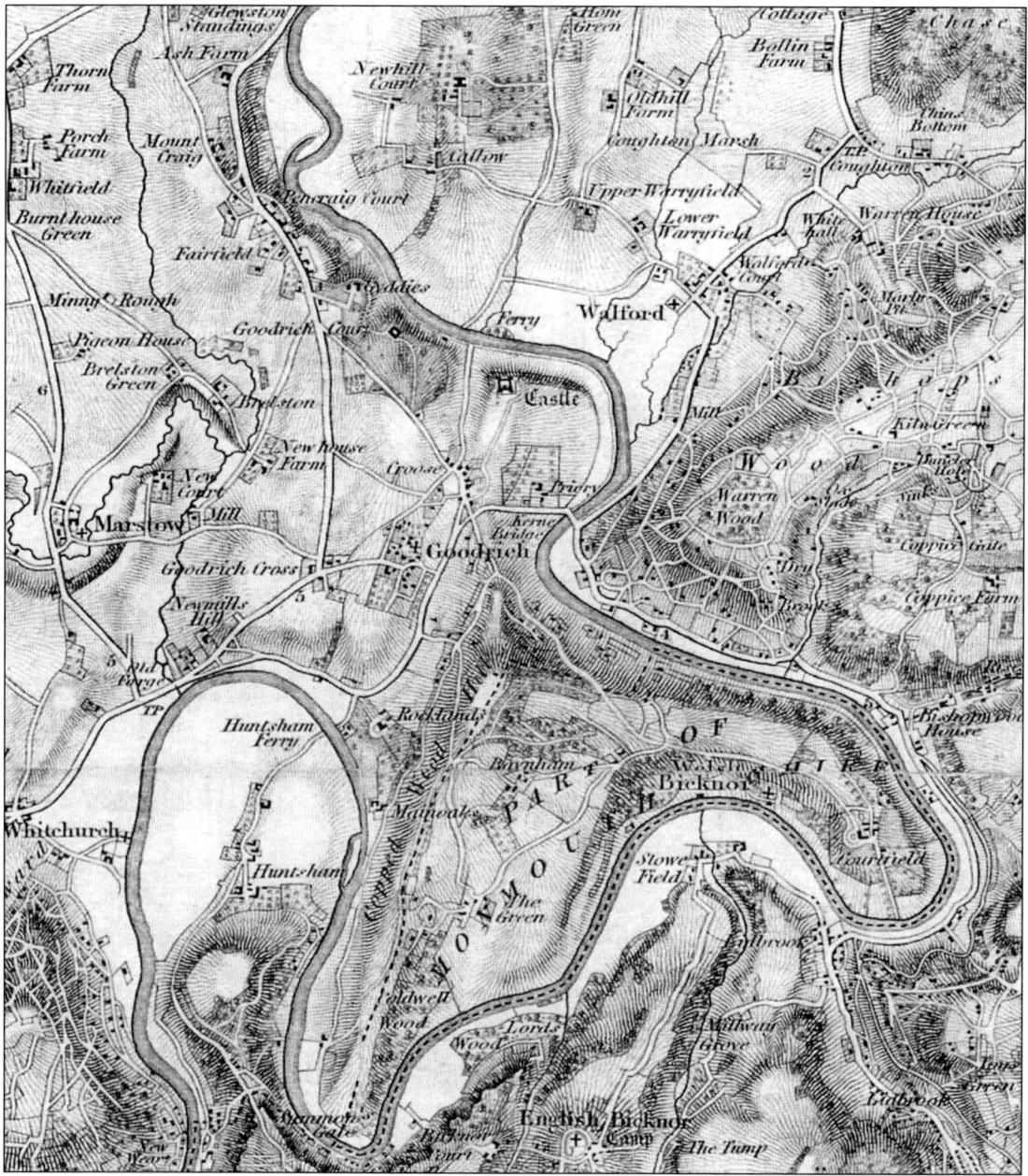

Fig. 1.2 The Goodrich area, c.1835, showing the ferry (on the site of the ford) to the north of the castle and Flanesford Priory by the site of the present Kerne Bridge

of a myriad of sizes of pebbles, comprised mainly of a white or glassy quartz, but with less frequent jasper and decomposed igneous rocks, all cemented together in a red-brown sand. It formed as flash floods swept across the arid landscape, dropping water-borne material quickly as unsorted sediments.

The succeeding rock unit is the Tintern Sandstone – the youngest of the Old Red Sandstones. It caps Coppett Hill, and can be found to the east of the Quartz Conglomerate crags at Huntsham Hill, Howle Hill and beyond. The rock can be described as a soft yellow, red to green-grey sandstone.

The flat ground south of Huntsham Bridge indicates the extent of the modern day floodplain of the River Wye. Huntsham Court lies on a slight rise in the ground, which continues towards the base of Huntsham Hill. This river terrace was a former floodplain level of the Wye.

The geological story of the area would not be complete without describing the formation of the Wye Gorge. It is very likely that the level of the land was once somewhat higher, the upper layers composed of rocks younger and softer than those that outcrop at present. Over time, these rocks were completely eroded by a large river meandering across the landscape. Once all these younger rocks had been eroded, the river started to cut down into the harder rocks of the Old Red Sandstone, as well as the hard limestones that form the edge of high ground of the Forest of Dean. The meanders of the river could no longer move across the landscape because of these relatively hard rocks and so the river cut downwards forming the steep cliffs of the Wye Gorge.

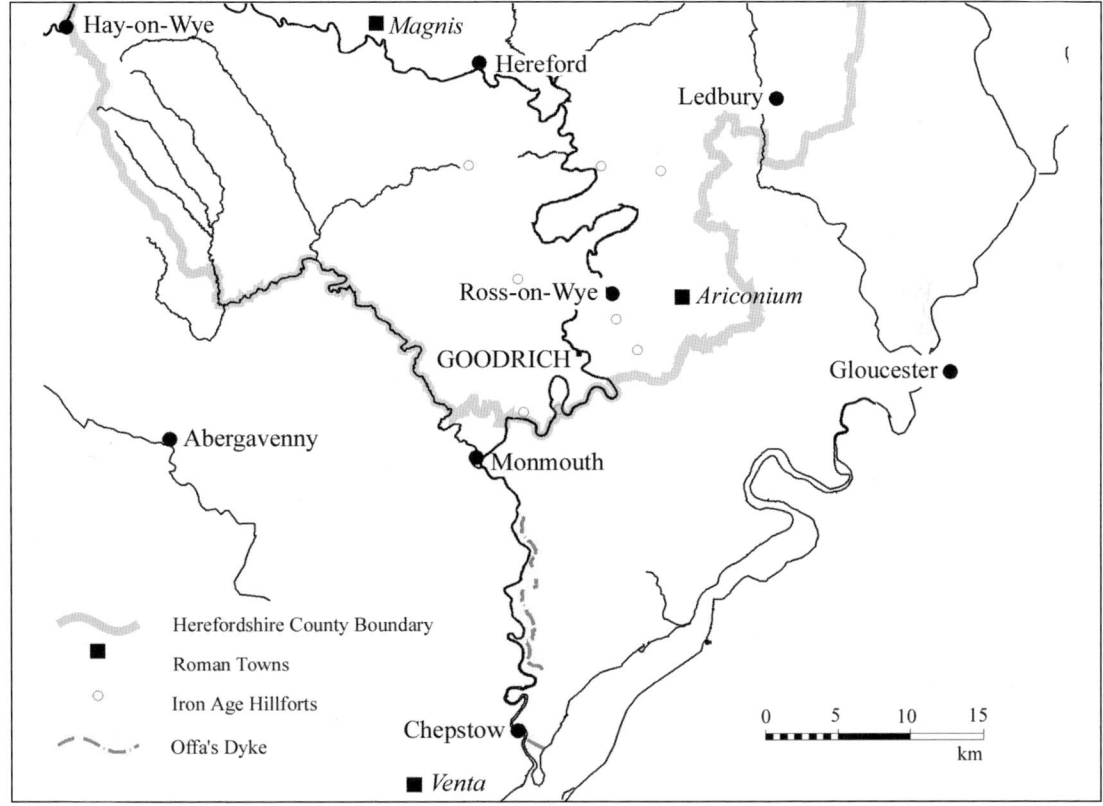

Fig. 1.3 The area around Goodrich

Prehistory (*by* Loretta Nikolič)

The numerous caves and rock shelters near Symonds Yat provide the earliest evidence of human activity in the area. They are found in the steep-sided gorge where the Wye cuts through the sandstone and limestone bedrock. These caves were repeatedly visited by humans (and fauna) from the Late Upper Palaeolithic and Mesolithic onwards into historic periods and may have acted as fixed points in a landscape for nomadic hunter-gatherers. Some have prominent views along the gorge and this characteristic may have been highly desirable to ancient hunters, allowing them to observe the arrival of their prey – herds of animals migrating along the gorge. The largest and most investigated of the sites is King Arthur's Cave in the limestone cliff above the Seven Sisters rocks (Fig. 1.4). It supposedly produced a skeleton in 1695, and was first excavated in the 19th century, when most of the interior deposits were removed. It is now a scheduled ancient monument.[1]

The evidence for early farmers in the region is scarce as the Neolithic is relatively invisible there in terms of material remains, especially standing monuments. However, several finds of worked flint, including arrowheads and polished axe and mace heads, have been found in the Wye Valley near Walford, Hentland, Welsh Newton, Linton and other locations.[2] The distribution of such remains provides some evidence for Neolithic settlement in the Wye area.[3]

The characteristic monumental structures normally associated with the period are found in the wider region – in the megalithic tombs of the upper Wye Valley and at the mouth of the river. These early Neolithic monuments are part of a wider geographic group known as the Cotswold-Severn tombs. Found over an area stretching from Oxfordshire to the Gower, they vary greatly in construction from simple 'dolmen' style structures to large trapezoidal mounds covering passages and chambers. Often located along river valleys, there are several in proximity to the Wye, such as Arthur's Stone above Dorstone, whilst others have views down the river. In the lower Wye Valley such structures are absent or have been lost – the nearest is at Thornwell Farm, located at the mouth of the Wye.[4]

The monuments of the Later Neolithic and Early Bronze Age are more visible. The monolith called The Queen Stone at nearby Huntsham is the last remaining representative of what was once a stone circle (Fig. 1.5).[5] It has unusual weathered vertical grooves in its top edge, and similar markings can be seen on the Devil's Arrows stone row in North Yorkshire. The purpose of the grooves has fostered several speculations

Fig. 1.4 King Arthur's Cave

about their use.[6] Other standing stones punctuate the wider landscape, such as at Staunton in the Forest of Dean and St Weonards, and Harold's Stones still stand in a row at Trellech.[7] Round barrows are well known from the Bronze Age and although no easily visible ones survive in the area, several have been identified from aerial photographs. One such discovery was made to the north-east of Goodrich, where the remains of a small barrow was found at Penyard Park, Weston-under-Penyard, after woodland was cleared.[8]

It is not until the Iron Age that the monument for which the area is well known – the hill fort – first appears. These earthwork constructions took advantage of the tops of hills and promontories and their elevated positions often made a statement in the landscape, or they may mark the edges of local territories. Whilst some were inhabited defended settlements, others were never permanently settled, or were known to hold stock or stores, and it has been speculated that others were gathering places.

At least nine hill forts are known in the lower Wye Valley, but they are not the only evidence of activity from that period. Aerial photography has revealed an Iron Age landscape that was widely populated.[9] At Dingle and Blakes Wood there is an area of open-cast iron ore mining which is thought to date back to the Iron Age. The small surface extraction pits and spoil heaps are still visible as earthworks and are known as the scowles.[10] An unusual Iron Age find was made at Linton during works at a local farm – a Janus-type sculpted head, sporting a drooping moustache that is now in the British Museum.[11]

Some 7km south-south-west of Goodrich, on the east bank of the Wye in Monmouthshire, is the well-defended fort at Huntsham. Enclosing some 2.6ha at the end of a promontory, the several ramparts and ditches go from cliff edge to cliff edge. Below it on the Huntsham plain are several rectangular-ditched enclosures that have also been dated to the Iron Age.[12] Only a short distance from the castle, on the opposite bank of the Wye, is Little Doward Camp. An early Iron Age fort was later rebuilt with more massive embankments and covering a larger area towards the north of the site, a low bank running across the southern section being part of the earlier defences.[13]

Fig. 1.5 The Queen Stone at Huntsham, photographed by Alfred Watkins when the base was being excavated in 1926

Fig. 1.6 Traces of what could be an infilled double ditch outside the present castle.

At Goodrich aerial photographs show features outside the castle ditch that could indicate earlier defences. An examination of all the available aerial photographs shows what appear to be two infilled ditches running from the southern side of the barbican (and probably cut by the barbican ditch) in a wide circle to the south and west around the present rock-cut ditch. Jim Pickering, who took some of the photographs, interpreted them as being of 'hill fort' type and therefore presumably of the Iron Age[14] (Fig. 1.6). If these earthworks do indeed represent some form of promontory fort, they would have enclosed an area a little larger than the castle and its ditch. It has been suggested that the hill fort would neatly cover what appears to be 'unoccupied territory' west of the Wye and east of the area assigned to Little Doward Camp.[15] It may be that existing Iron Age earthworks were reused in the primary ringwork phase of building the castle, and were later levelled prior to the construction of the masonry castle (see Chapter 11). They could have also formed the *vallum monasterium* of the church that is thought to have existed here (see pages 10-12 and 29-32).

The Roman Period (*by* Ron Shoesmith)
The Welsh border area was brought under permanent Roman control by Aulus Gallus, governor between 52 and 57 AD. To the south-east the Silures retained their independence for another generation, although Ostorius Scapula had conducted a punitive campaign against them as early as 47 AD. The territory of the Silures covered modern-day Glamorgan, Monmouthshire and the southern part of Powys – it may have extended into southern Herefordshire and thus included Goodrich. Whatever the case, the area of Goodrich is likely to have remained an uneasy borderland until the Silures were finally subdued by Sextus Julius Frontinus, governor between 75 and 78 AD.

It appears that during the Roman period iron ore was brought from the Forest of Dean and deposits of partially smelted ore, that had been discarded after recovery of malleable iron, indicate smelting sites which have been found adjacent to streams and rivers on many sites around Goodrich.[16] An earlier writer noted that 'Cinders ... are strewed over the surface of the fields, and if we dig a very little depth we find in many places a thick and apparently deep bed of them'.[17]

At Huntsham, below Symonds Yat, there was a Roman site of some 8ha on the gravel terrace situated just above the flood plain and below Huntsham Hill (Fig. 1.7). This was the central part of what must have been a substantial community that farmed this area for over 200 years. An aisled barn, two large residential buildings, and a precinct wall over 80m long have been partially excavated.[18] The archaeological work provided abundant evidence for early iron-working on the site, but this had ceased by the time that the main building (described as a villa) was built at the end of the second century. It may be that the establishment then concentrated on brewing, but there was also a water mill on the River Wye to the east of the main buildings, served by a stone-built weir and leat.[19]

About 18,000 Roman coins, deposited not earlier than 340AD, were found in three earthenware urns in Bishopswood near Kerne Bridge in 1895.[20] Close to this find spot a 'rectangular camp' is said to have been discovered along with some Roman pottery; unfortunately it was levelled for agricultural purposes. Another coin hoard was found in 1817 at the nearby Coppett Wood Hill.[21] To the west of the Wye a tessellated pavement and coins were found 'in a meadow

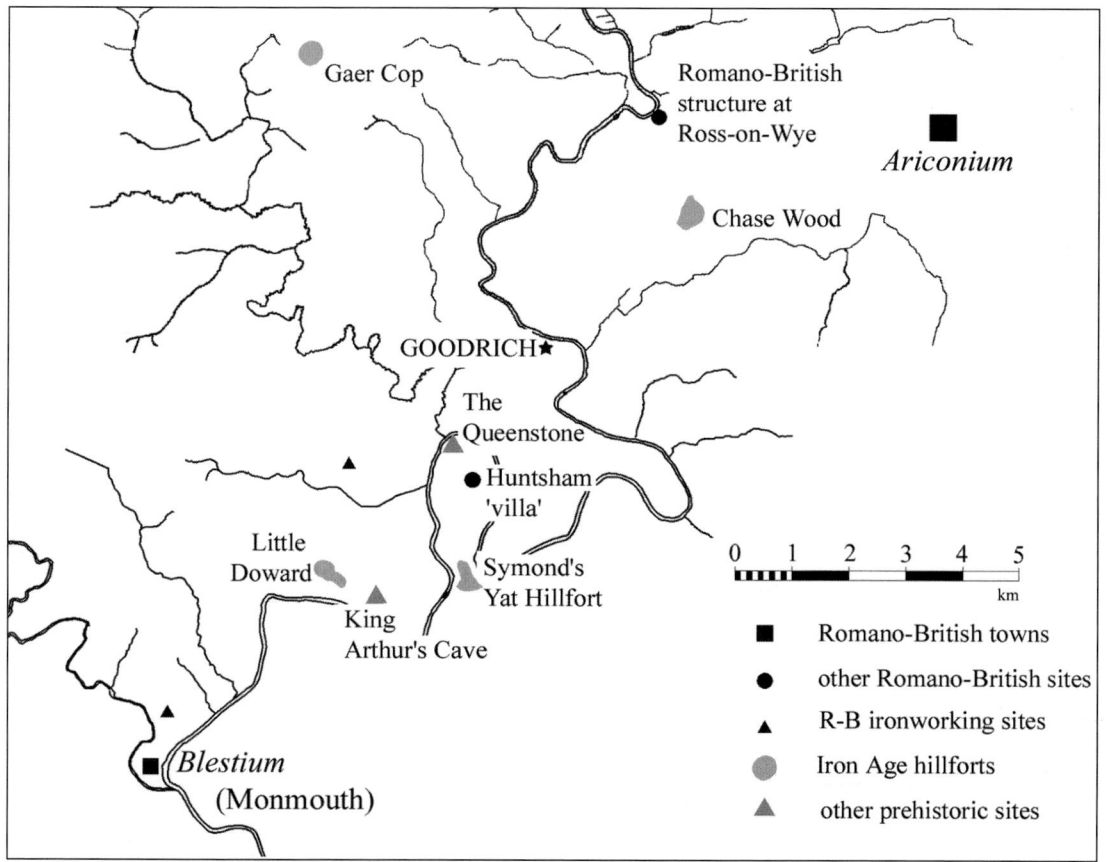

Fig. 1.7 Map showing the location of Prehistoric and Roman sites in the Goodrich area

on the boundary of the parishes of Whitchurch and Ganarew'.[22] Another local Roman site has been suggested in the grounds of Walford Court, where there is a poorly-preserved earthwork.[23] Two Roman coins, found at Goodrich Castle during the 1920s clearance works, are probably no more than accidental droppings during visits to this promontory above the Wye.

Although river transport was doubtless of considerable importance in the Roman period, road access was also a necessity and the ford below Goodrich Castle may well have been used. However, it has to be appreciated that Roman roads varied from well-constructed and maintained military routes down to basic farm tracks, and that there would doubtless have been many changes in the road structure during the 300 or so years of Roman settlement.

There were two main Roman roads that joined Gloucester to Caerleon – the southern route, crossing the Wye in the vicinity of Chepstow,[24] and the northern one which is included in the 13th Itinerary of *Antoninus,* where the distance from *Blestium* (Monmouth) to *Ariconium* (Weston-under-Penyard) is given as XI Roman miles – in good agreement with the actual distance of 12.5 miles.[25]

Several routes have been proposed for this stretch of road and all may have existed from time to time during the lengthy period of Roman settlement. The various routes all involve a crossing of the River Wye, and many of the fords in the area may have been used – Wilton, near Ross; Flanesford, near Kerne Bridge; and Goodrich Boat, below the castle site. It has been suggested that the Goodrich ford was much easier to cross than the one at Wilton,[26] and it certainly had much use in the medieval period. During 1955-6 a field survey and some limited excavations took place in an attempt to establish if a Roman road did cross the Wye at this point.[27] Approaching from the east, a track took up the line of Hom Lane and was apparent as a well-defined causeway leading down to the site of the ferry. However, a trench excavated across the causeway demonstrated that it was of 18th-century origin, and that there was no other road underneath it. No trace of any earlier road was found in the adjacent field. (This causeway, evidently part of the turnpike road from Ross to the ford built in 1759, has now completely disappeared as a result of ploughing.) Although no evidence for a road earlier than the turnpike was found on the left bank of the river, there must have been an earlier way down to the ford. The Roman road (if it did exist) and its medieval counterpart may have taken an angled course across the meadows towards the ford rather than a direct one. The field on the Goodrich side of the river is low-lying and the position of the ford may well have moved either up- or down-stream from time to time. Above the meadow, excavations established the presence of a road dating from at least the 13th century, but did not find a Roman predecessor. Towards Goodrich village there is a deep hollow-way so any remains of a Roman road are likely to have been lost as medieval and later cart-wheels cut deeper and deeper into the ground. An excavation in the hollow-way exposed a 19th-century road surface that overlay a well-kerbed edge, below which was a sherd of possible sub-Roman date.[28] The evidence for a Roman road at this point is therefore very flimsy and the idea of a Roman crossing at Goodrich Boat must remain in some considerable doubt.

The Early Medieval Period (*by* Bruce Copplestone-Crow)
The estate worked from the Roman civil site at Huntsham appears to have been known as *Garthbenni* in the post-Roman era. In the mid-6th century a church was built there by a

certain King Constantine who gave it to Dyfrig, a bishop in Ergyng (the post-Roman kingdom that covered most of southern Herefordshire),[29] 'so that it might be a house of prayer ... and an episcopal place forever'.[30] Dyfrig consecrated the church and left three of his 'disciples' as the nucleus of a monastic community: an abbot of *Garthbenni* is mentioned in two early-7th-century documents and 'monks' with lands at the mouth of the Gamber are mentioned in one dating from *c.*860.[31] The church could have been somewhere on or close to the castle site, its presence possibly accounting for the many Christian burials (see pages 29-32) discovered on the eastern edge of the castle ditch. It is clear from later evidence, however, that the king kept the ferry below the castle in his own hands, evidently not wishing to part with this valuable economic resource. The monastery and bishop-house of *Garthbenni* lasted until the late-9th century.

As a place-name, *Garthbenni* is thought to mean '[estate associated with] the promontory ridge',[32] the physical feature concerned probably being the ridge of high ground on which the Iron Age hill fort of Huntsham was built and below which was the Roman civil site. According to the highly tendentious *Book of Llandaff* (written at the behest of Bishop Urban of Llandaff [1104-34] and incorporating many early documents that he believed proved that his diocese once covered a much larger area than it did in his day) a document of the late-9th or 10th century, but apparently referring back to the 6th century, gives the boundary of this estate as extending from a 'Black Marsh' (now Huntsham Pool) in the south to 'the ferry of King Constantine ... across the Wye' (almost certainly the ferry below the castle) in the north.[33] Within these brief bounds the estate would have included all the modern civil parishes of Goodrich and Welsh Bicknor and perhaps other areas.

Ergyng took its name from the Roman town of *Ariconium* (Weston-under-Penyard). This town is thought to have been the site of the first church of which Dyfrig was bishop and, if correct, Constantine's removal of his seat across the Wye to *Garthbenni* can be seen as part of a general movement away from the town-based bishops of the Roman era to the rural, monastery-based, bishops of the so-called 'Celtic Church' seen elsewhere in western Britain at this time.[34]

Despite the longevity of *Garthbenni* as the site of a bishop's seat, the names of only seven of its bishops are mentioned in deeds and charters in the *Book of Llandaff*. Dyfrig has already been mentioned, and his successor seems to have been one Inabwy.[35] After this came Ufelfwy (early 7th century), Berthwyn (early to mid-8th century), Tyrchan (mid-8th century), Nudd (late 9th century) and, finally, Cyfeiliog (who the *Book of Llandaff* says died in 927).[36] Bishop Berthwyn was a contemporary of Aethelbald, king of Mercia (716-57), and in his day, in 722, a battle was fought at Pencoed in Ergyng. The Welsh were victorious, but only after the 'Saxons' had devastated the area and destroyed many churches.[37] If the flurry of grants made by local laymen to the church at *Garthbenni* in the mid-8th century was intended to assist in its rebuilding, then that church was one of these. Two of these grants were made in the (damaged?) church, one of them 'on the altar of St Dyfrig ... and into the hand of Bishop Berthwyn'.[38]

A battle at Hereford in 760[39] reversed the result of Pencoed and led to increasing English settlement in Ergyng. By Nudd's day this was sufficiently extensive for the English to have given the name Archenfield to the parts of the old kingdom of Ergyng west of the Wye. In 918 Bishop Cyfeiliog was captured in Archenfield by Vikings, and his ransom of £40 was paid, not by any Welsh king, but by King Edward the Elder of England, who evidently regarded Archenfield and *Garthbenni* as part of his kingdom.[40] By this time the seat of the local bishop had in any case been moved still further west, across the River Monnow into Gwent,[41] probably so as to escape English influence.

This move, possibly made in about 880, marked the end of monastic and episcopal life at the church in *Garthbenni*. The church itself, however, probably remained in use until the arrival of the Normans. However, in the 1050s Archenfield was laid waste by the Welsh, and many churches were destroyed.[42] One of these was the 'Church of the Twelve Saints' at Welsh Bicknor which, in the time of King Harold, Herewald (bishop in Archenfield) rededicated and brought back into use. Sometime later, 'in the time of [King] William and of Tewdos son of March' (i.e. after 1066) he transferred the clergy and traditions of Constantine's church to Welsh Bicknor, joining it to its own 'Church of the Twelve Saints' in the same cemetery.[43] In time the traditions of King Constantine's church were remembered better than those of the 'Twelve Saints' (perhaps not surprising, in view of its former status as a bishop-house) so that by the 12th century Welsh Bicknor church was being called solely 'the church of St Constantine of Bicknor' (King Constantine by now being confused with Saint Constantine).[44] The traditions, however, of King Constantine's church and monastery were revived in the 14th century, when Richard Talbot founded an Augustinian Priory in the chapel William de Valence had built at the castle (see Chapter 6).

Domesday Book, dating from 1086, is in agreement with the *Book of Llandaff* in naming *Taldus* or Tewdos as the owner of the *Garthbenni* estate at the time of the Norman conquest. By now, however, the English had given the name *Hulla* (meaning simply 'hill', i.e. Huntsham Hill) to the estate and this was in the hands of one Godric Mapson.[45] It was his taking over of *Garthbenni* or *Hulla c.*1070 from Tewdos that was the cause of the amalgamation of King Constantine's church (possibly on the site of the castle) with the one at Welsh Bicknor.

2 GOODRICH VILLAGE
by Ron Shoesmith

Goodrich Parish
Goodrich is a large parish some 5 miles south-south-west of Ross that extends along both banks of the River Wye (Fig. 1.2). Most of the parish is to the west of the river where it seals a long bend that includes the much smaller parish of Welsh Bicknor. On the west are Marstow and Whitchurch parishes whilst to the east, Kerne Bridge, completed in 1828, joins Goodrich to Walford parish (Fig. 2.1). To the south Huntsham Bridge, built in 1885, joins the two parts

Fig.2.1 Kerne Bridge

of the parish, the flat plain in the river meander leading up to and including the 450ft (147m) high Huntsham Hill, all being within Goodrich. The parish used to be even larger and included Glewstone and Pencraig to the north, both now in Marstow parish.

The village of Walford (whose place-name means 'Welshman's Ford')[1] is some three-quarters of a mile to the north-east of the castle. Although still in use by visitors to the castle in the 19th and early 20th centuries, the road that led from Walford to the ford and ferry has now totally disappeared, but for many hundreds of years it was one of the main routes between England and Wales.

Village Roads
The present village road leads down the hill from the main A40 to join into the road to Kerne Bridge (Fig. 2.1). This is partly due to the re-design of the village when Goodrich Court was

built, and partly to the re-arrangements as a consequence of the construction of Kerne Bridge itself. The earlier village road led up from the ford at Goodrich Boat to the centre of the village at Y Crwys (The Croose), and from there directly across the present road to follow the minor road to Goodrich Cross (the line of a postulated Roman road) where the Cross Keys Inn sits at the western extremity. Originally it was a linear village with several side tracks leading down to the south-east.

Flanesford Priory

Goodrich Castle stands on a bluff well above the River Wye, but the remains of Flanesford Priory lie half-a-mile to the south, on low-lying ground near to the river and close to the ford after which it is named. The road from Goodrich village to Kerne Bridge runs close to the priory buildings (Plate 5, p.60).

The Priory of St John the Baptist was a small house of Canons Regular of St Augustine, founded in 1346 by Sir Richard Talbot (see Chapter 6) with reasonable endowments. In 1446 the Bishop of Exeter granted indulgences towards the building of a church and to the support of the priory, suggesting that there was some need of repair. The church was probably to the north of the surviving medieval buildings. When the priory was dissolved in 1536 its possessions totalled £15 8s 9d. In 1538 it was given to George, 4th Earl of Shrewsbury, the owner of Goodrich Castle.

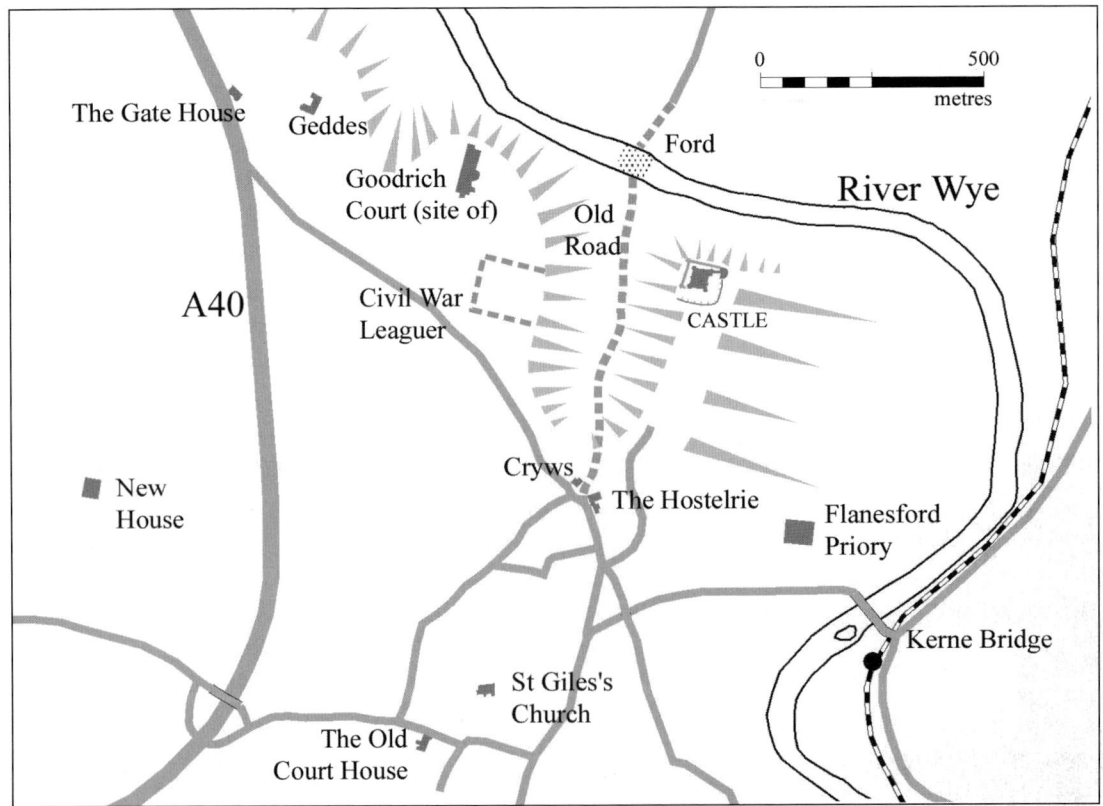

Fig. 2.2 A map of Goodrich and area showing buildings mentioned in the text

Fig. 2.3 Flanesford Priory has been converted to provide holiday accommodation

The main surviving building originally formed the south side of the cloister and was of two storeys (Fig. 2.3). The external north wall includes corbels, indicating an open cloister. It was long thought to be the refectory with an undercroft, in a common Augustinian form. However, the presence at first-floor level of a western doorway, and a fireplace half-way along the northern wall, means that this attribution is uncertain.[2] The building is now interpreted as a first-floor hall used as a guest house, with the prior's lodging in the two-storey south-eastern wing attached to the main range. The two buildings were originally connected at first-floor level by two doorways. There are indications of a lost range in the external east wall of this building – possibly the reredortor or lavatory. The west wall of the guest hall also had medieval buildings attached.

At the north-eastern corner of the main building there are indications of a wall running in a northerly direction which would have formed the eastern side of the cloister; the range associated with it may well have contained the chapter house and the dormitory. Other buildings presently within the complex include the late 18th-century farmhouse and a cider mill. A post-medieval barn, which adjoins the medieval building on the west, incorporates some medieval work in its north and south walls. During the 1980s, archaeological watching briefs found traces of several other buildings.[3] The gatehouse entry to the priory precinct was probably to the south, with access from the road that ran east-west to the ford at Kerne

Fig. 2.4 Flanesford Priory seen from Kerne Bridge, with the castle outlined on the skyline

Fig. 2.5 St Giles's Church

Bridge. The monks did not depend on the river for their fish – there are four fishponds that survive as earthworks to the south-west of the complex.

The main building was converted into a threshing barn in the mid-18th century with alterations to the entry. More recently, most of the buildings within the Flanesford complex have been converted to holiday accommodation (Figs. 2.3 & 4).

St Giles's Church (Fig. 2.5)

The parish church of St Giles is at the western end of the village and is approached by paths rather than roads. It is a large building consisting of a combined nave and chancel with a north aisle of similar width and length. The central part is 13th century, but the church was radically altered in the early-14th century when the nave was extended (or rebuilt) to the west and a two-bay chapel added to the chancel. The outer walls were then built (or rebuilt) to the present form. The tower and porch are mid-14th century.[4]

Goodrich Court (Fig 2.6)

Sitting on the opposing ridge to the castle, Goodrich Court was designed by Edward Blore 'to exemplify the style of architecture prevailing during the reigns of Edwards I, II & III'. The first stone was laid in 1828 and the building completed in 1831. This was the home of Samuel Rush Meyrick and the setting for his world-famous collection of armour from every corner of the earth.[5]

Louisa Anne Twamley, who visited the court and castle in 1838, described her impressions:[6]

> In going to Goodrich Court, you seem to step back a few centuries, except that modern refinement is combined with olden appearances. Fair gardens and terraces, which command extensive and varied prospects, with the castle ruins in front, surround the mansion. I enquired whence the stone was procured of which it is built; and Sir S. Meyrick immediately led the way to the quarry, which is now an exceedingly picturesque spot, directly below the Court, and overhanging the Wye. It is a compact red sandstone: the red colour being rather detrimental to the effect of the building, to my fancy.

It was in 1841, during his second visit to Goodrich, that Wordsworth saw Goodrich Court for the first time:

Fig. 2.6 Goodrich Court in 1906. It was built between 1828 and 1831, but was demolished after the Second World War

> I could not but deeply regret that [the castle's] solemnity was impaired by a fantastic new castle set up on a projection of the same ridge as if to show how far modern art can go in surpassing all that could be done by antiquity and nature, with their united graces, remembrances, and associations. I could have almost wished for the power, so much did the contrast vex me, to blow away Sir Samuel Meyrick's impertinent structure, and all the possessions it contained.[7]

It was to be 110 years before his wish was finally granted, the Court being totally demolished by 1951.

When Meyrick died on the 2nd of April 1848, at the comparatively early age of 65, the building no longer had the same sense of purpose. He left it to his cousin, Lt Col Meyrick, who carried out radical alterations by subdividing some of the larger rooms, adding a new service range and moving the entrance hall to the east side. In 1868 the collection of armour was put up for sale and dispersed.

The now elderly Blore, when shown photographs of the changes, wrote to Mr and Mrs George Moffatt, who had bought the Goodrich Court estate in 1871, commenting that 'Col Meyrick's addition is ... a very ugly protuberance and deserves all the censure you have so well bestowed on such a monstrosity'.[8]

George Moffatt and his son Harold also carried out extensive works at the Court, changing the external character of the south and west faces from castellated Gothic to neo-Elizabethan. Internally the conversion was even more extreme – the old Grand Hall had a floor inserted to become kitchens and servants' accommodation, whilst the old kitchen was opened up to become the new Great Hall with a brand new hammer-beam roof and a gallery containing an organ. The stables and outbuildings attached to the south side of the house were demolished to make way for a large forecourt and flower gardens leading to another main entrance. The work continued into the early years of the 20th century when Harold Moffatt's eldest daughter, Dorothy, married Guy Trafford from Hill Court, a short distance across the Wye from Goodrich Court.

At the beginning of the Second World War, Mrs Trafford, by then a widow, offered Goodrich Court, Hill Court and Pencraig Court to the Essex-based Felsted School, who occupied the buildings from May 1940 to March 1945.[9] Originally the boys had to travel by bicycle or bus from Goodrich across Kerne Bridge to Hill Court, but later they crossed the river by their own suspension bridge – built by the scouts – on the site of the old Goodrich Boat ford and ferry. After the war, the building fell into disuse, and in the first instance the fixtures and fittings were sold and then the entire building was disposed of for the stone. Although the Court disappeared, the Monmouth Gate, built in the same original style, still survives to surprise travellers passing along the A40 (Fig. 2.6).[10]

Fig. 2.7 Goodrich Court Gatehouse on the A40

Y Crwys (The Croose) (Fig. 2.8)
Y Crwys (derived from the Welsh for 'the Cross') is a stone building in the centre of the village described as a ruin in 1843 when it was obtained by Meyrick.[11] A mid-19th-century writer suggests that the lower part of

Fig. 2.8 Y Crwys (The Croose) from *The Goodrich Court Guide*, by Charles Nash (1867)

the building was of 14th-century date and that it was buried when the present road was built up such that the bottom level of the building now lies about 2m below the surface. The same writer noted that in re-erecting the upper part 'the arch of the principal window and one of the capitals of the doorway, all carved in stone, were found built up in the wall'.[12] During the work a cross was restored to the roof and the arms of William de Valence added. The building was apparently used as a gaol from the beginning of the 16th century until about 1800 and is shown as such on a 1718 map (Fig. 9.1).

Ye Hostelrie (Fig. 2.9)
At one time an inn called the Crown and Anchor, it was also called the Anker and was where manorial courts were held. The romantic part, with its tall Gothic chapel window and diversity of pinnacles, was built on the front of the building after Sir Samuel Meyrick bought it in 1845.[13]

Old Court House
The present building, which lies south-west of the church, includes timber-framed elements of the late-16th century.[14] Richard Tyler, who had already acquired the ancient farmhouse next to Y Crwys, bought the house in or shortly after 1626 (see also Chapter 7).[15]

Geddes (Giddis)
North-west of the castle, the central part of this building is of the mid-16th century, whilst the south wing was added in the early 17th century and substantially repaired towards the end of that century, probably following damage during the Civil War.[16]

Fig. 2.9 Ye Hostelrie in 1910

New House (Fig. 2.10)
Built by the Reverend Thomas Swift (the grandfather of Jonathan Swift) in 1636 in the northwest of the parish as a vicarage, this curious building consists of three ranges, each of three storeys and arranged radially as though to represent the Holy Trinity.[17]

Fig. 2.10 New House Farm about 1930 (RCHM)

Part Two

The Historical Background

Chapters 3 – 9

Chronological Table

Historical Date	National/Local Event	Ownership/ Resident at Goodrich Castle	Constructional Event
Possible Bronze Age/ Iron Age to 6th Century		King Constantine's church given to Dyfrig	Evidence of ditches visible on aerial photographs. Possible church and burials to east of rock-cut ditch
c.1070-1138	1066 Conquest William the Conqueror Henry I 1100-35	Godric Mapson William FitzBaderon c.1095-c.1125 Baderon of Monmouth c.1125-1138	Possible timber & earthwork castle First stone castle: Stone keep (early 12th century) Middle part of east curtain wall. Traces of other curtain walls. Well?
1138-76	Stephen 1135-54 Henry II 1154-89	**The Clare family:** Gilbert FitzGilbert de Clare, Earl of Pembroke 1138-48 Richard Strongbow (Gilbert's son) d.1176 **The Crown** 1176-1204	No work done
1176-1204	Richard I 1189-99 John 1199-1216	Granted to William Marshal, Earl of Pembroke 1204	Small garrison – no work done
1204-45	1216 Castle under siege by Welsh	**William Marshal and his sons**	No work done
1246-47		John de Mountchesney d.1247 leaving Goodrich to his sister Joan	No work done
1247-1327	Edwardian invasion of Wales 1276-67 Second Edwardian invasion of Wales 1281-83 South Wales risings 1287 & 1294	**The de Valences:** Joan m. William de Valence 1247 William de Valence d.1296 Joan de Valence 1296-1307 Aymer de Valence 1307-24 heirs of Aymer 1324-27	**The grand Edwardian castle:** Rock-cut ditches on east & south New curtain walls & corner towers North range & vestibule Gatehouse & Chapel towers Low status east building (? Stables) 1st Barbican
1327-1421	1346 Flanesford Priory founded 1348 Licence for gaol at Goodrich 1402 Owain Glyndwr raids	**The Talbots:** Richard Talbot, 2nd Lord Talbot 1327-56 Elizabeth, widow of Richard 1356-72 Gilbert, 3rd Lord Talbot 1372-87 Richard, 4th Lord Talbot 1387-96 Gilbert, 5th Lord Talbot 1396-1418 Angharad (d. of Gilbert) 1418-21	Alterations to chapel – balcony/ wall steps – upper room inside gatehouse for canons. New west curtain wall including the great hall and lobby. Replacement of SW tower with Great Tower. New south curtain wall with rooms around the keep including dungeon and kitchen. New east hall. Alterations to the barbican and improvements to the gatehouse.

Chronological Table

Historical Date	National/Local Event	Ownership/ Resident at Goodrich Castle	Constructional Event
1442-1590		**The Shrewsburys:** John, 6th Lord Talbot & 1st Earl of Shrewsbury John, 2nd Earl of Shrewsbury 1453-60 John, 3rd Earl of Shrewsbury 1460-73 George, 4th Earl of Shrewsbury 1473-1538 Francis, 5th Earl of Shrewsbury 1538-60 George, 6th Earl of Shrewsbury 1560-90	Addition of 1st floor to N range with galleries. 3-storey E range with galleries. Grand staircase hall in lobby Insertion of garderobe tower on E wall. Further extension eastwards of gatehouse. New windows in chapel. Formation of N & W wards with enclosing walls and towers. Stables in west ward and associated works. Piped water supply and alterations to kitchen.
1590-1642		Tenants of the castle under the earls of Shrewsbury & then the earls of Kent. Including Thomas Kery, John Talbot, Eustace Weisland, George Moore, Thomas Gwyllim, and finally Richard Tyler.	Extensive repairs 1631-32
1642-46	The Civil War	Occupied by Royalists 1644 – Sir Henry Lingen Castle under siege 1645-46 by Colonel Birch	Burning of the stables. Extensive damage culminating in the collapse of the north-west tower following mining – hardly a roof entire.
1647-48	After the Civil War	No occupants – the Countess of Kent paid £1,000 compensation	Castle slighted: removal of battlements Demolition of barbican & outer gatehouse Castle left as a ruin
1700 to early 20th century	Construction of Goodrich Court The Wye Tour 1828-31	No occupants – Castle bought by Admiral Griffin in 1755 on death of Henry Duke of Kent	Castle as a ruin
20th & 21st centuries		Ministry of Works Department of the Environment English Heritage	1915 – Scheduled as an ancient monument 1920 – Taken into compulsory guardianship following collapse of part of W wall 1920s – Clearance and repair works; shop erected in barbican 2008 – Shop in barbican removed; new shop/display area/café next to car park.

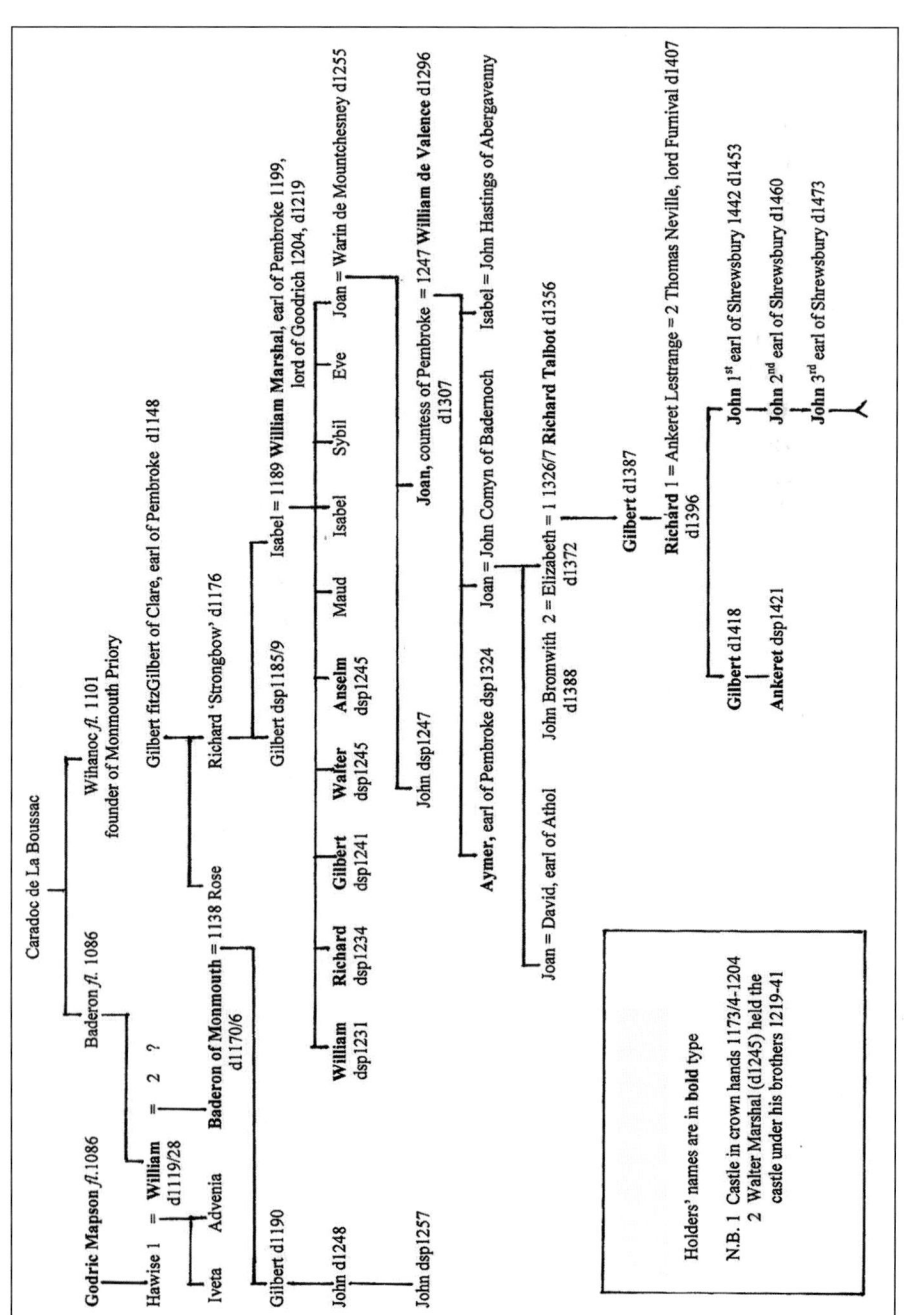

Fig. 3.1 Holders of Goodrich Castle c.1070-1473

3   **AFTER THE CONQUEST (1066-1204)**
by Bruce Coplestone-Crow

Godric Mapson (*c*.1070 to *c*.1100)
Godric's origins are unknown, but his surname, (which is perhaps derived from an Old English personal-name *Mappa*[1]), suggests that he may have been one of the Englishmen to throw in their lot with the Norman conquerors.[2] He attached himself to the household of William FitzOsbern, from whom he received *Hulla* in about 1070. To establish himself there he probably built the castle that bears his name. Although no castle is mentioned at *Hulla* in the 1086 Domesday Book,[3] this does not mean one did not exist. Part of the reason that he took so little profit from the estate at that time (only £2 per annum) may be that he was still incurring the substantial expense of both building and maintaining a castle. However, the impact Godric made on the estate saw it very soon taking his name as its own, and part (perhaps the greater part) of that impact must have been the building of a castle. This early castle was probably a simple ringwork with a timber tower over (or perhaps beside) the entrance (see Chapter 11).

Godric's manor of *Hulla* lacked both Welsh Bicknor and the Goodrich Ferry with its associated lands on both banks of the Wye. Earl William FitzOsbern retained both of these when he gave *Hulla* to Godric, and they became appurtenances of the castle he built at Monmouth. Both the ferry and the manor continued to belong to the Monmouth lordship until its abolition in 1536, and then to the county of Monmouth until 1844, when they were transferred to Herefordshire.[4]

Nothing more is known of Godric Mapson, apart from the probability that he is the Godric who, according to a charter of Monmouth Priory, had land in Monmouth. He seems to have left a daughter, Hawise, as his heir. As the daughter of a tenant-in-chief of the crown, wardship of her and of her lands passed to King William II (Rufus) (1087-1100) after her father's death, and it appears that he gave her in marriage to William FitzBaderon, lord of Monmouth, for upon FitzBaderon's marriage to an otherwise unidentified Hawise, he was granted Goodrich (see below). It is possible that there had been a private arrangement between Godric and FitzBaderon concerning the marriage that the king allowed to proceed.

William FitzBaderon (*c*.1095-*c*.1125)
William was nephew and heir to Wihanoc de La Boussac (a Breton), to whom the Conqueror had given the lands that William FitzOsbern and his son Ralph had originally had at Monmouth

before Ralph had forfeited them in 1075 having rebelled against the king. By 1081, Wihanoc had founded Monmouth Priory as a cell of the abbey of St Florent at Saumur in Anjou. Sometime in the next five years William acquired his uncle's lands at Monmouth, including the castle and the outlying members at Goodrich Ferry and Welsh Bicknor.[5] Rufus's grant of Goodrich to William FitzBaderon upon his marriage to Hawise is mentioned in a charter FitzBaderon issued to Monmouth Priory:

> William FitzBaderon and lady Hawise his wife and his daughters Iveta and Advenia gave to God and St Mary the Virgin at St Florent and the monks there, one carucate of the land which king William gave to Hawise in marriage; and the church of Goodrich Castle and all their tithes, namely, of the carucate of land, honey, mills and … [reading uncertain] … And this gift and grant was placed on the altar by the hand of the said William and of his wife Hawise, with Iveta and Advenia the daughters.[6]

The deed is undated, but its witness list shows that it was made on the same day as another charter of William's, which also had the consent of his wife and daughters:

> In addition, William FitzBaderon gave to St Florent and to St Mary of Monmouth and to the monks the land of *Cachebren* which is near the mill of Goodrich Castle. And this gift was made on the third day before the solemnity of our Most Holy Father Benedict which is kept in Lent [18 March] in the presence of the abbot of St Florent, who had then come to Monmouth. Hawise wife of William with Iveta and Advenia their daughters confirmed the gift. …[7]

The 18th of March was the day on which the monastic church of St Mary at Monmouth was dedicated by bishop Hervey of Bangor (during a vacancy in the See of Hereford) in the presence of the abbot, William of St Florent, and Bernard, the king's chaplain. The year must be 1101, since Bernard was given custody of the Hereford See in January 1101 and Flaad FitzAlan (one of the witnesses) had been succeeded by his son, Alan, by the following September.[8] Together, the deeds show that what FitzBaderon gave to Monmouth Priory – the church at Goodrich and land at *Chachabren* (now New Court Farm in Marstow) – he had by right of his wife, whose marriage had been granted by King William Rufus.

FitzBaderon had no sons by Hawise, who must have died not long after 1101. He was still living in 1119, but by 1128 had been succeeded by Baderon (known as Baderon of Monmouth) – his son by a second wife.[9]

Baderon of Monmouth (*c.*1125-1138)

It was probably Baderon who built the keep and other stone defences at Goodrich. His reasons were as much connected with the fact that the Welsh were still raiding their Anglo-Norman neighbours of the March of Wales and their English neighbours of Herefordshire in the period 1139-48 as a letter of the abbot of Gloucester to the bishop of Hereford dating from that period shows,[10] as they were with the need to safeguard both his route into England and his revenues from the ferry.

Baderon's time as lord of Goodrich extended into the reign of King Stephen (1135-54). This was the time of a civil war (generally known as 'The Anarchy'), which had its origins in Stephen's seizure of the English throne on the death of Henry I, against the interests of his cousin Matilda (Maud), Henry's daughter and designated heir. She had been married to the emperor of Germany (hence her preferred title of 'Empress'), but was currently the wife of Count Geoffrey of Anjou. The Empress's principal allies in the war were her half-brother Robert, earl of Gloucester and an illegitimate son of her father by a lady of the Gay family of Oxfordshire, and the sheriff of Herefordshire – Miles of Gloucester. The lands and interests of both of these magnates lay mainly in the west of England and in south Wales.

The civil war began in Herefordshire in 1138, when a disaffected baron seized the royal castle at Hereford. Stephen swiftly brought up an army to retake it and it was during the resulting month-long siege and its aftermath that the future of Goodrich was decided. A few days after Pentecost (22nd of May) the king received the letters of defiance issued by Earl Robert that marked the formal opening of warfare. At this juncture the line of the River Wye gained considerable strategic significance to the king as Earl Robert's greatest concentrations of power lay either side of it – at the castles of Bristol and Gloucester, and at the lordship of Glamorgan in Wales that he had gained through marriage to the heiress of Robert FitzHamon. It was, therefore, in Stephen's best interests that the major crossings of the Wye (ones able to take large quantities of men and material) between Gloucestershire and Glamorgan – those at Hereford, Goodrich and Chepstow – should be controlled by him. The Hereford crossing he was busy securing for himself, but the other two also needed placing in secure hands. To this end he allowed Gilbert FitzGilbert of Clare (a man whose star was very much in the ascendant at Stephen's court, who was with him at the siege of Hereford[11] and to whom he now gave the earldom of Pembroke) to inherit Chepstow Castle and its associated lands that had belonged to Walter FitzRichard of Clare, Gilbert's uncle who had died childless earlier in the year (Fig. 3.2).[12] Then, having successfully concluded the siege of Hereford, he arranged for Goodrich, with its brand new keep and defences, to also be placed in Pembroke's hands. He had no reason as yet to suspect Baderon of Monmouth's loyalty to the crown (though he was to become one of Stephen's most dedicated opponents only a year later), and to compensate him for the loss of Goodrich arranged a very advantageous marriage to a daughter of the illustrious new earl. The wedding took place at Chepstow on the 1st of November 1138, and ten days later, having travelled up the Wye to Monmouth, the couple confirmed to the priory there a gift they had made on their wedding day.[13]

Gilbert FitzGilbert of Clare, Earl of Pembroke (1138-1148) and Richard 'Strongbow' of Clare (1148-1176)

In the event, the arrangements Stephen had made at Hereford in 1138 concerning Chepstow and Goodrich had little of the effect he must have expected. In the autumn of 1139 Miles of Gloucester, castellan of Gloucester under its earl, went over to the Empress's side and he was followed by almost all the lords of the March of south Wales. Six months later Hereford Castle fell to Miles, and this, and the fall of Worcester to the Empress's forces in 1141, meant that for nearly ten years Stephen's forces were denied access to lands beyond the Severn. There is no evidence that either Chepstow or Goodrich was taken by the Empress's forces during this time, which probably means that Earl Gilbert's castellans at these places must have been among the castle-holders who (according to William of Malmesbury) 'kept safe within their fortifications and watched how things would turn out'.[14]

Fig. 3.2 The seal of Gilbert FitzGilbert de Clare, 1st Earl of Pembroke

Nothing is known of Gilbert's activities at Goodrich, but his possession of the castle brought it within the barony he had inherited from his uncle. Besides Chepstow and Nether Gwent, this barony contained over 60 manors in England valued at £381 in Domesday terms. To this barony Stephen had added several other manors so that Goodrich came into the hands of a baron whose income was probably much more than their Domesday value of about £1,200 *per annum*. Situated on them, moreover, were 206 knights' fees (129 in England and 77 in Wales), and these and his great income made him the most powerful baron at King Stephen's court.

Goodrich and all the rest passed to Gilbert's son Richard 'Strongbow' (Fig. 3.3) after his death on the 14th of September 1148. However, with the accession of King Henry II in 1154, the Earldom of Pembroke (given by his predecessor) was, under the terms of peace made between the two factions at Westminster in the previous year, revoked, which meant that Strongbow had to exist on much reduced resources. To improve his prospects, he embarked on an invasion of Ireland in 1170 that brought him both great riches and the kingdom of Leinster (Plate 7, p.61). This was not to Henry's liking, however, and he himself over-wintered in Ireland in 1171/2

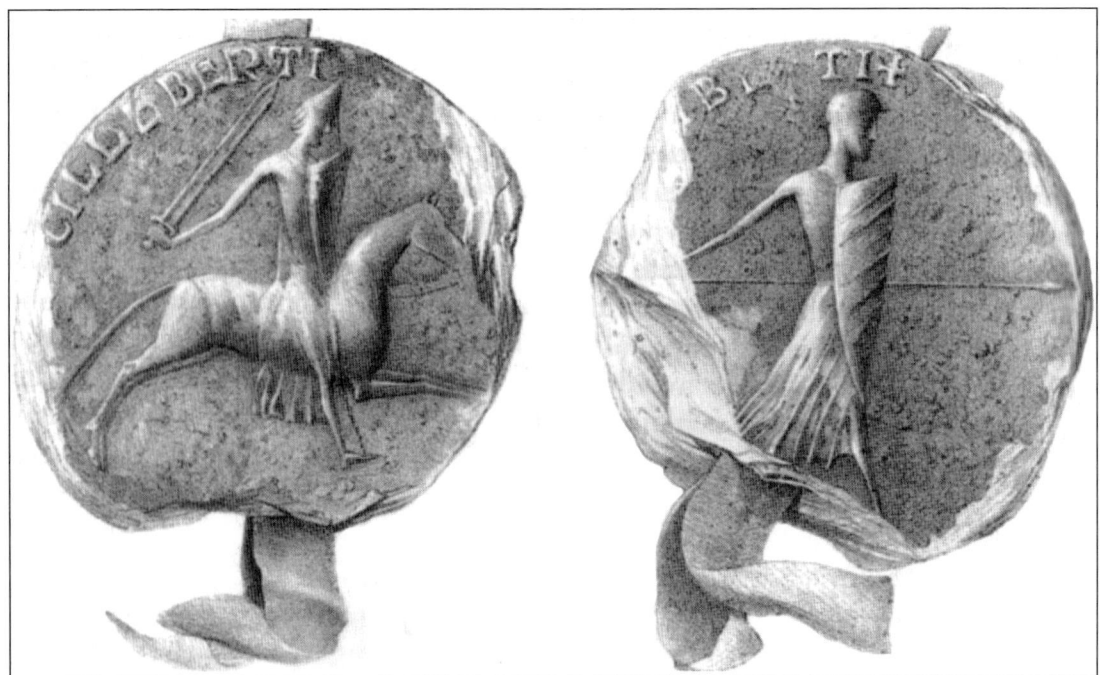

Fig. 3.3 The seal of Richard Strongbow

28

to ensure that what Strongbow had there was by his gift (one that could be revoked) and not by right of conquest.

Richard Strongbow died in Ireland at the end of May 1176 and was buried in Holy Trinity Church, Dublin (Plate 8, p.61). By his wife Eva, daughter of Dermot MacMurrough the exiled king of Leinster whom Richard restored to his throne, he left two under-age children – Isabel, born in 1172, and Gilbert, born a few years later. As Gilbert was under age, all his lands were taken into King Henry's hands. In the following year the men of *Castello Godrici* and Trewen (its outlier in Llangarron) accounted for five marks of a tax levied on lands in the king's demesnes.[15]

The Crown 1176-1204

Goodrich remained in royal hands for nearly 30 years after the death of Strongbow. This was probably because of the political situation in south Wales; for over 40 years until his death in 1197, Rhys ap Gruffudd, prince of Deheubarth, either led the Welsh of the region, or inspired them, in attempts to overcome Anglo-Norman possession of large tracts of their land. The security of the south Welsh border was frequently in danger either from him (despite a pact with Henry II that made him his justice in south Wales) or from other prominent Welshmen. Keeping hold of Goodrich may have been seen as a way of guaranteeing that security.

Gilbert, Strongbow's young son, died before reaching his majority, probably in 1185. In the following year, when the sheriff of Herefordshire answered for the judicial fines of his county, half a mark (6s 8d) each was paid by Theodoric and Juliana of Goodrich for withdrawing their pleas (subject unknown) in the county court.[16] In 1187 the 'men of Goodrich Castle' owed 40 shillings of a tax levied on lands currently in the king's hands.[17]

Christian Burials at Goodrich Castle (*by* Ron Shoesmith & Bruce Coplestone-Crow)

In 1976 part of the outer side of the castle ditch, close to the south-east corner, collapsed – it was described at the time as a landslip. Examination revealed a quantity of human bone amongst the soil and rock fragments. It was carefully collected and an analysis of the skeletal material indicated that the remains of at least three adult individuals were represented, based on the presence of three thigh bones and parts of three large skulls.[18]

In 1988 a trench for an electricity supply to the castle was dug alongside the access path, close to the top of the castle ditch.[19] It was about 0.8m deep and 0.3 to 0.6m wide. From the south-eastern corner for a distance of some 35m on the eastern side of the ditch, the excavation exposed a series of grave cuts and burials (Figs. 3.4 & 5). All the graves were orientated approximately east-west and appeared to be well arranged in rows. Altogether some 25 grave cuts were identified, but only in two or three cases were human bones exposed. Where this occurred the electricity cable was lifted slightly so that the burials remained undisturbed. Apart from occasional stones set on end, there were no traces of either stone or wooden coffins and the bodies appeared to have been laid directly into the ground. It was evident that some of the graves cut into or through earlier ones, and it was apparent from this and from the regular layout that the burial ground had been in use over a reasonably long period of time and was not the result of a single event. Due to access problems there was little time to examine the trench in any detail.

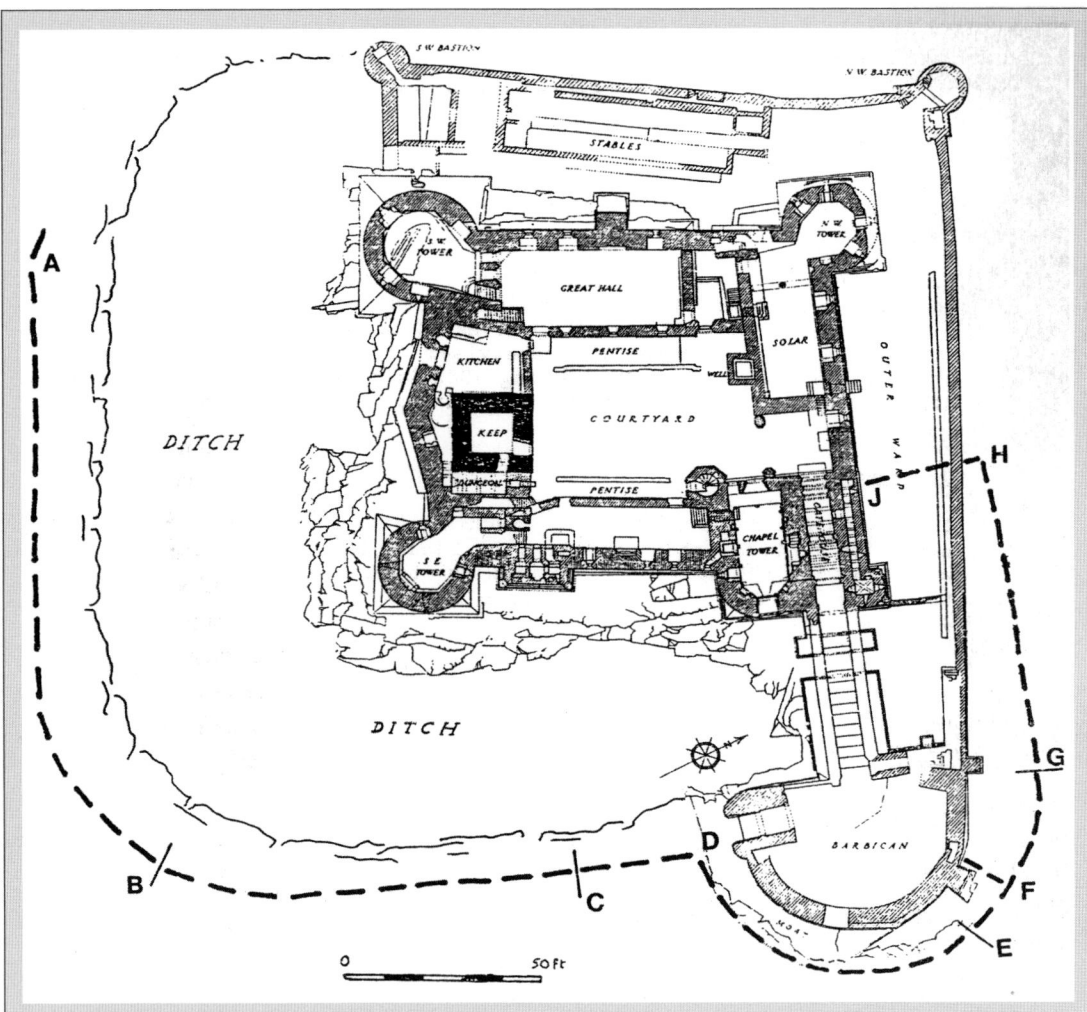

Fig. 3.4 Plan showing the line of the electricity cable trench. Grave cuts were seen between B and C. The section from C to D could not be examined

The presence of articulated leg bones, the identification of the eastern edge of several grave cuts in the side of the ditch, and the human remains from the landslip, all indicate that the burial ground extended westwards at least as far as the rock-cut ditch edge. The shallow nature of the burials may have been due to the proximity of the bedrock to the surface (as is evident in the sides of the ditch surrounding the castle), but it is also possible that the ground level in this area has been lowered at some time in the past. Samples from the right femurs of three different individuals from the bones collected after the 1976 landslip were sent for radio-carbon dating. The 2013 report concluded that:

> … they could have died at the same time or within a relatively short period of each other, most probably in the late twelfth or early thirteenth centuries cal AD.

Building a castle on the site of a pre-existing burial ground and probable church may seem a little odd (not to say sacrilegious) to modern eyes, but it was often done by the Normans and their Anglo-Norman heirs in Britain. The royal castles at Lincoln, Oxford and Cambridge were built on such sites soon after the Conquest and there were certainly many others. Some of these churches may have become the private chapel of the king or new lord, but most seem to have retained their former parish use.

Fig. 3.5 Part of one of the burials exposed within the electricity cable trench

To a certain extent, it is not surprising that this should have happened during the initial stages of conquest and subjugation. After all, what better temporary fortress could there be in a land virtually without castles than an unroofed (to reduce fire-risk) and barricaded stone-built church? Use of it would then continue until a more permanent earth and timber castle could be built, as close as possible for the sake of security. Two generations after the Conquest the lord of Wigmore in Herefordshire was being 'exhorted and counselled' by his friends not to allow the completion of a church being built at the entrance to his lands '… in case his enemies should make inroads into his territory and find there a refuge and stronghold in spite of him …'.[20] At Earl's Barton in Northamptonshire, where an Anglo-Saxon church and cemetery stands on the end of a promontory of land, a ditch was dug across the promontory and a motte ('Berry Mount') thrown up in the graveyard between the church and the ditch. The prominent west tower of the church, which still stands, probably acted as an additional strongpoint, and burials continued there into the modern era.[21] The bailey of the Norman castle at Hereford contained the Old English church of St Guthlac and its burial ground. When the castle was besieged in 1140 a ditch was dug through the cemetery that disturbed the rotting corpses of many recently buried townsmen. The priory church and its burial ground was later moved outside the walls of Hereford.[22] Recent excavations at Narberth in Pembrokeshire have shown that the outer bailey of the castle included part of a pre-existing cemetery.[23] As Narberth was the site of one of the 'chief courts' of Dyfed in the early middle ages it is likely that this cemetery surrounded a church. Finally, but by no means exclusively, at Trowbridge in Wiltshire the Norman castle included a late-10th-century two-cell church and its burial ground within its inner bailey. Both church and graveyard continued in use, some of the later burials being placed close to the foot of the motte. Burial ceased there when the church was put to secular use in the early 13th century.

As burials continued to be made in the Goodrich Castle graveyard into the 13th century, this probably means that the church they were associated with continued to be the parish church of the people of Goodrich (as, indeed, it had been for centuries past). There is no suggestion that the 'church of St Giles of Goodrich Castle' mentioned in 1144[24] was ever a private chapel. The same thing seems to have happened at Narberth, where burials stopped when the castle was rebuilt by Robert III de Mortimer (1247-82) and a new parish church was provided on a hill opposite the castle. Mortimer held Narberth under William de Valence as lord of Pembroke when the latter was rebuilding Goodrich Castle. There are certain similarities in the way the two castles were rebuilt, although only Valence had the income to do the vast work at Goodrich. It is possible that the same thing happened at Goodrich as at Narberth for nothing in the present church of St Giles, built on a hill opposite the castle, predates the mid-13th century.[25]

The number of intercutting burials found at Goodrich indicate that the cemetery was in use over a considerable period of time, perhaps going back to King Constantine's day (see pages 10-12). Its full extent is unknown, but it seems to have been confined on the east by the banks and ditches of the Iron Age fort. Refurbished for the purpose, one or other of these defences may therefore have formed the *vallum monasterium* of the monastery, marking the division between the sacred and the profane worlds.

4 WILLIAM MARSHAL, EARL OF PEMBROKE, & HIS SONS (1204-45)
by Bruce Coplestone-Crow

William Marshal, Earl of Pembroke (1204-19)
William was a younger son of a Berkshire knight who gained fame and fortune on the tournament circuit in France and through conspicuous loyalty to the kings of England. Marshal stood steadfastly beside Henry II through the various revolts of the royal sons against their father who had promised him a marriage to Isabel, Strongbow's young heiress. However Henry died in July 1189 before it could be arranged. Nevertheless, Richard I allowed the marriage to go ahead and William and Isabel were wed before July was out. Through his wife he now acquired the lordship of Chepstow and a claim to the earldom of Pembroke her father had lost in 1154. This earldom was eventually granted to him by King John immediately on his accession to the throne in succession to his brother Richard in 1199. With his wife he also had a claim to the kingdom of Leinster in Ireland (which was not realised until 1199) and acquired a part share of the Giffard barony in England and Normandy, the latter including the important and valuable castle of Longueville in the Pays de Caux. Thus, when Philip Augustus, king of France, completed his conquest of Normandy from John early in 1204 William was among the many Anglo-Norman lords with lands on both sides of the Channel who stood to lose their English (and Welsh) possessions to John if they chose to remain in Normandy and so become a subject of the French king. Conversely, if they chose to remain loyal to John, they would lose their Norman holdings. Since William chose to stand by John, Longueville was to all intents and purposes lost to him early in 1204 and it is against this background that we must view the English king's grant to him of Goodrich – probably as some form of compensation for this loss. In the event, so high was the regard in which Marshal was held by King John that he allowed him to negotiate a private treaty with Philip Augustus that saw him retain his hold on Longueville and the rest of his Norman possessions. This was in the future, however, and for the present John's grant of Goodrich to William on 1st April 1204 was in the following terms:

> Be it known to all men that we have given and by this charter conferred on our beloved and faithful William Marshal, earl of Pembroke, Goodrich Castle, together with all the rights appurtenant to it, to have and to hold to us and our heirs by him and his heirs in fee and inheritance, by rendering to us the service of two knights for all services. On which

account we will that the said earl and his heirs shall have and hold the said castle and all its appurtenances, well and in peace, free and quit, whole and complete, in wood and in field, ways and footpaths, meadows and pastures, water and mills, fishponds and fisheries, in moor and marsh, with all liberties and free customs appurtenant to that castle, by the said service. Dated by the hand of Simon the priest, at Marlborough, 1 April in the fifth year of our reign.[1]

Although the grant does not mention it by name, Trewen (the manor's outlier in Llangarron) was certainly included in the gift, for in 1212 it was stated specifically that William Marshal had Goodrich and Trewen by gift of King John.[2] Later in 1204 the earl was granted a weekly market on Thursdays at Goodrich, and in 1211 he paid scutage[3] on the two knights' fees he had there.[4] The gift should not be seen in isolation, however, as Richard I had already given him the keeping of the Forest of Dean (with its castle of St Briavel's)[5] and the office of sheriff of Gloucester, the boundaries of both Forest and county coming up to the Wye close to Goodrich. The Forest of Dean had long been noted for its iron-working industry and there can be little doubt that, once it was in his hands, Earl William exploited this resource to his own material and financial gain (see Chapter 6).

Goodrich Castle came under attack during the war between King John and his barons, Pembroke's loyalty to John making it a prime target for the rebels. The attack came shortly after the king died on the 19th of October 1216, and was probably made by Llywelyn Fawr, Prince of Gwynedd, and his son-in-law, Reginald de Braose, Lord of Brecon and one of the rebel barons.[6] King John had left Henry, a nine-year-old boy, as his heir, and on the 28th of October the young boy and Marshal were at Gloucester for his coronation (London being in the hands of the rebel barons and their French allies). As Marshal was about to take his seat at the coronation feast, a messenger from his constable at Goodrich burst into the hall and announced before all present that the castle was under siege and that his help was needed to repel his foes. Marshal quietly despatched a relieving force before sitting down to get on with the celebrations.[7] Later in the year he assumed the regency of England on behalf of the young king. He was at Goodrich Castle on the 4th and 5th of July 1217, whilst campaigning against the last remnants of the insurgency in south Wales, from where he sent letters to the sheriff of Nottingham and Thomas of Gravenall.[8]

As earl of a large lordship at Pembroke – in the march of Wales and so an area where he could exercise all the rights of an independent sovereign – Marshal was well aware of the financial advantages that flowed from its location beyond the reach of the English king's writ. It comes as little surprise, therefore, to learn that while in charge at Goodrich he took active steps to withdraw both Goodrich and Trewen from the royal hundred of Wormelow (or Archenfield) to which they belonged. By 1221 the jurors of that hundred were able to claim that Trewen 'belonging to the Earl Marshal' had once performed its services at their hundred-court, but that they were now withheld, and if Trewen had thus been moved beyond the king's writ it would appear certain that Goodrich itself had also been removed.[9] The wood of Doward (in Ganarew and Whitchurch) was also in the lordship of Goodrich later in the 13th century and this can again probably be put down to the earl.[10] The result of this policy was that in 1245 the manor of Goodrich Castle was said to be, quite simply, 'in Wales'.[11] William de Valence, who later held the Goodrich estate, was twice called upon to explain to Edward I and to his justices the liberties he claimed at Goodrich (though no curbing of his powers was attempted). Great man though he undoubtedly was, William Marshal was not above feathering his own nest. Some or all of the extra income that these actions gave him was probably put to use on the structure of Goodrich Castle. It goes without saying that the crown never accepted the situation at Goodrich and, in general, the perception of the position depended very much on the status of its holder and the strength of the royal administration.

Besides expanding and consolidating what he held at Goodrich, it was probably William Marshal who provided the castle with an honour or barony owing its feudal services there. This he did by re-assigning to it certain castle-guard services originally due at Chepstow Castle, whose own barony owed the service of over 65 knights' fees to the crown. These Chepstow knights were well familiar with the needs of a castle on the Welsh border and, of those that fitted the bill, Marshal chose men who had a personal connection with Goodrich. It was a relatively small barony, consisting of about nine knights' fees, but, if the usual period of 40 days free castle-guard service was observed, it was sufficient to provide one knight at the castle for nearly every day of the year free of charge. If the knight was required for longer, William would, of course, pay him at the going daily rate. With the constable of the castle, this knight would lead a largely non-feudal garrison paid from the Marshal's own resources and probably consisting of a mixed force of sergeants (men-at-arms) and archers. The feudal knight, with his expensive-to-maintain horse and armour, was by this time more of a liability than an asset in castle-guard service.

The earliest record of this barony is in the 1324 *inquisition post mortem* on Aymer de Valence, Earl of Pembroke, when it was said that there were eight and a half knights' fees held as of the castle of Goodrich.[12] This *inquisition*, together with earlier evidence, shows that these knights' fees were based on lands in Bedfordshire, Gloucestershire, Hampshire and Hertfordshire, and possibly lands at Llanwern in the lordship of Chepstow. Although Llanwern was not formally added to the barony until 1247, long after Marshal's death, there may have been an informal association between Llanwern and Goodrich dating from his day.

William Marshal, Earl of Pembroke and Regent of England, died on the 14th of May 1219 and was buried in the Temple Church at London, where his effigy still remains. His heirs were his five sons.

The Sons of William Marshal (1219-45)
On the great earl's death all his possessions in England, Wales, Ireland and Normandy passed to his eldest son, William (William II) Marshal, although under the terms of his will his other sons (Richard, Gilbert, Walter and Anselm) were to hold various parts of the inheritance from William II. Goodrich was the share of Walter, the second youngest, who was under age and in the care of the king. Thus, on the 4th of August 1219, the king was able to instruct his sheriff to carry a tun of wine (252 gallons) 'found on the land of Walter Marshal at Goodrich' to the royal cellars at Hereford.[13] William II died without issue on the 6th of April 1231 and his lands and titles were given to his brother Richard, although Goodrich remained in royal hands because Walter was still under age. William II's revenues have been estimated to have been in the order of £3,500 *per annum,* half of it coming from his lordship of Leinster. This placed him among the half-dozen wealthiest men in the kingdom.

Goodrich was eventually conveyed to Walter on the 11th of July 1231, but the keeping of it was still in the hands of John of Monmouth, the royal agent in south Wales, in the following year.[14] In September 1233 Walter joined the rebellion of his brother, Earl Richard, against King Henry III and the foreign favourites at his court. Henry brought an army into south Wales while, at the same time, Goodrich was besieged by forces under the leadership of the sheriff of Herefordshire and Emery de St Amand (constable of St Briavel's Castle and warden of the Forest of Dean). By the 4th of November the garrison had negotiated a truce and had given hostages for their future good behaviour. On the same day the sheriff, who had placed his own men in the castle, was instructed to let John of Monmouth have it and its two hamlets of Huntsham and Trewen.[15] A week later Earl Richard forced the king to retire from Grosmont, after raiding his camp at dawn. On the 12th of November Nicholas de Molis was told to restore to the men of Goodrich Castle the oats and fodder taken from them for the munitioning of St Briavel's Castle, since this had occurred after they had made a truce with Emery.[16] The revolt ended when Earl Richard died in Ireland in April 1234. On the 31st of May John of Monmouth was mandated to deliver the castle to Walter Marshal, the king having received him into grace and restored to him the lands taken while in rebellion.[17]

With the death of Earl Richard without direct heirs, the Marshal inheritance passed to his brother Gilbert, who died in 1241 (he fell from his horse in a tournament and was dragged to his death by a stirrup), also without direct heirs. The legacy now devolved on Walter Marshal, lord of Goodrich. He died at Goodrich on the 24th of November 1245 and on the 3rd of December the constable was told to hold the castle for the king until Anselm, the fifth and last brother, came to do homage.[18] Anselm, however, died on the 22nd of December and immediately afterwards Emery de Chanceaux, sheriff of Herefordshire, took Goodrich into the king's hands and appointed Robert of Boulsdon as his bailiff. Robert valued his bailiwick of Goodrich at £10 *per annum*.[19]

John de Mountchesney (1246-47)

With the death of the last of the five brothers, the Marshal inheritance was divided between their five sisters and their husbands. In the final division, made in July 1246, Goodrich Castle was assigned to John de Mountchesney, the son of Joan (one of the sisters) and Warin de Mountchesney of Swanscombe in Kent. At the point when John was to receive them, Goodrich and its appurtenances were valued at £57 10s 6d yearly, plus 20 marks (£13 13s 4d) for the right to appoint priests to the churches of Goodrich and Whitchurch.[20] However, in 1247 John died childless before taking possession of Goodrich, leaving his sister, Joan, called Countess of Pembroke, as his heir. On the 31st of July 1247, the king wrote to Robert Walerand, keeper of Goodrich, instructing him to deliver the castle to William de Valence, half-brother to King Henry, then aged somewhere between 16 and 19 and, within a few days of this, Valence married Joan de Mountchesney. Against the conventions of the time, perhaps, this proved to be a love-match. In December the king told the sheriff of Herefordshire to let de Valence have the revenues and profits arising from Goodrich Castle for the period since he had given the castle to his half-brother.[21]

5   THE VALENCES (1247-1324) & THEIR HEIRS (1324-27)

by Bruce Coplestone-Crow

William de Valence (1247-96)
William was the fourth son of Hugh, count of La Marche and Angoulême and lord of Lusignan, by Isabel, daughter of Count Aymer of Angoulême, widow of King John and mother of Henry III. He was thus a half brother of Henry III and at the king's invitation came to England in 1247 where he was laden with lands and revenues, with promises of more to come. In fact, by the time he was obliged to quit England for the Continent in 1258 for refusing to submit to the Provisions of Oxford (an attempt to control the king's actions), he was among the wealthiest men in the kingdom. He returned early in 1261 and in April was readmitted to the king's peace and full restitution made of his lands.[1] However, after the king's defeat by Simon de Montfort at the battle of Lewes in 1264, he again fled to the Continent and the victorious Earl of Leicester gave the castle and manor of Goodrich to Humphrey de Bohun junior.[2] In May of the following year de Valence landed in Pembroke (which he had in his hands via his wife) and went on to assist in the defeat of de Montfort at Evesham on the 4th of August 1265. Humphrey de Bohun junior died of wounds sustained in that battle and Goodrich was returned to William de Valence. A change came over him after the events of that year so that, whereas:

> Before this date he had done little of value in England; he had taken all from his adopted country and shown the utmost ingratitude for the gifts [made to him by the king]. But after 1265 William became far more lawful in his ways, and in later years served Edward I and England faithfully at home, in Wales and in France.[3]

William de Valence bought the manor of Moreton Valence near Gloucester from William de Pont l'Arche in 1252, perhaps with a view to it taking any overflow of people and horses from Goodrich, where he may already have begun rebuilding the castle. In the same year he obtained oaks from the Forest of Dean for building a new hall at Moreton and for repairing its mill.[4] On his return from exile in 1261 he had 15 oaks from Dean specifically 'for the work on Goodrich Castle'.[5] This was followed in April 1266 with a further 10 oaks for the same purpose, but after this there seems to have been a break in building activity of nearly nine years, for three of which he was in the Holy Land with Prince Edward. In 1275 he was granted 12 oaks from Dean followed by another 12 in 1277,[6] two in 1280 (when Robert Cockerel was constable of Goodrich Castle) and six in 1282.[7] There was then a break of 10 years, before further oaks were granted, six being given in 1292. In the following year 12 were given specifically for the repair of the castle.[8]

In all William de Valence obtained 100 or so oaks, the majority from the Forest of Dean, presumably for the building or repairing of Goodrich Castle. Doubtless, the increasing power of Llywelyn ap Gruffudd in Wales was the initial reason for commencing reconstruction works at the castle, and it is perhaps significant that few oaks were provided after Edward I's final conquest of Wales in 1283. On the basis of the number of oaks required, it would seem that the castle was radically transformed between 1261 and 1282.

The revenues William had at his disposal with which he could fund the rebuilding of Goodrich Castle were considerable, though not as extensive as some barons on his social level. Through his wife he had one fifth of the revenues of the Marshal earldom of Pembroke, which was about £700 *per annum*. In 1247 King Henry granted him a double-fee of 500 marks (£333 6s 8d) annually for life, and, at a later date, £500 *per annum* for life. His total revenues were estimated to be about £2,500 yearly in 1272.[9] This had to cover the administration and upkeep of all his manors, payments to local officials, the expenses of household officials when he was away, and many other items.[10] The money he had available for work at Goodrich was, therefore, considerably less than £2,500 – and well below the income of his Marshal predecessors.

Hand-in-hand with the rebuilding of the castle, William strove to keep the lordship of Goodrich within the March of Wales, where he could have the full judicial and financial rights that had been enjoyed by his Marshal predecessors. In 1292 William had to explain why, 20 years previously, he had withdrawn the services of 'five men of Goodrich Castle [who] used to go in the king's army for 15 days at their own cost' and also a man to attend the hundred court of Wormelow.[11] In 1276 it was said that William's bailiffs at Goodrich Castle would not permit the king's bailiffs to execute their office there. In 1282, when a case arose in Gloucestershire concerning the theft of money by one John Crump (who was held in the prison at Goodrich Castle on that charge), the king's justice could only go to a spot 'near the said liberty [of William de Valence] within the king's jurisdiction' to have the case heard, and then only by a jury summoned by the bailiff of Goodrich. If, however, Crump was to be found guilty by that jury he was to be handed over to the bailiff for hanging 'as justice requires'.[12]

As a man claiming all royal rights within his liberty of Goodrich, William de Valence fell foul of proceedings which were designed to discover which of the crown rights had been usurped by barons and 'by what warrant'. When neither William nor Joan his wife appeared at Hereford in 1292 to answer the plea, (as he did not regard Goodrich as being part of the kingdom of England, de Valence felt no need to receive the king's writ and, not having received it, did not feel answerable) order was given to take their 'liberty' into the king's hand. However, in August the sheriff was ordered to return Goodrich Castle to de Valence, and no more is heard of the plea.[13]

In 1277 de Valence played an important role in Edward's invasion of Wales, being joint leader with Edmund (the king's brother) of the army that set out from Pembroke to reach Aberystwyth on the 25th of July. There de Valence was responsible for building the castle and town wall, spending over £1,600 in all (Fig. 5.1).[14] Experience he had already gained in rebuilding Goodrich Castle probably recommended him for this task. In Edward's second and final invasion of Wales in 1282 he was again established at Aberystwyth. The castle had

Fig. 5.1 The remaining part of a mural tower at Aberystwyth Castle

cost about £3,900 when finally completed in 1289. An uprising in south Wales in 1287 resulted in the bailiffs at Goodrich Castle being told to assemble William's horse and foot at Monmouth on the 28th of July for service in south Wales.[15] Another rebellion in 1294-5 saw him again serving in person in Wales, but by then he was an old man. He went to France on the king's behalf early in 1296, but died at his manor of Brabourne in Kent on the 16th of May and was buried in Westminster Abbey (Fig. 5.2).

His lands at Goodrich Castle in Archenfield were reviewed and valued in the castle on the 29th of June. The valuation found that his estate consisted of the castle with a garden, dovecot, mill and vinery; arable, meadow and pasture land; various rents, a market, and a fishery. The whole was worth £28 10s annually and was held from the king for the service of two knights' fees. His heir was his son Aymer.[16]

Further building work was being carried out at Goodrich Castle at the king's expense soon after William's death. This was probably a result of the 1294-5 rebellion of Madog ap Llywelyn, which saw several bands of marauding Welshmen roaming the Wye Valley.[17] At the end of May 1296 the king paid for clerks and workmen to be accommodated at Marstow, within the lordship of Goodrich,[18] and it is possible that these men were making repairs to the castle following an attack by these warring bands. The work seems to have been completed by his widow, Joan, after she took up residence at the castle probably in November 1296. She was aged about 60 when her husband died.

Fig 5.2 Tomb of William de Valence in Westminster Abbey

Joan de Valence, Countess of Pembroke (1296-1307) (see also Chapter 19)
The dower of Joan de Valence, Countess of Pembroke, consisted of the castle of Goodrich (with 'all the lands that [her husband] acquired in the manor of Goodrich Castle'), the lordships of Pembroke and Wexford, and several manors in England. There was considerable wrangling over the English manors that had been assigned to her as dower, but her son seems not to have objected to her having his father's rebuilt castle at Goodrich.[19]

She was at Goodrich on several occasions during her widowhood, but extensive details of these have survived in her Household Roll for the year from Michaelmas 1296 to Michaelmas 1297.[20] The Roll shows that she was at Goodrich from Sunday the 18th of November 1296 until Wednesday the 8th of May 1297, but as the accounts relate to her travelling household and not to the household of Goodrich, they give little information about the structure and manning of the castle after the great rebuilding by her husband.

On arrival at the castle she ordered half a hogshead of wine (about 25 gallons), half a pig and five sides of pork to be brought from the castle's store for herself and her household. On the following day she was approached by the reeve of the village of Goodrich with a gift of eight fresh salmon. Her household consisted of her gentlewomen, Beatrice de Valence (the wife of her son Aymer) and Mary, an unnamed steward (who kept the accounts), Edward Burnel (her clerk of the chapel), Humphrey (her chamberlain), John (of the Wardrobe), an unnamed laundress, John of Wendogeda (her butler), John Cely (the pantler), Druet (the doctor), Roger (the cook), Walter (the farrier), John (the baker), Isaac (the larderer), Ralph (the saucerer), Walter (her usher, possibly Walter Gatelyn, a native of Goodrich),[21] Simon (the doorkeeper), John (the groom), Hamon and Davy (her coachmen), and Aymer Walters (the carter). Looking after her spiritual needs was Dom Thomas (her chaplain), who had under him three clerks. Also part of Joan's household were William de Mountchesney, a relation of hers who was probably a squire, and Busser (or Boucher) the messenger. The lady Beatrice also had a small household to look after her needs.

The countess's upper household, therefore, consisted of some 30 people, many of whom would have had their families with them. In addition there was a lower household of about 15 pages, valets and grooms to wait on her and to look after the horses. All these people are in

Fig 5.3 A drawing from the Luttrell Psalter of the type of waggon that Joan de Valence might have used to travel between London and Goodrich

addition to any laundresses, cooks, farriers, bakers, clerks and such like who were either already at the castle or came from the neighbouring district. About 30 horses were normally stabled at Goodrich, with a similar number at Moreton, although this number more than doubled when her son Aymer came to visit. Thus on Easter Day there were 62 horses at Goodrich alone. A Dom Clement, who is occasionally mentioned, may have been the castle's own chaplain. In 1306 she presented Matthew of Tibberton, a priest, to the living of Goodrich Castle.[22]

Once installed at Goodrich, her household quickly organized the supply of its everyday needs. The provision of food and drink for herself, her household and her visitors was an enormous logistical task for her steward, butler and pantler. Food was either bought in or provided from one of three principal stores – the travelling store, a store at Moreton Valence, and a much less important store at the castle. From the latter came wine (the daily consumption averaged about 25 gallons, corn (for baking), oats, bacon, mutton, salmon, lampreys, a ray-fish, peacocks, fowls, beef and geese.

After about the middle of March, when stored hay ran out, this was regularly purchased from Huntsham. Litter for the animals came from the bishop's manor of Walford, just across the river. 'Confectionery' and candles were bought at Hereford, while from Gloucester, Chepstow and Southampton came some of the 13,300 herrings eaten during Lent. Beer was regularly bought at Monmouth even though the Goodrich brewery produced 400 gallons at a time – the daily consumption being about 60 gallons.

Transporting a 'pipe' of wine (about 100 gallons costing £3 6s 8d) bought at Bristol posed a considerable problem. John, the butler, was sent to fetch it and received 2d daily for his trouble. The hire of a boat for 11 days to bring the wine from Bristol to Monmouth cost 4s. Thereafter, to cut out the time-consuming bends of the Wye, it was brought by road to Goodrich by Joan's own transport.

Whilst at Goodrich Joan received a steady stream of visitors. The most important was her son Aymer, who was there in December 1296 and the following Easter. Joan also received Gilbert of Clare (the son and heir of Gilbert IV of Clare, Earl of Gloucester) who was then only five or six years old. Gilbert came on the 4th of February and two days later he was joined by his mother, Countess Joan of Acre, a daughter of Edward I, and both stayed for several days. Robert III de Vere (who had just succeeded his father as Earl of Oxford) came to dinner in April, to perform homage for lands he held of Joan.

Joan's friends from the district – Matilda de Grandison (prioress of Aconbury), Lady Bluet of Raglan, Lady Cecilia de Mucegros of English Bicknor, and Thomas of Berkeley – visited on numerous occasions. On one occasion the prioress brought Lord John of Barry, who held the lordship of Manorbier in Pembrokeshire from Joan. John of Hastings, her son-in-law, came with Aymer at Easter, together with Roger of Inkpen, a knight who served both Joan and her son.

Visitors who were associated with Joan in Pembroke included Sir Thomas de la Roche, who held the barony of Roche, and Sir Thomas de Braybeof. Richard Symonds of Simpson in the barony of Roche 'and others of the county of Pembroke' came late in April to escort Joan from Goodrich towards London on the 8th of May.

The total number of people resident at the castle at any one time during Joan's stay is difficult to estimate. This is because although the names of the most important visitors are known, they often came with all or part of their own households. However, if the doubling of the number of horses stabled at the castle during Easter is anything to go by, then it can be assumed that her guests would have at least doubled the number of people present to around 80. Assuming that Joan's upper and lower household, with their dependants, totalled approximately the same, this would suggest that there could well have been in excess of 150 people at the castle on Easter Day. It is unlikely that all these people were housed within the castle buildings and many (especially the lower orders) must have lived in temporary wooden huts and tents. The feast provided on that day was indeed enormous, consisting of one and a half beef cattle, three pigs, half a boar, half a salmon, mutton, kid goats, nine bucks, two calves, 17 capons and hens, 24 pigeons, cheeses and 500 eggs. The Christmas Day meal was slightly smaller – one and a half beef cattle, two pigs, 12 ducks, 18 pullets, two peacocks, cheeses and eggs, plus fish for 'Aymer and the priest'.

Joan was at Goodrich during the coldest season of the year, so vast quantities of firewood had to be supplied. By early December there had been 17 days wood-cutting in Bishop's Wood at Walford (where there were 10 woodcutters and 15 horses and grooms for transport), and six days in Lady's Wood at the Doward (involving seven wood-cutters and 38 grooms with their horses). A week later 60 horses were carrying firewood cut at Doward and 18 horses and a boat were transporting firewood from Bishop's Wood.

The lady Joan's normal daily routine seems to have been to tend to her business in her chamber and then to go out riding, either on horseback or in her coach. A new carriage had been bought in London in October and there are frequent records of repairs to it and its horses' harnesses, suggesting that it was well used. She made a daily provision of dole or food for at least 20 paupers, and on the Feast of St Catherine she catered for 61 paupers. In addition, four gifts of food or money were made to the Carmelite friars at Gloucester.

Her business affairs and correspondence kept her messenger, Busser, and other staff constantly busy. A selection of these activities gives an impression of her position at Goodrich and her involvement both locally and nationally. Letters were sent to the sheriffs of Hereford and Gloucester, while others were concerned with the distraint placed on her manors during her dispute with her son as to precisely which manors she should have as her dower.

The bailiffs and others at her manors in England regularly received communications from her. During December letters were sent on a regular basis to London, and to Sutton Valence in Kent (a 12-day return journey), and many times to Moreton Valence where Walter the farrier was looking after his mistress's horse. In April, John of the Wardrobe went to Bristol to purchase white vestments for the countess and her household against the coming of Pentecost.

Her men of the county of Pembroke received more correspondence than anyone else. There was a flurry of letters in March (when Busser took eight days to get to Pembroke), and on the 9th of April a letter was sent to summon Richard Symonds 'and others' to escort her to London. A letter to her Westminster house on the 2nd of May was 'to make provision against the arrival of the mistress there'. Three days later a barrel was bought to carry lampreys to London, and on the 8th of May she left the castle to head to the capital.

Joan's expenditure for 1296/7 was just over £413, but this was purely for her travelling household. It does not include any costs arising from the permanent staff at her various castles, lordships and manors, or any capital costs. Her widow's one-third of her husband's income should have given her about £800 annually, the remainder of which was presumably spent on her permanent households.

Joan de Valence died in September 1307, aged about 70. Her *inquisition post mortem* showed that she held Goodrich Castle and other separate houses with gardens, arable land for growing rye, four acres of meadow, rent of 36 free tenants and nine customary tenants, a watermill, a fishery, and pannage for pigs. The whole was worth £13 10s annually and she held them of the king, her heir being her son Aymer, said to be 36 years of age.[23] Since her husband's death 11 years previously there had been a decline in the value of Goodrich of just under 52% (from £28 10s to £13 10s). This was on top of the decline of 50% during William's own tenure of the castle and manor (from £57 in 1245 to £28 10s in 1296).[24] William's rebuilding of the castle evidently caused overuse of the estates resources in his day, but under his widow the likelihood is that her expenditure exceeded her income, causing it to decline further.

Aymer de Valence, Earl of Pembroke (1307-24)

On the death of his mother Aymer assumed the title of Earl of Pembroke in her right.[25] As he was constantly in the service of the crown and moved in the very highest circles at home and abroad, he had little time for his English lands, and this shows in the paucity of records of his dealings with Goodrich. Although he frequently visited his mother there, there is little to show that he ever visited afterwards. However, on the 27th of February 1320, having received a complaint from Adam of Orleton, Bishop of Hereford, he wrote from London to John of Sutton, his constable at Goodrich, instructing him not to cut more firewood in the Bishop's Wood across the Wye than was allowed by ancestral custom.[26]

Aymer died in France on the 23rd of June 1324. As he had no living issue his inheritance devolved on his two nieces, Joan and Elizabeth, daughters of his sister Isabel by John Comyn – the 'Red Comyn' who had famously been murdered by Robert the Bruce before the altar of the Greyfriars Church in Dumfries in 1306. The title of Earl of Pembroke died with Aymer. The *inquisition post mortem* on his lands at Goodrich is illegible,[27] but when the estate was made over to Elizabeth Comyn in 1325 it was said to be worth £41 1s, a big increase on the figure for 1307. Nevertheless, it represented only about 5% of the total value of Aymer's lands, which have been estimated to be worth about £3,000 *per annum*.[28]

The Heirs of Aymer de Valence (1324-7)

As Elizabeth Comyn was fatherless and unmarried at her uncle's death, she became a ward of the king. At the end of 1324 King Edward II gave her guardianship to his favourites, Hugh Despenser the Elder and Hugh Despenser the Younger (father and son),[29] who attempted to force money and also lands (including Goodrich) from her. They were partly successful in this in regard to Goodrich, such land grabs being part of Hugh Despenser the Younger's policy of consolidation of his already enormous landholdings in Wales and the Marches. The Despensers' triumph was short-lived, for in September 1326 Edward II's estranged queen, Isabella, and her paramour, Roger de Mortimer, seized control of England. The hated Despensers were swiftly captured and executed, Hugh Despenser the Younger being hung, drawn and quartered on a 50 feet high scaffold outside Hereford Castle.

In the confusion attending the downfall of the Despensers, Richard, 2nd lord Talbot, son of Gilbert, 1st lord Talbot of Eccleswall in Herefordshire, married Elizabeth Comyn and seized the castle (where they found some of the Despensers' possessions)[30] in her name.[31] There is a romantic story that Richard had heard of her predicament under the Despensers and, taking an armed band, rescued her from their manor of Pirbright.[32] This could be true, but there is no supporting evidence. It is perhaps more likely that he had gathered a band of men for the seizure of Goodrich Castle in her name, since it was said many years later that he and his wife had 'entered upon the castle' while the Despensers were still alive.[33]

6   THE TALBOTS, EARLS OF SHREWSBURY (1327-1590)

by Bruce Coplestone-Crow & Pat Hughes

From 1327 to 1473 (*by* Bruce Coplestone-Crow)

Richard, 2nd Lord Talbot (1327-56) and Elizabeth, his wife (1356-72)

Though their occupation of Goodrich had been somewhat irregular, Richard and Elizabeth's position there seems to have been recognized by the new administration of Edward III and in March 1336 the king issued letters patent annulling what had passed between Elizabeth and the Despensers.[1]

In 1338 Richard took the first steps towards the founding of a college or priory of secular canons at Goodrich. In July he had a licence to grant various lands and buildings to certain chaplains just appointed to celebrate divine service within the liberty of the castle.[2] Such foundations were an essential element of the greatest late medieval castles,[3] their purpose being to pray for the souls of their founder, his ancestors and successors. The earliest was at Kenilworth, licensed by the pope in 1318.[4] The greatest was St George's Chapel, Windsor, founded by Edward III in 1348.

These chaplains or canons were given the chapel of the castle as their church and Richard evidently intended them to be a permanent feature. He may, in fact, have seen their presence as a revival of the traditions of an earlier church (King Constantine's church) that may have been on the castle site. Stairs which were inserted in the thickness of the north wall of the chapel led to a gallery from which a doorway in the west wall provided access to a first-floor room above the extended gate passage, possibly for use as a dormitory (see Chapter 16). The eastern two-thirds of the chapel were screened off for use as a priory church and altars were set against the screen to serve the people of the castle in the remainder of the chapel.

However, it must soon have become clear that life in a castle was unsuitable for members of an ecclesiastical house. This had been demonstrated long before at Salisbury in 1220, when the cathedral, hitherto in the outer bailey of Old Sarum Castle, was moved to its present site, the chapter citing the fact that they were dominated and oppressed by the castellan and soldiers and that they could not go in and out without the castellan's permission.[5] A more extreme case concerned the priory church of St Guthlac, which stood in the bailey of Hereford Castle. When the castle was besieged in 1140, its graveyard was dug up (recently buried and rotting corpses notwithstanding) and its church polluted with blood, resulting in the priory being moved to a new site outside the walls of the city.[6]

Fig. 6.1 Flanesford Priory in 1798 (Bonner)

If Richard was receiving similar complaints from his canons to those voiced by the clergy at Old Sarum, then the profits he was making in the king's wars in France enabled him to move them out of the castle. In 1342 Richard captured one Geoffrey de Charney in France and sent him to Goodrich Castle for imprisonment.[7] Charney was released after paying a ransom, and later in that year Richard founded and endowed a priory at Flanesford 'with a church and diverse offices for a prior and several canons'[8] (Fig. 6.1). His foundation charter was probably issued at this time.[9] In 1343 the pope appropriated the church of Westbury-on-Severn 'to the priory of Flanesford [Richard] has founded in the diocese of Hereford'.[10] Even so, it seems that a grant of the hundred of Archenfield and the manor of Wormelow, including all the revenues and profits the king had there,[11] was required before Richard was sufficiently confident of his revenues to seek the royal licence. This came in December 1346, although the foundation stone had been laid and the first prior installed in October.[12]

The grant of Archenfield and Wormelow greatly enhanced Richard's power and influence in southern Herefordshire. All the rights he and his predecessors had exercised (or claimed to exercise) in the lordship and manor of Goodrich were now extended to cover the whole of Archenfield. With this much greater area in which to exercise his rights, Richard needed a gaol, and a licence to build one at Goodrich Castle was duly given on the 6th of September 1348.[13]

Richard died on the 23rd of October 1356 and was buried at Flanesford Priory. His *inquisition post mortem* showed that he held the manor of Goodrich Castle jointly with his wife and this was valued at £13 6s 8d. He also had the manor of Wormelow and hundred of Archenfield, valued at £24.[14] His heir was his son Gilbert.

Goodrich formed part of Elizabeth's dower in her husband's lands. She died on the 20th of November 1372, her *inquisition post mortem* showing that she held the castle and demesne of Goodrich of the king. In the castle were various buildings and the whole was worth only

£1 yearly after outgoings. It also found that she had various meadows, pasture and woodlands in the area, and a mill and weir on the river, both of which had been damaged.[15] Another *inquisition* held on the following day found that she also held the hundred of Archenfield and manor of Wormelow as part of her dower. The lands now passed in full to her son, Gilbert.[16]

Gilbert, 3rd Lord Talbot (1372-87), and Richard, 4th Lord (1387-96)

Like his father before him, Gilbert was much involved in the king's foreign wars. He was abroad, in Gascony, when his father died and was still there in February 1357. By the end of 1358 he was indebted to the crown in the great sum of £1,102 13s 4d which he was allowed to pay off in annual instalments in consideration of the good service rendered by himself and his father.[17] He died in Spain in April 1387, leaving his son, Richard, aged 26, as heir.[18]

Richard married Angharad, daughter of John Lestrange of Blackmere in Shropshire, and died in September 1396 leaving his son Gilbert, then aged 13, as his heir. Shortly before his death, Richard had granted the office of constable of Goodrich Castle to Philip More for life, with £5 annually and the profits and customs attached to the office.[19] Angharad, his widow, retained one-third of Goodrich for life.

Gilbert, 5th Lord Talbot (1396-1418), and his daughter, Angharad (1418-21)

As Gilbert was a minor when his father died, the king kept him and his lands in ward. In May 1397 the king committed the keeping of Goodrich Castle and the other properties to the Earl of Nottingham, to hold until Gilbert was of full age and rendering £80 yearly to the Exchequer, provided he maintained the buildings and supported all charges.[20] In September 1396 the king gave to John Scudamore of Kentchurch the office of constable of Goodrich Castle to hold during the minority of Gilbert. Scudamore retained the constableship until at least 1413.[21]

In July 1399, during the disturbances which attended the deposition of Richard II, Edmund, Duke of York and guardian of England, told the sheriff of Herefordshire 'to take such order that Goodrich Castle be safe kept until further order to the use of the king and none other'.[22] In November, Hugh Waterton (an old retainer of Henry IV, the new king) replaced John Scudamore as keeper of Archenfield and Goodrich, though not as constable of the castle.[23]

With the 1402 rising of the Welsh of south Wales in support of Owain Glyndwr, the security of Goodrich came under increasing threat. Waterton had his keeping of two-thirds of Archenfield and Goodrich renewed in June of that year, with a new clause allowing him to set off against his annual rent 'all sums or monies duly and necessarily expended in the repairing of the castle'.[24] In September Gilbert's mother married Thomas Neville, Lord Furnival, and by her right he was allowed to take possession of one third of Goodrich and Archenfield. That same month Richard Kingston, archdeacon of Hereford, reported to the king that:

> there were come to our county more than 400 of the rebels of Owen Glendower and many other rebels besides from the marches of Wales and they have captured and robbed within your county of Hereford many men and beasts in great number …[25]

As a result, the king moved to Worcester where he planned to assemble an army to take to Hereford. He wrote from there to Thomas Neville, Lord Furnival, giving him strict orders, under pain of loss and forfeiture of Goodrich Castle:

> ... to take such order for the furnishing and safe guard of the said castle [of Goodrich] with fencible men, victuals, armour, artillery and all other thing needful for the purpose, that no damage or peril shall arise by his fault or negligence or by careless guard thereof.[26]

The following day he gave Gilbert Talbot possession of all the castles, manors, lordships, etc., of Richard his father.[27]

In June 1404 the Welsh invaded Archenfield, bringing with them two weeks' supply of victuals. The terrified sheriff and gentry of the county wrote to the king's council:

> The Welsh rebels in great numbers have entered Archenfield and there burnt houses, killed the inhabitants, taken prisoners and ravaged the country to the unsupportable damage of the county. We pray our sovereign lord that he will come in his royal person, otherwise we shall be utterly destroyed, which God forbid.[28]

The revolt continued into 1405, although Glamorgan and Gwent began to return their allegiance to the English king, so lessening the danger to Goodrich. Gilbert had been in the forefront of the royal campaigns in Wales and the Marches and at the end of 1405 he complained to the king that he was greatly in debt due to the 'great expense he had sustained in the service of the king and of the Prince of Wales'.[29] In 1406 Bishop Robert Mascall made a list of the many churches of Archenfield which had suffered so badly at the hands of the Welsh. However, it seems that neither Goodrich Church nor Flanesford Priory were damaged,[30] probably due to the care that Furnival and Gilbert took over the fortification and manning of Goodrich Castle.

Thomas, Lord Furnival, died in March 1407, his one-third of Goodrich Castle and the land and hundred of Archenfield remaining in the hands of Angharad, his widow.[31] She died in June 1413, at which point her lands passed to her son Gilbert, then aged about 24.[32] Gilbert died

Fig. 6.2 Rouen in the early 1400s

in October 1418 at the siege of Rouen leaving an infant daughter, Angharad, as his heir. Three days later, the king, Henry V, who clearly thought highly of Gilbert's military prowess, paid £16 13s 4d to brethren of different orders for 2,000 masses to be said for his soul and that of Edward of Mortain.[33] Angharad died in December 1421, aged about five, her heir being her uncle, John Talbot, second son of her grandfather, Richard Talbot, and younger brother of her father.[34]

John, 6th Lord Talbot and 1st Earl of Shrewsbury (1421-53) (Fig. 6.3)

John Talbot married Maud, sole daughter and heiress of Thomas Neville, Lord Furnival, in 1404. On Thomas's death John became, by right of his wife, Lord Furnival and lord of the barony of Hallamshire, centred on Sheffield Castle. From then onwards Goodrich took second place to Sheffield in the Talbot affections, chiefly because of the vast profit that could be made from his Yorkshire coalmines. His possession of Blackmere in Shropshire and its associated lands formed the basis for John's title of Earl of Shrewsbury which was given in 1442.

In 1418 John was made king's lieutenant in Ireland and in May 1419 he captured Donat MacMurrough, King of Leinster. Donat was first imprisoned in the Tower of London, but in 1424 was handed over to Talbot for confinement.[35] He was finally released in July 1427, apparently after paying a ransom.[36] It is entirely possible that during his three years in Talbot's hands he was kept at Goodrich. Silas Taylor, writing *c*.1655, quotes a tradition that:

> the keepe of the castle was by way of ransome built by one Macbeth or Macmac, an Irish commander, who with his sonne was taken prisoner by John Earle of Shrewsbury in Ireland, and here imprisoned, and to this day it is called Macbeth's Tower, and to our times were alsoe kept in this castle the memorialls of this atchievement; viz. the two great head-pieces of father and sonne, of that vastness and capacity that the one would hold half a bushel of graine; the less was very thicke, and both very ponderous.[37]

The name Macbeth, which probably only dates from Shakespeare's day, can be discounted, but 'Macmac' may well be a garbled form of MacMurrough. The Irish king's ransom cannot have been used for building the keep, but the rest of the tradition concerning him seems to be based on truth.

John Scudamore of Kentchurch seems to have been succeeded by William Thomas of Somerset, esquire, as constable of Goodrich Castle. William received £5 annually for life from the lordship of Archenfield and manor and hundred of Wormelow by gift of Gilbert Talbot in 1417.

In April 1423 Talbot sailed to France where, under the terms of the treaty of Troyes, the infant English king, Henry VI, had been monarch since the death of Charles VI in October 1422 and where large areas were under full English control. Maud had died in 1422 and in Paris in July 1424 John Talbot married his second wife, Margaret Beaufort, only daughter of the earl of Warwick.

Despite sporadically successful opposition from the French, the English had maintained their ascendancy since Agincourt in 1415. After taking Rouen (where Gilbert had died in 1418) they had completed the occupation of Normandy. In 1428 they launched a major offensive in the Loire Valley capturing forty towns and laying siege to Orléans. In December 1428 Talbot arrived to take joint command (with the Earl of Suffolk) of the besieging force, and a few months later received envoys from the city opening negotiations for surrender. But the siege of Orléans was the beginning of the end for the English. On the 3rd of May 1429, in her first action, Joan of Arc led a relieving force into the city and five days later the last English troops before Orléans demolished their siege works and withdrew. In the first concerted French campaign in a generation, Joan rapidly struck east, west and north of Orléans, clearing the English from the Loire Valley. She won battles at Jargeau on the 11th and 12th of June, Meung-sur-Loire on the 15th of June and Beaugency on the 16th and 17th June. On the 18th the vanguard of her army annihilated the English at Patay, where Talbot was captured.

He spent four years in captivity before a prisoner exchange returned him to England in May 1433.[38] After a brief stay, he returned to France in July where he quickly re-established his reputation as an aggressive general and gained the epithet 'the English Achilles'. In 1434, the Duke of Bedford, English regent of France, created him count of Clermont, but in the following year the English alliance with Burgundy came to a bitter end. In January 1436 Talbot repulsed a French force which had advanced to Ry near his headquarters at Rouen. The citizens of Paris rebelled and forced the English garrison to surrender. Although a daring rapid march by Talbot captured Pontoise, 20 miles from the city, and he raided as far as Paris itself, the French capital was permanently lost.

In October 1440 Talbot recaptured Harfleur, taken by the French five years earlier, and his audacious campaigns made him a national hero. In May 1442, he took the title Earl of Shrewsbury. But the wars in France were not given sufficient resources by an English court distracted by political intrigue and the commanders were constantly short of money and men. One of Talbot's earliest acts after being created earl was to request sums due to him as 'Marshal of France'.[39]

Even with Normandy lost, so great was Talbot's reputation in the field that his death, aged 65 or more, at the battle of Castillon on the 17th of July 1453, marked the end of all hopes the English crown had of retaining any lands in France, apart from Calais. A soldier's soldier at the end of what was seen as a chivalric age,[40] the French built a chapel on the spot where he fell.[41] In his will he bequeathed most of his castles, lands and manors to Margaret and his children by her, but the lordships of Goodrich and Archenfield were willed to his 'son and heir', John, eldest surviving son of Maud. He also stipulated that John Gye was to have the office and fee of constable of Goodrich Castle for life.[42]

Bordeaux had been under English rule for three hundred years, an association which led to the English attachment to 'claret', as they call the wines of the area. The well-known *Quatrièmes Cru* (fourth growth) Bordeaux, Chateau Talbot,

Fig. 6.3 John, 6th Lord Talbot and 1st Earl of Shrewsbury

is from the property of that name in the commune of Saint Julien. The estate belonged to John Talbot and, like the rest of the English lands in France, was lost after his death.

John, 2nd Earl of Shrewsbury (1453-60), and John, 3rd Earl (1460-73)

John, the 2nd Earl of Shrewsbury, was killed at the battle of Northampton in 1460, fighting on the Lancastrian side. His heir was his son John, aged 11. In May 1461 William Herbert of Raglan and others were commissioned to take into the king's hands the castles and lordships of Goodrich and Archenfield of John, Earl of Shrewsbury, 'rebel'. On the 3rd of February 1462 the Yorkist king, Edward IV, granted the same properties to William Herbert, for good service against the Lancastrian king, Henry VI. In August 1464 John, Earl of Shrewsbury, though still under age, was licensed to enter into any of his father's lands, lordships, castles, etc., not already granted to William Herbert.[43] Goodrich, therefore, remained in the hands of Herbert (who was made Earl of Pembroke in 1468, renewing the ancient connection between Goodrich and Pembroke). However, Herbert was on the losing side at the battle of Banbury in 1469 and was taken by the victorious Earl of Warwick to Northampton for execution. By July 1469 Goodrich was finally in the hands of John, 3rd Earl of Shrewsbury, then aged about 20.[44] He had been knighted by the Prince of Wales in 1461, after the second battle of St Alban's. The 3rd earl died on the 28th of June 1473, his heir being his son George, a minor.

From 1473 to 1590 (*by* Pat Hughes)

George, 4th Earl of Shrewsbury (1473-1538)

George Talbot was born in 1468 at Shifnal in Shropshire, one of the Talbot family's many holdings and, at the age of five, inherited vast estates in Yorkshire, Derbyshire, Nottinghamshire and Staffordshire in addition to those in Herefordshire.

In October 1473 the king granted to Richard Croft, knight, the office of receiver of the lordships of Goodrich and Archenfield and of all other lordships and lands in Herefordshire, held by John, late Earl of Shrewsbury, to hold during the minority of his heir.[45] His accounts for Michaelmas 1481 to Michaelmas 1482 show that his receipts totalled £27 17s 5½d, while his disbursements included £10 to Thomas Grey, Lord Ferrers, steward of the Court of Goodrich and constable of the castle, and £6 1s 8d to John Benet, porter of the castle, each year for two years. Croft also accounted for 14s of repairs 'this year done and incurred on divers houses in the castle'.[46]

On the 29th of September 1474 the king appointed George's mother, Katherine, daughter of Humphrey Stafford, Duke of Buckingham, to look after the castle, lordship and manors of Goodrich and Archenfield and, as long as they remained in the king's hands, at a yearly charge of £53 6s 8d. On the 11th of January 1484 Richard Williams, the king's servant, was given the dual offices of steward of the lordship of Archenfield and constable of the castle of Goodrich.[47]

From the age of 19, George Talbot was involved with the politics of the day, fighting on the side of Henry VII at the battle of Stoke Heath. By the beginning of the 16th century he was well established as the 4th Earl of Shrewsbury.

With the accession of Henry VIII in 1509, his career took on a new impetus. He became Lord Steward of the Royal Household, a Privy Councillor, and one of the Chamberlains of the Exchequer. He undertook a number of diplomatic missions and, in 1520, was one of those present at the Field of the Cloth of Gold.[48] In 1529 Talbot supported Henry VIII in the divorce crisis and subscribed to the articles against Cardinal Wolsey.

As a soldier, George's introduction to the unruly Scottish borders was less than splendid and he was quickly superseded by the Earl of Surrey. However, his later conduct in the suppression of the Pilgrimage of Grace – the northern counter-reformation rising in 1536/7 – was of great value to his king. It is evident that he had a hand in most of the great affairs of his age.[49]

Like his father, George Talbot made Sheffield his main residence, but his official duties (he was Justice in Eyre for various Lordships on the Welsh Marches,[50] and Constable of both Wigmore and Radnor Castles) took him into Shropshire and Herefordshire and it would be surprising if he did not visit Goodrich from time to time. George married twice. His first wife, Ann, daughter of Lord Hastings, died in 1507 having borne him 11 children. His second wife, Elizabeth, bore him one daughter who married William Herbert, Earl of Pembroke. George Talbot died in 1538.

Francis, 5th Earl of Shrewsbury (1538-60)

A letter from Francis, George's eldest surviving son, to the people of Goodrich when he inherited the estate in 1538,[51] suggests that custom dictated that the lord ought to visit his property, that his predecessors had all spent time at the castle, and that the Goodrich tenants still expected that their lord should take a personal interest in them. After acknowledging 'the sume of twentye markyes graunted to me by my loving frindes and tennantts of my Lordship of Goodrich', he went on to say:

> I perceyve also that my said tennanttes be in dowte lest the payment of this said some shuld be prediciall unto theym in tymes comyng considering that I come not thyere myself before the payment of the said money which they cleame by their custome that I shuld do.[52]

It seems that, unlike his father, Francis had no intention of visiting the castle – his interests lay in the north of the country where, in the late 1540s and 1550s, he was president of the Council of the North, and spent a considerable part of his life on military duties on the Scottish border.[53] His interest in the Goodrich area centred solely on its resources. This is shown by an undated peremptory communication which demanded that all available men from Goodrich, complete with horse and harness, should report to Sheffield 'on Sunday fortnight' to serve his Highness against the Scots.

Francis' lack of personal involvement with his Welsh border possessions did not prevent him from taking the opportunity to buy Flanesford Priory from the crown when it became available at the Dissolution, despite his apparent Catholic sympathies. Later evidence suggests that the priory buildings effectively became the 'home farm' for the castle.

The estate continued to provide the absent owner with a steady income. Timber management was, perhaps, the most important element in the estate's economy and the woodlands at Coppett Hill, Longrove and Doward produced a regular cash crop, the earl keeping two foresters to direct his assets. The court rolls contain numerous entries regarding the woods – among them, dating from the early 1540s, are a series of fines levied on those who felled trees without permission.[54] The woods were also used by pig keepers – in 1557 payments for swine pastured on the earl's woodland were made from many of his possessions. Either pig-farming was big business or suitable woodland was becoming scarce. Difficulties over fishing rights in the River Wye are recorded in the court rolls with sufficient regularity to indicate the economic importance of this industry to the Goodrich estate.

The whole of south Herefordshire and the Forest of Dean had long had a name for iron working, and the Goodrich estate shared in this industry, with several forges operating during the 16th and early 17th centuries. The Earls of Shrewsbury, who already had important iron workings on their northern estates, were active in promoting the industry. What seems to have been the oldest of the forges on the Goodrich estate stood where the River Garron meets the Wye, at a spot still known as Old Forge. In the mid-16th century it was not rented out, being operated for the direct profit of the earl. At least one other forge, that at New Mill, had started up by the mid-16th century. Indeed, the name New Mill appears first in 1588.[55] All these natural and industrial resources were exploited by the Talbots.

Although the ford and ferry were just below the castle, they were outside the jurisdiction of the estate and continued to be part of Monmouthshire. Nevertheless, proximity dictated strong links with the castle and in the 1540s the ferryman was known as 'boatman of the castle lands' and the Goodrich manor court regarded the ferry as within its jurisdiction. Far from being an asset, the constant passage of travellers across the ferry and up Boat Lane may well have been a drain on local resources, for the landowners whose property adjoined the lane had to maintain the highway at their own cost.[56]

George, 6th Earl of Shrewsbury (1560-90)

When Francis Talbot died in 1560 his son George became the 6th Earl and inherited the vast family estates. By the time of his father's death he was already well established at court and remained a loyal servant of the crown throughout his life. It was to George Talbot that Elizabeth I entrusted the custody of her cousin Mary, Queen of Scots, and it was on his estate at Sheffield that Mary spent much of her imprisonment.[57] The constant financial drain of a busy public life made it all the more necessary that the Talbot estates should be well managed and yield maximum profits. The extant correspondence indicates that the new earl was only too anxious to ensure that his estates were efficiently run.

In this, the Goodrich manor and its guardian castle were not forgotten. Indeed, at a time when interest in the past was becoming fashionable, the antiquity of the castle itself seems to have been a source of some pride to the family. When negotiations were in hand for the marriage of Francis, George's son and heir, to Ann, daughter of William Herbert, Earl of Pembroke, in 1561, the earl wrote to the Master of the Rolls: 'I am contented that they shall have my Castle of goodrich in harfordshire which is both comodyouse, and most ancientist house I have'.[58]

Subsequent correspondence suggests that, in offering the castle to the newly-married couple, the earl had an ulterior motive. The long absences of the fifth earl seem to have resulted in slackness that played havoc with the administration of the manor and no doubt George would have appreciated having his son on the spot to ensure that the officials were doing their job properly. However, this was not to be, for the young couple chose instead to

Shrewsbury, says plaintively that neither he nor Mary realised that they were expected to stay at Goodrich for the winter. The letter continued with estate business. The earl wanted to charge his tenants for swine grazing the hedgerows – Gilbert pointed out that the swine were all in the woods where the tenants had grazing rights, but he offered to have the pigs driven out and impounded so that the rights could be challenged in the manor court.[69]

The struggle with tenants on the Goodrich estate was only part of Shrewsbury's difficulties, Gilbert also being employed by his father to negotiate with tenants in Derbyshire in 1575 and '79.[70] Even so, he continued to manage the Goodrich estate and to live in Goodrich Castle for at least part of the year. He was there in March 1579, when he wrote to his father asking for instructions about the sale of woods near the castle, and in 1583/4 when he issued instructions that two horses were to be brought into the castle from Talbot's meadow. The rest of the time responsibility for the day-to-day running of the place must have been in the hands of the constable, Godfrey Wigfall, who also had charge of the prison.[71]

When his elder brother, Francis, died of plague in 1582 leaving no sons, Gilbert became the heir. In 1587, he gave up the stewardship of the manor and probably ceased to reside at the castle.[72] It seems likely that this was due to his father's increasing ill health and the necessity of the heir taking a more active part in the ordering of the family business. George Talbot died in 1590 and Gilbert became the 7th Earl.

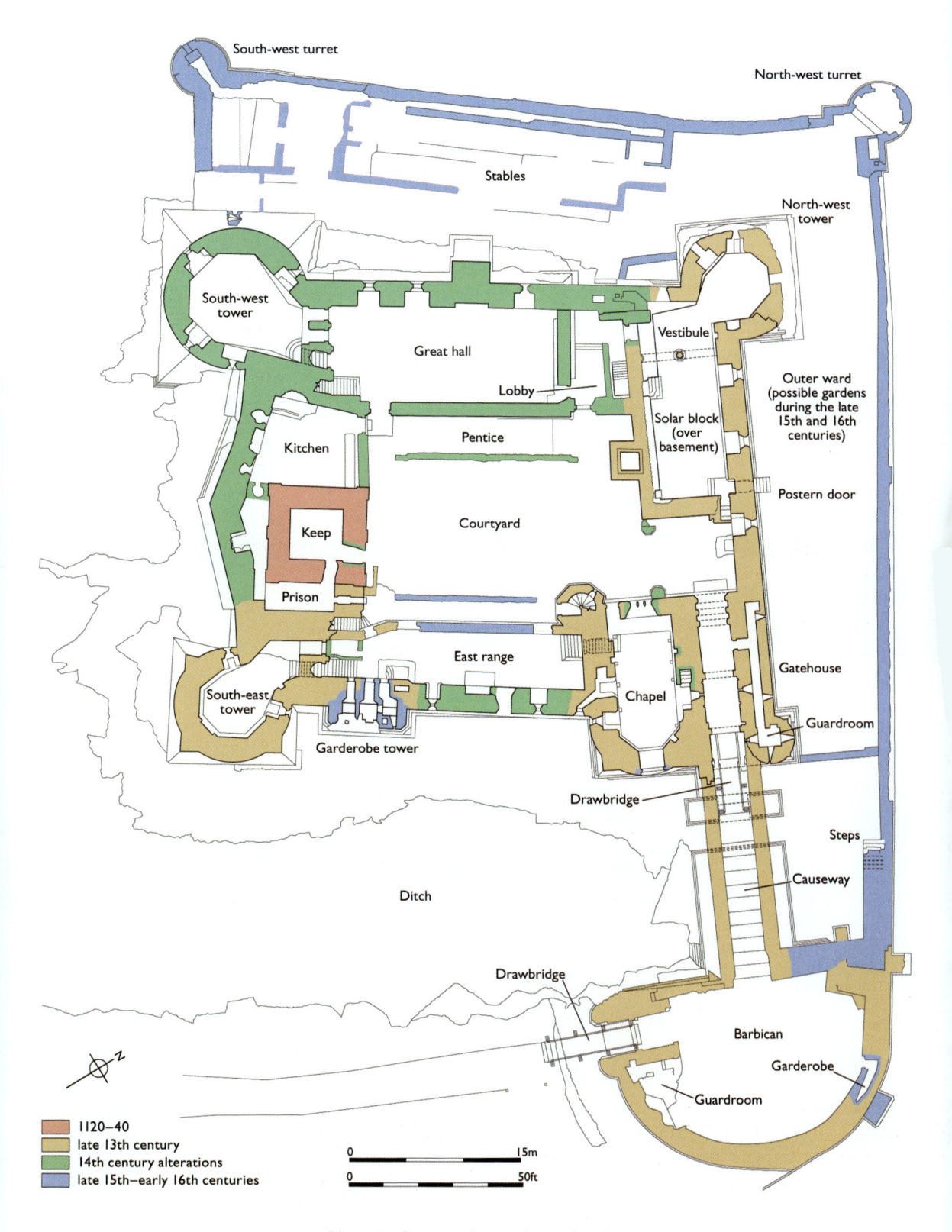

Plate 1 Ground Plan of the Castle

ABOVE: Plate 2 The castle from the east
BELOW: Plate 3 The castle from the north-east

Plate 4 A painting of the castle from the east by Liam Wales

ABOVE: Plate 5 Goodrich Castle and Flanesford Priory in the bend of the River Wye
(photo Herefordshire Archaeology)
BELOW: Plate 6 The Goodrich Ferry and castle in 1797 by Samuel Ireland

ABOVE: Plate 7 Marriage of Aoife (Eva) and Strongbow.
This marriage gave Strongbow his claim to Leinster
Below: Plate 8 The supposed tomb of Earl Richard 'Strongbow' in Dublin Cathedral, but the armour is of a later period and the shield bears three crosslets, not the Clare three chevrons. The original tomb was severely damaged when part of the nave wall collapsed in 1562 and a replacement effigy was used in the repair (courtesy of Paul R. Davis)

Plate 9 The stained glass window in the west wall of the chapel commemorating the Radar Research Squadron in the Second World War

Plate 11 The custodian's hut in the barbican, now demolished

Plate 10 The stained glass window in the east wall of the chapel celebrating the millennium

Plate 12 The new visitor centre

63

Plate 13
The window on the west elevation of the keep, showing the different colours of the stone as depicted in plate 14 below. Malcolm Thurlby argues that the hollow roll mouldings on the window jambs and the positioning of the chevroned string course at cill level suggest a relationship with the Herefordshire School of Romanesque Sculpture. Note, too, the chevron jambs (courtesy of Malcolm Thurlby)

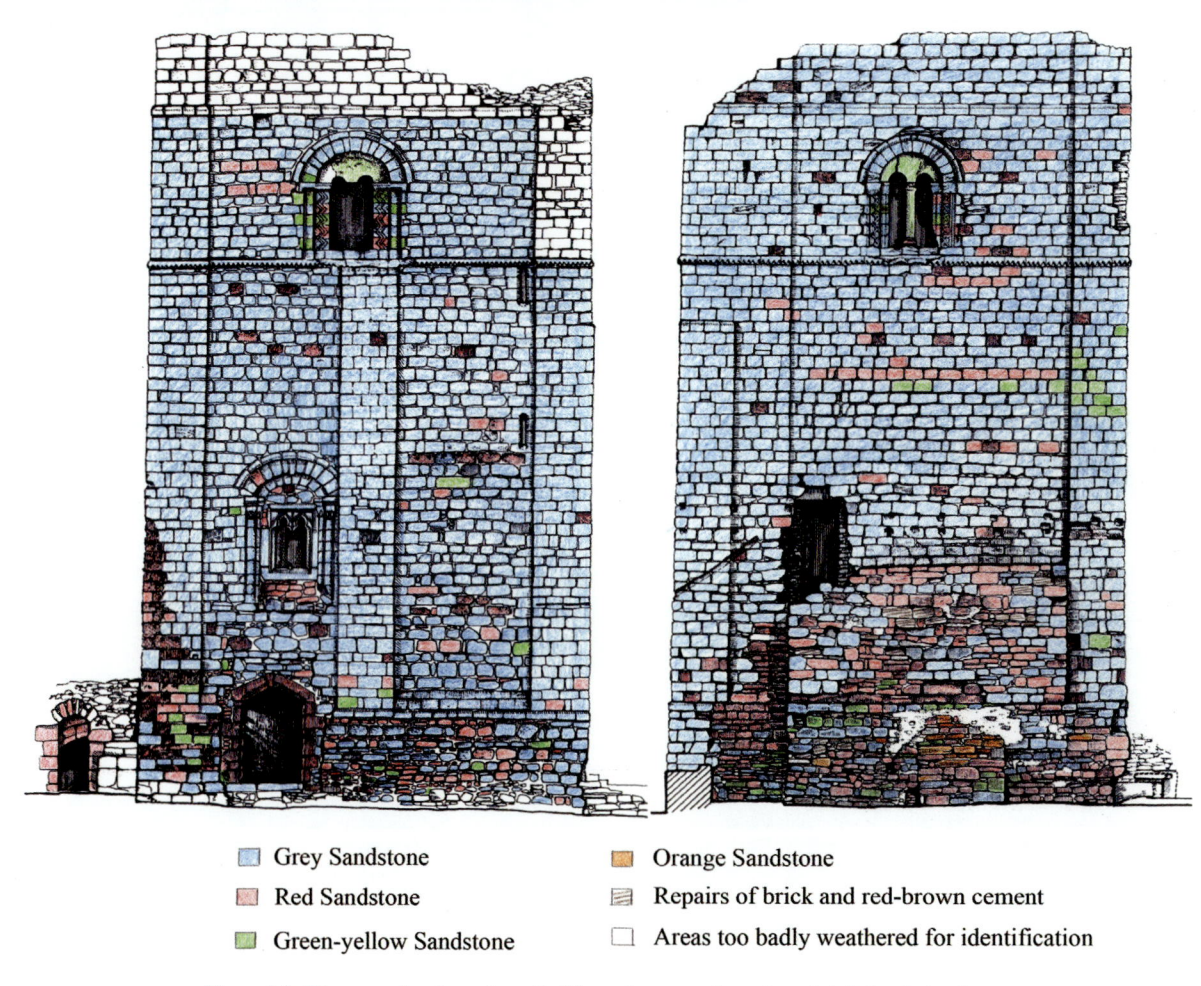

- Grey Sandstone
- Red Sandstone
- Green-yellow Sandstone
- Orange Sandstone
- Repairs of brick and red-brown cement
- Areas too badly weathered for identification

Plate 14 The north elevation (left) and west elevation (right) of the keep showing the use of different sandstones

64

7   The Castle & its Tenants: 1590-1645
by Pat Hughes

Having modernised the castle and put it into a habitable state, Gilbert Talbot, the 7th Earl of Shrewsbury, made strenuous efforts to find a suitable tenant. The first was Mr Thomas Kery (*sic*), Clerk to the Privy Council, probably the son of John Kerry, who was mayor of Hereford in 1555 and founder of the Kerry almshouses.[1] John Scudamore had known him for many years and persuaded the earl to adjust the rent to accommodate such a good tenant – 'careful in reparinge the castle and other houses orchards and gardens adionyng'. However, he stayed less than two years, and in 1593 indicated his intention of giving up the lease. He was followed by John Talbot of Grafton in Worcestershire, a cousin of the earl who was still there in 1594.[2] It appears, from a rather obscure reference, that a 'Lord Herbert' recuperated at Goodrich, for a letter reported that 'Goodrich hath done a great cure'.[3] It is not clear whether this was Lord Herbert, Earl of Pembroke, who had been very ill in the September, or his son, who was suffering from poor health in the autumn of 1599.

The first years of the 17th century are chiefly remarkable for the well-documented and acrimonious exchanges between the Earl of Shrewsbury's officials and his tenants over the conflicting interests of the iron works and the fisheries. Iron working was of major importance and the fisheries were also big business, but the weirs that created the fish pools were a hazard both for the iron-working and to navigation on the river. The problems rumbled on without any satisfactory solution and at this distance in time the rights and wrongs of the case are impossible to sort out.

In 1606 Eustace Wenland, a lawyer from St Weonards who acted for the Talbots, requested a lease of the revenues from the Goodrich estate 'at such a reasonable rate as others may have it' noting that the iron works – which prevented the disposal of the whole of the demesne – 'doe still endure'. He also asked for 'some roomes in the Castle, garden grounds, orchards cow pastures and such commodities as your Lordship may best spare'.[4] Thus there were clearly some lodgings available in the castle for a tenant to occupy, at a time when much of the castle was still set aside for the entertaining of official guests. It also seems that the farmland, orchards and cow pastures surrounding the priory went with the tenancy – a circumstance confirmed by later evidence. The request includes the second post-medieval reference to gardens at the castle, probably in the north and west wards, where the outer north-western corner tower is more characteristic of a 'banqueting house' than a fortification (see Chapter 18).[5]

The next tenant, George Moore, who arrived in 1609, also acted as constable and agent to the earl, supervising the iron works and the woodland and involving himself in the long-running saga of the weir and the fishing rights. Showing himself as a zealous defender of the privileges of the Lord of the Manor, he inquired into the customs of the manor and into tenants' rights at Longhope, Huntley and Doward and took issue with the sheriff of Hereford, whose claim to have jurisdiction over Goodrich manor was a continuing irritation.[6]

A number of letters written by Moore concern the sad case of George Bonner, a Goodrich man, who was committed to Gloucester assizes on a charge of murder. The sheriff of Hereford, pre-judging the issue, made an attempt to impound his wife's goods, on the grounds that they were the property of a convicted felon. He actually removed a pewter dish as an indication of his intentions. Here Moore took a hand, for not only had Bonner not yet been convicted, but Archenfield law, operative in Goodrich, allowed the heirs of a felon to inherit his property, contrary to normal legal practice. Moore therefore made an inventory of Mrs Bonner's remaining goods and marked the cattle before housing them at the priory, by then used as farm-buildings. The sheriff, undeterred, fetched them out and, apparently in a fit of bravado, drove them up to the castle gate, where a number of the Goodrich tenants were assembled. The tenants pleaded with the sheriff, offering security if he would leave the cattle at Goodrich, and Mrs Moore also joined them from the castle, pledging her support for the case, but the sheriff was adamant and the cattle were driven off to Hereford by his men.[7] Three months later, the charge against Bonner was agreed by two judges to be manslaughter and he was acquitted. The sheriff was forced to eat his words; he returned the cattle by two of his 'cheffest men in levarry' and acknowledged the wrongful removal of Bonner's stock. It is worth noting that George Bonner, after his ordeal, felt it worth making the long journey to Sheffield to present his case to the earl in person. The frequency with which letters went from Goodrich to Sheffield, often several in a week, indicates the extent to which the earl must have been in close touch with the affairs of both castle and manor.

George Moore's name features in the surviving correspondence and the Court Rolls for two years only. No other tenants are noted for the five years before Gilbert Talbot's death in 1616. The castle was left to Mary, Dowager Countess of Shrewsbury, who made William Scudamore her agent, with power to administer the iron works and to take what fuel was needed from the woods. Brief returns for the estate, sent by William Scudamore to the countess, exist for the years 1617 to 1619.[8] However, in 1619 the crown claimed Goodrich in settlement of a huge debt of £20,000 owed by the countess. The castle was then let to the Earl of Pembroke who, in 1620, sublet the estate to William Purfrey of Drayton, Leicestershire and Benjamin Hale of Flitton, Bedfordshire. Despite some confusion, all the indications are that there was some sort of accommodation made with the crown, since the Lord Chamberlain was involved. The heiress to Goodrich, Elizabeth (daughter of Gilbert, Earl of Shrewsbury and Mary) and her husband, Henry, Earl of Kent, were also party to the transaction. Presumably Purfrey and Hale acted as agents, managing the estate finances and paying an agreed sum to the Crown.[9]

Some of Purfrey's rent rolls survive and they, together with property deals, show that between 1623 and 1629 a Thomas Gwillym styled himself as being 'of Goodrich Castle'.[10] He may have been the 'Thomas Gwillym de Whitchurch, Armiger' who is listed among the suitors at the manor court between 1624 and 1628.[11]

In 1631, the then tenant, Richard Tyler, an attorney, negotiated a new lease of the castle, outhouses and lands with the Kents, paying £71 rent every three years for nine years. This implies that the priory and its surrounding farmland still comprised the 'Home Farm'. Certainly farmland formed part of the contract, for the tenant was to be allowed to:

> cutt, work and carry away all such regular corne as shalbe growing upon the premises …
> then paying iid for every acre whereupon such winter wrie shalbe growing.

There are indications that Richard Tyler had been in the district since at least 1631 (and possibly as early as 1623) and may have already been tenant of the castle. However, it is more likely that he took over the castle, and the responsibilities that went with it, sometime in 1627/8.[12] Although Mr Purfrey, as agent, seems to have stayed at Ross on his earlier visits, Tyler, in an account dated 1632, claimed entertainment expenses on the grounds that Purfrey had, for the last four years, been 'coming twise a yeere at the lest and staying there [at the castle] a fortnight at a tyme'.

The 17th-century rent rolls survive in the papers belonging to John Selden, a lawyer and scholar who was closely associated with the Earl and Countess of Kent. Some of them appear to have been written by John Bridgeman, the steward for Goodrich; others may have been written by, or addressed to, Selden himself. In particular there are pages of rough notes, reminders of jobs to be done or questions to be asked. They show that during 1631 and the early part of 1632, considerable activity took place on the manor of Goodrich, with new leases being issued to many of the Goodrich tenants, including the one to Richard Tyler.

The Accompt of Money expended in and about the Necessary repayer of the Castle of Goodrich sithince the 8th of July 1631 to the 20th of January 1631 following viz:

Impris

paid for 6 semes of Lyme for mending the seelings and other places	iii s
paid unto James fyllye for plastering about the rooms of the Castle as severall tymes 6 days	vi s
pd to a mason for teking downe an ould stonnwall at the Pryorye 5 daies	v s
pd to the same Masone for mending of decayed places about the Castle & pitching uner the gatehouses and mending the hastles of the Chymneys 8 daies and a half	viii s vi d
pd to the same Masone for making of 100 perches of Stonnwall in needfull places about the pryery & castle of the ould stones which before did noe service att the rute of 3d the perche	xxv s
To the glazier of Monmouth for mending the glass about the Castle	x s ix d
For nailes to mend severall places about the Castle	ii s vi d
Pd for 16 (blot!) new locks and keyes and for mending other locks and keyes for the doores about the Castle	xv s i d
pd for squaring a treei in penyard and for quartering the same and for making a sawpit, to mend the gallery and other places about ye Castle	xv s vi d

In the accompt I doe not accompt any thinge for my owne labour and traveyle, nor any of my servants attendance nor the labour of my plowes drawing of stones, nor any other thing, but the very money which went out of my purse.

per me Richard Tiler

Fig. 7.1 Repairs to the Castle from July 1631 to January 1632

The most probable reason for all this activity is that the Goodrich estate had been put into the control of the Kents following the death of the Countess of Shrewsbury in 1632. However, this cannot be the whole truth, for Richard Tyler's new lease was not only made out in September 1631 (predating the countess's death), but was also granted by the Earl of Kent rather than the Countess of Shrewsbury. It seems, therefore, that for some reason the estate had passed to the Kents before the death of the countess.

One of the most interesting documents in the Selden papers is a set of building accounts for the repair of the castle in the six months between July 1631 and January 1632 (Fig. 7.1).[13] Since the terms of Tyler's lease required the earl to pay for repairs, these entries were sent to John Selden by Tyler. Another set of accounts, for June to December 1632, in the same hand and following the same format, has also been found (Fig. 7.2). Running parallel to both these accounts is the set of memoranda, previously mentioned, in which the writer, either Selden or a secretary, noted various matters that had to be attended to and questioned their value.[14]

Among the first items entered in the 1631 account are repairs to the fabric, using stone from Flanesford Priory; in other places fallen stone was reinstated (Fig. 7.1). A glazier from

The Accompte of Money laied out uppon the Reparaccions of the Castle from the 15th of June 1632 to the first of December 1632 following			
Imprimus	li	s	d
paied for mendinge the Locke making a newe keye and making a little locke for the Castle Gate	0	2	6
paied for ii seames of Lyme to mendinge the Castle Walles	0	5	0?
paied for sawiers for saweinge of Tymbar to mend the gallery	0	10	0
paied for makeinge a double dore for a backe into the Castle and for a Locke and hinges for the same	0	4	0?
paied to William Drake the mason for makeinge upp a walle with Lyme and stone under the pillars of the Gallery and mendinge the Foundacone of the Castle in maney places 22 daies	1	2	0?
paied for servinge the masone with stone and mortar at 8d the day	0	14	8
paied for cleeving of three thousand of Lathes to mend the Gallery and other places aboute the Castle	0	10	6
paied for mendinge the park pales at severall tymes by George Bonner	0	6	0
paied for a newe Locke for the Conduite house Lockes hinges and staples and the setting one	0	3	6
paied the Plumer Thomas Hughes for making tweentye yerdes of pippes of Leade for the draweinge of the water to the Castle for placeinge of them and mendinge all the Reste of the pippes to bring the watter home for 2 newe Cockes for 80 pownd of Souder at 9d the pownd and for a Labourers hyer that helped the plumer to uncov[er] the pippes and bringinge Claye and Coveringe of them againe and doeinge all thinges belonginge thereunto	10	4	6
paied to William drake the Mason for making 17 perches of drye walle from the Ryver of Wye to the upper end of the Sheaperds hill betwixte the Commons Called Copped Wood and the Castle grownd a Worke very necessary to be done at 4d per perche	2	16	8
And for digginge breakinge and Carridge of stones to doe the same at the Rate of 6d the perche	4	5	0

Fig. 7.2 Repairs to the Castle between June and December 1632

68

Fig. 7.3 Reconstruction of the courtyard looking north-east towards the gatehouse in the early 17th century

Monmouth was employed to mend the glass and was paid 10s 9d. Since glass was charged at 6d a square foot, this represented a considerable amount of work. James Fyllye, the plasterer, was only paid one shilling a day and, as lime is the only material mentioned, it would appear that this was plain and not ornamental work. Sixteen new locks and keys were ordered and other locks repaired at a total cost of 15s 1d.

By September 1631 the repairs were sufficiently advanced to allow the entertainment of an influx of official guests, being the Commissioners of the Countess of Kent, who stayed for a fortnight. They included Mr Claxton and '3 that came with him' and Mr Isham and his son. They were apparently concerned with a September audit, and were inquiring into the running of the estate on behalf of the countess. Not only did the Commissioners have to be accommodated in the castle, perhaps in the re-plastered rooms with their new locks, but the Goodrich tenants and local gentry, who came to 'dispatch business' with the Commissioners, also had to be entertained and their horses stabled and fed.

On the 9th of April 1632, while building work was still under way, Thomas Duck and Benjamin Hare, as agents of the Kents, visited the castle in person 'and tooke possession of the said Castle of Goodrich' on their behalf.[15]

Once the castle and manor were officially in the hands of the Kents, Richard Tyler was made both constable of the castle (with charge of the prison) and agent for the estate. The archives of the manor also seem to have been his responsibility, and copies of official papers were kept at the castle. One entry 'A book of survey which was att Goodrich Castell ... of great consequence', emphasises the importance of the Goodrich archive. Unfortunately nothing further is known of this book of survey.[16]

Repair work continued during 1632 and included further work to the gallery and the water supply (Fig. 7.2).[17] One of the problems with the gallery seems to have been the state of the arcade posts, which had become rotten at the bases. These were cut off and under-built in stone by William Drake. This stub wall still survives along the courtyard side of what was the eastern range (Fig. 7.3).

The substantial amount of timber needed for the repairs suggests that the rest of the building was in very poor condition and that the hesitation over the work was justifiable. The 10s 10d quoted in the account as paid to the sawyers represents just under 600 feet of sawn wood.[18] Some was no doubt used to mend floors, but some may have replaced studs in the front walling, where the plasterwork was also renewed. Three thousand laths were needed for the gallery and other places around the castle and it is the use of laths, rather than wattle and daub, that suggests that the gallery front was close studded.[19] Some of the laths may have been used for ceiling repairs.

As repairs continued, new locks and keys were provided for the castle gate and new double doors were made. More work was done on the castle foundations, and palings and walls built and replaced in the park.[20] The piped water supply from a spring on the opposing hill (probably installed in the castle in the 1580s) had been in place long enough to need a thorough overhaul. This was an expensive business – the whole, including £3 worth of solder, came to £10 4s 6d.

The scattered and fragmentary nature of the surviving documentary sources makes it unlikely that this is the complete story of the restoration of Goodrich. Indeed, in the first account Richard Tyler emphasised that there were other costs not included.[21] Enough survives, however, to give an indication of the extent of the work and to fill out the picture of Goodrich Castle in the 1630s. It would seem that by the end of the work the castle was once again in good repair – a busy modernised unit that functioned as a combination of estate office, home, prison and hotel (Fig. 7.3).

Within this complex of buildings, Richard Tyler entertained the agents, lawyers and representatives of the Kents for up to a fortnight at a time and at considerable expense. He also acted as gaoler, kept the manorial papers, and administered the business of the estate and its valuable woodlands.[22] As part of his appointment he must often have undertaken commissions for his patrons, such as the 'gloves and kidskins' bought for her ladyship, probably from Ross, then a centre of the gloving trade.[23]

All told, Richard Tyler was involved with Goodrich for more than 30 years, bringing up his family there, until two years before his death in 1663.[24] During that time he was to suffer hardship, to lose his home and to witness the destruction of the castle he had worked so hard to restore.[25]

8   THE CIVIL WAR & SLIGHTING OF THE CASTLE (1642-1665)
by Pat Hughes

From a 21st-century point of view it is surprising that Goodrich, secure in its rural fastness, should have taken any part in the 17th-century Civil War. However, several factors contributed to its strategic importance. Firstly it commanded an important crossing of the River Wye – a main route into south Wales. Secondly it had the misfortune to lie close to the route between Charles I's base at Shrewsbury and Raglan Castle in Monmouthshire where, at the very outset of the Civil War, Lord Herbert and his father (both devoted Royalists) had amassed quantities of troops and armament ready to support the king.[1]

Early in October 1642, hoping to prevent the Raglan levies from reaching the king, the Parliamentary forces under the Earl of Stamford first took Hereford and then attempted to consolidate their position by fortifying the surrounding area. Goodrich Castle would have been an integral part of that fortification.

As the 9th Earl of Kent continued the family allegiance to Parliament, and the family lawyer, John Selden, was a member of the Long Parliament, it is likely that their trusted tenant at Goodrich Castle, Richard Tyler, was of the same persuasion. Tyler either had the Parliamentary garrison billeted on him, or at least vacated any rooms that he used in the castle and retired to one of the properties that he owned in Goodrich.

It is clear from the following tale, reported by the Royalist propagandist broadsheet, *Mercurius Rusticus*, that Goodrich was occupied by Parliamentary supporters at this early stage of the war and used as a base for marauding troops. At the beginning of the Civil War the vicar of Goodrich was the Revd Thomas Swift, a fervent Royalist, of whose loyalty to the crown there are many tales. He lived at the New House in the west of Goodrich parish (see Chapter 2), together with his wife and a brood of ten children. The broadsheet recounts a chilling story of how, while Swift was in hiding, the family home was plundered and his family threatened. If the pamphleteer is to be believed, the attack was one of deliberate malice, with the only possible motive being to terrorise the local inhabitants into compliance with the military authorities.

Mrs Swift, having had warning of the army's intention, made a special journey to Hereford to beg that her house and goods should be spared. When the Earl of Stamford answered her request by tearing up her petition and promising that she should be plundered the following day, she rushed home to secure what she could of her possessions before disaster struck.

In the morning Captain Kyrle of Walford Court, with some 70 horsemen and 30 foot-soldiers, based at Goodrich Castle, descended on the parsonage. They took away the parson's corn and what food and household stuff they could find. They even emptied the feather beds so that they could fill the ticks with malt, and finally commandeered the cart and six horses to carry everything away. Lacking protection from the earl, Mrs Swift applied directly to Captain Kyrle for a 'Protection'. He charged her 30s for the paper and graciously allowed her to buy back four of her own horses, for £8 10s. Thankful that some of her goods might be spared, Mrs Swift returned home, retrieved her scattered belongings from her neighbours and 'rejoyced that she had not lost all'.

However the 'Protection' proved valueless, the poor lady being subject to a series of demands for oats, cider, corn and foodstuff, either directly from Kyrle or from the garrison at the castle. When she finally refused to send what was demanded, troops broke in through a window and proceeded to ransack the place. They took books and clothes, even stripping the clothes from the children's backs and the covers from the baby in the cradle. The four remaining horses were again removed, with metalware and poultry and the soldiers threatened to 'plunder all under the Petty-coat, and other immodest words, not fit for them to speak'. Shortly afterwards another group of soldiers came bringing teams to remove heavier articles and took all the food in the house. The miller was threatened that if he gave food to the household, they would grind him in his own mill, other neighbours receiving similar threats. It was another 36 hours before one neighbour dared to take provisions to the stricken family.[2]

Meanwhile, the king had not waited at Shrewsbury to be joined by the troops at Raglan, as had been expected, but had moved southwards towards London, being met at Edgehill by the forces of the Earl of Essex. The engagement, on the 23rd of October 1642, was inconclusive, but had the effect of concentrating the Parliamentary forces to the east of the Severn, leaving Stamford isolated in a hostile county. He eventually withdrew to the comparative safety of Gloucester and Goodrich was left un-garrisoned, having been occupied from the beginning of October to the 3rd of December.

For some months Herefordshire was out of the conflict, but in early April 1643 the county again became involved. Parliamentarian Sir William Waller, invited by gentry who objected to the domination of Raglan Castle, left Gloucester and marched via Ross and the crossing at Goodrich to Monmouth. As there seems to have been no resistance, it is unlikely that Goodrich Castle was garrisoned by Royalists at this time. Although Waller was speedily driven back across the Severn, he did not stay there, for learning of the weakened state of Hereford's

Fig. 8.1 Sir Henry Lingen

defences, he marched on the city which surrendered after less than a day.[3] Waller was not able to keep Hereford, and within a fortnight he had left and the Royalist grip on Herefordshire was temporarily complete. The Goodrich area was not threatened so there would have been no pressing reason to garrison the castle.

However, an enquiry into the treasonable activities of neighbouring gentry, instituted by Parliament in 1650, makes it clear that Sir Henry Lingen (Fig. 8.1) was using the castle at some time in 1643, 'when William Probin, servant of Benedict Hall, rode among the king's forces under Sir Henry Lingen and Commissary Lingen [Sir Henry's brother] of Gutheridge Castle'. After the king's forces failed to take Gloucester in August/September 1643, the situation gradually changed, and at the beginning of 1644 Goodrich was once again garrisoned, this time for the king. The fact that Richard Tyler's personal possessions were purloined by the Royalist garrison implies that he was once again living there.

The castle was certainly garrisoned by Royalists under Captain Cassie in May 1644, when Massey, the Parliamentarian commander of Gloucester, marched on Ross. John Corbett, Massey's chaplain, wrote that he attacked Wilton Bridge, guarded by musketeers from Goodrich, 'took the captaine, slew many of his men, and tooke the rest in the chase almost up to the castle'.[4]

For the rest of the summer of 1644 fighting was focused in the midlands and the north, but in September, two months after the decisive defeat of the Royalists at Marston Moor, Massey turned his attention to the Wye Valley. He attacked and defeated Prince Rupert at Beachley, once again threatening Herefordshire. With Massey at Monmouth, Goodrich was once more in the front line.

It must have been at this juncture that Sir Henry Lingen took over Goodrich Castle as his headquarters, as distinct from merely billeting soldiers there. In a paper written after the siege in 1646, to acquaint the Parliamentary Commissioners with his losses, Richard Tyler stated:

> … the tyme Sir Henry Lingen and his brother Commissary Lingen contynued the Government of the castle of Goodrich … began at the feast of St Michael 1644 and ended about August 1646 followinge being almost the space of two years.[5]

The full text of this account gives a good impression of the scale of the losses that Richard Tyler suffered at Lingen's hands. During the two years of occupation the little orchard at the priory, gates, rails, walls and hedges were destroyed, and some of the priory buildings burned – either by vandalising troops or during the later siege. Of greater consequence was the damage to property and woodland and the enforced payment of rents to the Royalists, rents which had to be paid a second time to the Countess of Kent.

Tyler seems to have had some warning of the occupation by the Lingens, for he managed to sell his beasts before they were requisitioned but, inevitably, he was imprisoned and his goods and furnishings purloined for the use of Lingen and his officers. Without knowing the quality of the goods lent by Tyler, it is difficult to estimate what is represented by the £24 14s which he claimed for 'Certeyne goods … lent by Inventory to Sir Henry Lingen'. Comparison with values given in probate inventories of that general date suggests that the sum was probably sufficient to furnish private rooms for Sir Henry and his brother. All in all Tyler reported losses in the region of £300, albeit the figure may include claims on behalf of the Countess of Kent.[6]

Sir Edward Powell of Pengethley, about six miles from Goodrich, was regarded as a Parliamentary sympathiser and had forfeited his goods and his rent rolls in 1643.[7] During the remainder of 1644 and 1645 demands were made of his steward, Anthony Grubb, for more hay boards. One such letter signed, your 'Loveing Frend Hen Lengen' demanded 'your Longest size of Boardes for I am informed that you haue very Longe ones'. To add insult to injury he was also charged with delivery.[8]

Local Royalists gave voluntary support to the king's cause, and were later prosecuted by Parliament for their contributions. Benedict Hall, Rudhall Gwillims of Whitchurch,[9] Anthony Drew of Torrington, Captain Clement Ludford, and Richard Buckley of Longdon in Worcestershire, who had joined the Goodrich garrison, were all subsequently arraigned and fined for their sympathies.[10]

Meanwhile Colonel Massey, having retaken Monmouth, was preparing to take Chepstow Castle, thus again bringing Goodrich into the line of fire. One skirmishing party under Parliament's Colonel Broughton reached the Goodrich area and garrisoned a house nearby. The house was later fired by Royalist forces from the castle and the garrison captured and taken to Hereford.[11] It is suggested that this house was Flanesford Priory, as Richard Tyler's sympathies were with Parliament and the house could certainly be claimed to be 'near' the castle. Alternatively, the house in question might have been Geddes, three-quarters of a mile to the north-west of the castle, as the old part of the house shows the scars of burning and the rest was rebuilt in the latter part of the 17th century[12] (see Chapter 2).

Throughout the moves and countermoves that took place in 1645 Lingen was establishing himself at Goodrich. Richard Tyler complained that his fields were spoiled and stripped of turf to make bulwarks for the castle, while '81 greate ocks beside coppice woods' were demanded from him. The coppice wood, like the fences and gates taken from his farmland, were probably used as fuel, but oak timber of that quality was probably needed to reinforce the already formidable defences.[13]

The natural defensive position of the castle, high on its rock and commanding the ford and ferry, could hardly be bettered and there is no official record of any attempted attack during this period. However, tradition asserts that such an attack was made, and was foiled with heavy casualties, helped by the Revd Thomas Swift who caused the ford to be seeded with caltrops.[14]

The summer of 1645 saw the formation of the New Model Army and the Royalists' defeat at the battle of Naseby. The king, having spent 12 days in Hereford, where he knighted Henry Lingen, escaped to the west in the hope of raising a new army in Wales. In his wake came a Scottish Presbyterian army led by the Earl of Leven, who, at the end of July, encamped outside Hereford and laid siege to the city. After a five-week stalemate, word was brought of a relieving army advancing from Worcester with the king at its head. On that news the siege was lifted and the Scots retreated to Gloucester.[15]

During their stay in Herefordshire the Scottish troops had made themselves hated in the surrounding parishes by the rapacity of their plundering, taking over £31,000 worth of supplies. However, the Goodrich garrison was probably not withdrawn during the Hereford siege, as the local village escaped the worst plunderings. Miles Hill, the solicitor charged by Parliament with provisioning the Scots, published a pamphlet itemising the damage. In Goodrich parish alone goods worth £38 3s 6d were taken.[16] By comparison, the parish of

Ross lost £1,189 18s. Lord Leven wrote a letter to Parliament in vindication of his troops. He claimed that they had been promised £200 a day in money and provisions from Herefordshire and the surrounding counties, but that 'They never received a farthing, but for the most part have been left to their own shift, and constrained to eat Fruit and the Cornes that were growing upon the ground …'. It would appear that not only the innocent country folk but the Scots soldiery themselves were to be pitied. However, there seems to have been little violence and no loss of life.[17]

When, in mid-November 1645, Massey's troop was ordered to withdraw from Monmouth it was forces from Goodrich, among others, who were called on to retake the town for the king.[18] However, by the autumn of 1645 the efforts of the New Model Army had begun to bear fruit – Cardiff and Bristol fell to Parliament, and Chepstow and Monmouth were recaptured. Then, at the end of the year, Hereford fell to Colonel Birch (Fig. 8.2). Sir Henry Lingen, in the city at that time, and the governor, Sir Barnabas Scudamore, escaped across the frozen Wye and reached Goodrich.[19] Here there was a garrison of over 100 men, with at least 60 horses housed in the stables within the outer defences. From this base, Lingen and his troop of horse rode out to harass and forage in the surrounding countryside. Colonel Birch noted with irritation that no passenger was safe between Hereford and Gloucester while the ferry was controlled from Goodrich, and he could not leave Hereford for fear of the city being plundered.[20]

Fig. 8.2 The figure of Col John Birch on his memorial in Weobley Church

Lingen's marauding activities depended on his supply of horses and forage, so Birch determined simultaneous surprise attacks on the stables and on the troops in the 'Boat House' (probably the ferryman's cottage) who guarded the crossing. Several accounts of this attack survive.[21] Roe, Birch's secretary, explained the position of the stables:

> One great stable, within the outward wall of Gutheridge Castle; the backe of the stable being it selfe part of the wall … being as neere the castle wall that only a carte loaden could pass between the castle it selfe and this outer counter scarfe.

Birch left Hereford with 500 men during the night of the 9th of March 1646 and arrived at Goodrich before dawn. Roe described the attack: 'The castle it selfe, hearing soe great a noyse about the gate, supposed the danger there, therefore applied all their force thither'. Meantime a second party with ladders had scaled the walls, breached the rear stable wall and led out 76 of the horses, before firing the stables.[22]

Fig. 8.3 Aerial photograph showing traces of the Parliamentary encampment or leaguer on the hill to the west of the castle. Inset: an indication of the shape and size of the leaguer

Birch, in a letter to the Speaker, reiterated the main action, and added:

> In the mean time I fell on their out-Guard, in a place called the Boat-House, which was within Pistoll shot of the Castle [much more than a pistol shot!] which held out two houres untill it was digged thorow; then they desired quarter for their lives; wherein was Major Pateson, Commander of the Horse, and Major Benskin and 15 Gentlemen more and Troopers, whom I brought to Hereford. This success it pleased the Lord to give me with little losse, which is very advantageous.[23]

The guard at the Boat House was intended to protect the castle from attackers using the ferry or the ford, and would have hardly been expecting a surprise attack from the castle direction. Even so, their dogged defence of the guard-post tied down some of Birch's troops for two hours before the final surrender.

Nevertheless, it is evident that Colonel Birch's plan worked perfectly. The men defending the stables were captured or slain and the horses seized, while the defenders at the gate were too preoccupied with what they saw as the main attack to notice what else was happening.

The foundations and paving of the stables survive on the west side of the castle (see Chapter 18) with a driving way separating them from the main part of the castle and built against the outer works, just as described by Roe. The outer wall would have had only a slight defensive function and, since it could be scaled using a 13-rung ladder, would have been no more than 3.5 metres high. Some of the stabling may well have been built by Lingen using some of Tyler's 81 great oaks and Sir Edward Powell's long boards in its construction. Such a large stable is unlikely to have been needed in the post-medieval history of the castle except during the Civil War.

Sir Henry Lingen, far from being crushed by the loss of his horses, set about replacing them. With typical bravado and within weeks of the loss, Lingen and a party of 30 horsemen attempted to storm Hereford in Birch's absence, counting, in vain, on the citizens to rise in their support.[24] At that time Colonel Birch was active in other areas, notably Worcestershire and Ludlow. In late May 1646, with Worcester and Oxford both under siege, Birch placed 'a body of horse and foot and two mortar pieces and other equipage'[25] around Goodrich and settled down to blast and starve out the garrison.

Tradition says that the first action of the Parliamentary forces was to cut the water pipes, so recently repaired by Richard Tyler, and this may well have been the case. Samuel Meyrick, writing in the 1840s, claimed:

> Their first movement was to cut off the supply of water which issued from four springs on the hill on which Goodrich Court now stands and after passing along a stone gutter was conveyed by leaden pipe down to the valley and up again into the castle. The party sent for the purpose were fired on in their march to effect this as a [?] lb. ball was lately dug up in what must have been the route. Having effected that object, which was important as there was no well at the Castle, they took up position about halfway between the Croose and the castle, which they immediately entrenched.[26]

Meyrick was incorrect in saying that there was no well at the castle, but in his time its whereabouts had become unknown and it was not found until clearance work by the Ministry of Works in the 1920s brought it to light again (see Chapter 10).[27] The Parliamentarian encampment or leaguer was apparently on the same hill as the springs (which later were used by Meyrick to supply his own house, Goodrich Court). Traces are apparent on an aerial photograph which outlines a large rectangular area that appears to include triangular corner bastions that are a standard feature of a classic 17th-century layout (Fig. 8.3). The surrounding ditches would have been backfilled after the siege was over, to ensure that they could not be used again should there be another uprising.

At the end of May more cannon was needed at Goodrich: 'Colonel Birch begs the committee to let him have some battering cannon for Godrich, else I may sit long enough before it', and the Governor of Gloucester was required to 'furnish him speedily with two whole culverin'.[28] One of these, a great iron culverin, was sent from Gloucester, and two were obtained from Ludlow.[29] On the 1st of June, the 'pioneers' began to make 'approaches' – dog-leg trenches – towards the castle. The aim was to bring their mortar pieces close enough to the castle so as to shoot grenades over the walls.[30]

In an attempt to resolve the siege, Colonel Birch wrote to Sir Henry Lingen on the 13th of June, expressing 'great desire for his welfare' in view of the fact that Oxford had surrendered, and urging him to do likewise. Lingen refused, claiming that he expected relief, and that as the king had entrusted the castle to him he was unable to deliver it up without the king's express command. On receiving this reply Colonel Birch resolved 'never to parley more; and thereupon sent them in six grenadoes and tore down a piece of one of their towers'.[31] On the 18th of June, Birch wrote to the Speaker of the House of Commons:

> I am approached on all sides so near that they annoy me with throwing stones. I find the thing in itself very strong, and the defendants (being excepted persons and papists) very desperate. They have made many sallies, insomuch that they have lost several times 100 horse, and now they have not above 5 remaining. They have not killed one above 24 men in all, and never took one prisoner, though divers times we have been at hand blows, and I find my batteries, mortar pieces and mining, being the three ways we now put in execution, having cast a mortar piece here which carries a shell of 200lbs weight. I shall spend more powder than is here to be had, and for want of which I shall not be able to go on, if not supplied; my humble request therefore to the Parliament is for 80 barrels of powder for the service of this place and county; the magazine at Hereford being very small, with which assistance I question not to give you an account of this.

This letter appears in no fewer than three versions,[32] the fullest, (that quoted from the *Perfect Occurences* by Meyrick) being the one just transcribed. The grenades apparently came from the Forest of Dean.[33] The mortar, which was described by Roe as the 'great mortarpiece you made there', was most likely cast at Goodrich Old Forge located at the bottom of New Mills Hill, only 1½ miles from the castle, the furnace at Whitchurch (another possible site) probably not being in use at this time.[34] It is assumed that the mortar piece is the one called 'Roaring Meg', which now stands in the courtyard at the castle (Fig. 8.4). Faintly discernible on the casting is the line: '16 Co. Jo. B. 46'.[35]

The new mortar seems to have been a success and together with the other guns did considerable damage. A letter written from Goodrich on the 4th of July reported that 'there is great execution done in the castle by those shots we have made; that many parts of it are torn'.

Birch sent for two more big guns and it seems that they were forthcoming for on the 14th of July:[36]

> Our guns, have made a breach in the upper part of the wall, and the granadoes have done much spoil in the castle; yet they take no more notice of it, than if no enemy were before it, acting very little against us.[37]

According to Roe's account, Birch himself fired 19 of the 22 grenades that were shot into the castle from Roaring Meg.[38] The iron balls were hollow, filled with gunpowder and with a fuse attached. The secret was to provide sufficient length of fuse to avoid the grenade detonating in transit, but not so much as to allow the defendants time to put it out. Roe maintained that 'the enimy was terified, much of the inner part of the castle ffallen down'.[39] Efforts seem to have been concentrated on the north-west or Ladies' Tower, which was seen as the weakest point. One grenade was found, many years later, inside the well (see Chapter 10).

Fig. 8.4 Roaring Meg in the courtyard of Goodrich Castle.
Inset: one of the exploding shells or grenades found at the castle and now on display

As the mortars battered the upper face of the tower, the sappers tunnelled towards the outer curtain wall from the side of the valley to the west. The going was slow; the mine 'went heavily on for ten yards at least through ffirme rocke'. A dip in the ground just outside the wall and not far from the north-west tower may well indicate a collapse along the line of the mine – openings were still visible in the 19th century alongside the path leading up from the ferry. The 'Cavaliers' are said to have jeered at the pioneers hacking their way through the rock, saying 'they cared not for being blown up, they could from the sky laugh at the flourishing of the Roundheads'.[40] But, in spite of the difficulties, by the 18th of July the mine was 'in very good forwardness'.[41]

Lingen was not content with jeering; he set his men to dig a countermine from inside the Lady Tower. Birch responded – according to Roe, 'in the night you beat downe a tower of the castle into the mouth of their countermine; the tower falling so furiously that they could no wayes defend their mine'.[42]

Birch followed this up with the intention of storming the castle. One of his officers wrote:

> And all things were in so faire a way that wee were almost ready to storme; then which the Souldiers desired nothing more, so that all both Colonel, Officers and Souldiers, should not have needed to have been hastned, had not the worke been shortned in another way. We were so neere the storme, that Colonel Birch had drawne up the Horse and Foot, and was ordering them into a posture for falling on. But the enemy in Gotheridge Castle perceiving in what posture wee were in, and seeing how they were on all sides surprized, their hearts began to faile them, so that they took a most fearfull Alarm; and … being unwilling to endure a storme … they desired a parley, but my Colonell would not grant that, though much importuned for it: insomuch as when they saw we would not admit of any delay, they tooke in their Standerd Colours, and held out their white Flagge of Truce, and begged that they might march out Honourably to their owne homes, and some to garrisons.[43]

This request also was disregarded – all Birch was prepared to offer was 'mercy for their lives'. They were required to surrender and to forfeit all the arms, ammunition and provisions remaining in the castle. According to a letter from Nathaniel Kyrle to William Scudamore, they 'are to march out this day att 12 of the clock leaving all things behind them butt what they carry in theyr pocketts'.[44]

Local tradition claims that the garrison, with Sir Henry Lingen at their head, marched out of the castle to a tune called by his name, but in fact they left as prisoners. The tune 'Harry Lingen's Folly' was retained as a dance in the 18th century, but by the time that Webb was writing in the mid-19th century it was lost.[45]

Various versions are given for the numbers of surviving officers and men. Roe claimed that there were 60 officers and gentlemen, but does not specify the common soldiers; 'N.H.', writing from the Parliamentary leaguer, believed there were about 50 gentlemen and 120 soldiers and offered to send a list of names. Meyrick, working from *Perfect Occurrences*, named 37 officers and gentlemen, plus a supposed priest, and estimated 60 soldiers. He also listed what they left behind – two hammer pieces, four barrels of powder with match and bullets, and 120 arms, 'fixt and unfixt'. The lack of ordnance and powder may explain why there was so little retaliation from the besieged garrison.[46]

The defenders also left behind 30 barrels of beer, great stores of corn and meal, 150 bushels of peas, a hogshead of claret and another of wine, half a hogshead of sack and plenty of butter, cheese and beef. Excavations in the last century uncovered a heap of coal and a skillet embossed with the slogan 'C. U. B. LOYAL TO HIS MAGISTEIE'[47] (Plate 24, p.198) (see Chapter 20). It would appear that throughout the siege provisions could be obtained from the surrounding countryside and the castle was well stocked.[48]

With Goodrich Castle in Parliamentary hands, only Raglan Castle, where the massing of troops had first brought the Wye Valley into the conflict, remained as a Royalist stronghold in the area. The victors of Oxford, Worcester and Goodrich united against this last enemy stronghold and, 19 days after the fall of Goodrich, Raglan Castle also fell.

Although there is little direct evidence for the state of Goodrich Castle after Sir Henry Lingen's troops had been marched into captivity, all the indications are that it was in a poor state. Some of the damage can be estimated from the reports of the siege: '… the upper part of the walls were damaged and much of the inner part of the castle [is] ffallen downe, and the roof spoyled and there was noe whole roome left in it'.[49] It seems likely that the main attack and the greatest damage was on the west side of the castle, where the guns, situated on the opposite hillside had the most impact. The damage to the north-west tower is still obvious, only the basement walls surviving. On the south side, the wall close to the keep seems to have been another casualty, although the section next to the south-east tower survived well into the 19th century.

It is very likely that the damage to the inner part of the castle mentioned by Roe affected the timber-framed gallery and rooms along the east side of the courtyard. Although the roofs were 'spoyled', they were not necessarily damaged beyond repair. Indeed, if the building still afforded reasonable shelter to the Royalist defenders (and to the later garrison), it is likely that some parts of it were still habitable.

Although Birch was called away almost immediately to other projects, he left behind skeleton forces at both Goodrich and Hereford. It also seems that Richard Tyler returned to live at the castle.[50] No doubt the complaint he drew up was the product of long hours checking his own and his patron's property. Whilst this was happening, the future of the castle remained uncertain. On the 1st of March 1647 it was reported that Parliament had decreed that it was to be slighted. The order was repeated in July, with the addition that 'works made sithence these troubles dismantled' and the castle 'disgarrisoned'.[51] This order was carried out, as Colonel Birch's regiment, which occupied both Hereford and Goodrich, was disbanded and paid off in July 1647.[52]

The Dowager Duchess of Kent was the then owner of Goodrich Castle. The new Earl of Kent, a somewhat distant cousin, was a fervent supporter of Parliament and it was obviously something of an embarrassment to the government that military strategy demanded the destruction of property belonging to their own side. In August, Parliament sent John Selden to explain the matter to the countess. Selden was a suitable choice to break the news. Not only was he a Member of Parliament, but he had also acted as legal adviser to both her and the late earl, and was a close personal friend of the countess, administering the Herefordshire estates on her behalf. Indeed, rumour had it that they had secretly married.[53]

The matter was left in the hands of Richard Tyler, the constable of Goodrich, who arranged for the dismantling of the building that he had spent so long renovating; the work was completed by July 1648. Since the troops had by this time dispersed, it appears that the demolition was in the hands of local workmen, who had to be paid. This is borne out by an order made by the Committee for Herefordshire and Gloucestershire stating: 'Ordered that the T[reasu]rer to the Committee doth forthwith pay unto Richard Tyler gent Tenn pounds for the pulling downe of Goodrich Castle'.

Payment was made in two instalments of £5. This must have been a contribution towards the demolition expenses, but can hardly have covered the whole. It is likely that the sale of building materials was also used to defray the cost of the work, since it seems that all the post-medieval features, such as the fireplaces, staircases and door-cases that belonged to the 17th-century domestic quarters were removed, leaving merely the vestiges of the surrounding stonework. The castle seems to have been systematically stripped of everything of value.

The extent of actual slighting is more uncertain, but probably included the removal of crenellations and other wall top works, the dismantling of the main defensive features of the gatehouse including the portcullises and the drawbridge, and the razing of the barbican (which had no other function apart from adding to the defence of the castle).

A clue to these events comes from the writings of Captain Silas Taylor, who commanded a troop in Birch's regiment and was probably present during the siege. He was based in Hereford between 1649 and 1657 as one of the team of sequestrators in Herefordshire. These officers were appointed by Parliament to fine the Royalist 'delinquents' and confiscate their lands. Despite his unenviable job, Silas Taylor was a likable character who got into trouble with his own side for undue sympathy to his opponents. He was also an antiquarian and, as part of his notes for a history of Herefordshire, wrote an account of Goodrich Castle in 1655. What is particularly interesting is the way he refers to the castle:

Fig. 8.5 The entrance gateway and drawbridge pit in 1798 (Bonner)

> About a quarter of a mile or thereabouts [from the church] is the castle of Godrich, a very strong pile, a mighty deep trench being hewen into the maine rocke, where it wants the steepnes of the hill wch it hath upon 2 sides and part of the 3rd. The entrance into it, through a strong gatehouse, is over a little neck of land borne up on both sides with stonework, and is towards the east; it is noe great circuit. It is almost square in the figure, having 4 great round towers for its defence at the four corners of it. When you are passed the strong gate of the castle, the first thing on your left hand is a chapple, wth the picture of a Talbot on the south wall, with the garter of St George about it, and an Earles crownett upon it.

Fig. 8.6 Samuel and Nathaniel Buck's depiction of the castle in 1732

The Lady's [sic] Tower was battered by Coll. Birch. It is reported by many witnesses that ye cellars of the castle were floored with Irish earth, for that whenever they brought a toade into them and laide it on ye earth it would dye, and this they did to preserve their cellars from venome, and it is thought that the very timber came alsoe from Ireland, for there was not either spider or cobwebbe to be seen, but it is reported that in Monmouthshire there is a little spott of land of that nature.

The Hall was on the west side of the castle, where was observable a beame of oake intire without knott or knarle of 66 feet long, and held 20 inches or 2 feet square the whole length. The hall itself was 60 feet, allowing three feet for the beame in the wall.[54]

His description suggests that he knew the castle both before it was slighted and after demolition had taken place, fitting the suggestion that his troop was part of the besieging force. His description of the entrance, over 'the little neck of land' and through 'the strong gate of the castle', surely refers to a time before the slighting. The removal of the timberwork that spanned the 'deep pit' at the entrance, visible in the 1790s drawing by Bonner (Fig. 8.5), meant that this way into the castle was effectively blocked. It was presumably in the 1650s that Taylor was able to see the huge beam that had supported the hall ceiling, which would not have been visible until the ceiling panelling had been removed.

The general slighting of the castle is evident to some extent on the illustration of the ruins produced by Samuel and Nathaniel Buck in 1732 (Fig. 8.6). The outer parts of the gatehouse had evidently been dismantled, but the engraving suggests that only the upper parts of the towers and walls had been taken down, leaving the entire castle roofless with vegetation already strongly rooted on top of the walls. The only significant change may be that the top of the chapel tower appears to be more complete than it is now.[55]

In 1796 Charles Heath visited the castle with Christopher Llewellyn, then 93 years old. Llewellyn had always lived in the area and had worked as a navigator or boatman on the Wye. He declared that the only difference to the castle since he was a boy was that the insides of all the rooms had been 'neatly whitewashed', but that 'none of the roofs or floors of the rooms were in existence in his day, any more than at present'. Heath assumed that the post-Civil War slighting had been responsible for the general state of the buildings and considered that this was a reasonable assumption as Llewellyn would have known the castle in the early 1700s when the building had only had some 50 years of ruin.[56] Bonner and King, writing at much the same time, noted that the wheel which worked the portcullis had been seen within the memory of someone living in 1788, and that the hinges of the great entrance gate were still in place but little else remained of the fittings.[57]

Although the local committee paid promptly for the dismantling, the countess had to wait for compensation. On the 20th of June 1649, there was an 'Order in Parliament that the Council of State consider a former order as to demolishing Gooderich Castle and as to satisfaction to the Countess of Kent in respect thereof'.[58] In July it was reported to the House of Commons that '£1,000 ought to be allowed the Countess of Kent in respect of the demolishing of Gooderich castle to be paid out of revenue'.[59] Although no record has been found for the actual payment to the countess, there is no doubt that it was made, for five years later it was used as a pretext for a later claim by the Earl of Lincoln, who was demanding compensation for the destruction of Tattenhall Castle.[60]

In 1651 the Countess of Kent died, leaving most of her personal property to John Selden, whom she had appointed as her executor. The estate was in a bad way financially, no doubt due to the war. There was not sufficient revenue from the Goodrich and other Herefordshire and Gloucestershire estates to cover the £2,000 intended for legacies and funeral expenses, and Selden and his fellow trustee had to advance money out of their own pockets. The Goodrich estate passed to the 10th Earl of Kent, grandson of the countess's husband's cousin.[61]

Tyler continued to act for the family, collecting rents for the manor and receiving letters from the countess's trustees addressed to him at Goodrich Castle.[62] It is not known for certain where Tyler was living during the occupation of the castle and the destruction of much of the farm, although, after 1648, he may have moved to Flanesford Priory which for many years had been used as the home farm for the estate. In 1655 Silas Taylor described the priory as 'the beginnings of a religious house called Flanford a very sumptuous hall was finished, the foundations of a large church layd yet to be seen and nothing else done to it'.[63] This could either mean that there had never been a church on the site, or that the farmhouse was one of the 'priory buildings' destroyed during the siege.

However, by the time of his death in 1663 Tyler had moved to a large house in the village with five rooms on each floor. Both his will and the probate inventory make it clear that he was farming on a large scale. Tyler had managed the castle estates for the lords of Goodrich manor for at least 30 eventful years, possibly more as he may have worked for the Shrewsbury/Kent family from as early as 1611 when he was living at Eccleswall, another Shrewsbury manor.[64]

9   The Castle as Ruin & Tourist Attraction (1690-1915)
by Pat Hughes & Ron Shoesmith

The Castle as a Ruin (*by* Pat Hughes)
Although the castle was no longer in use as a residence, the Grey family, earls of Kent, kept the ruin in their own hands and when, at the end of the 17th century, they leased out the priory (or Castle Farm as it was then called) they did so with the exception of:

> All that Castle called Goodrich Castle together with the Scite of the said Castle and all the walls and outbuildings and ground and land belonging to the same which has been used of late with the same.[1]

The only part of the castle site that continued in use was the pound, which lay under the castle wall and is evident on the 1718 Lawrence map (Fig. 9.1). The coppice woods called Castle Grove and Prior's Grove were also excluded from the lease, together with 'a Cart Coach or Wayn way to the said Castle, and a footway' both of which seem to have led to the castle from the crossroads at Y Crwys.

The determination of the Grey family to keep the castle in their own hands resulted in the preservation of much of the remaining fabric. Although parts of the walls eventually succumbed to the ravages of time and weather, there is no evidence that the castle was used as a quarry for building materials as happened at many other similar sites. The stones stayed where they fell and although Heath stated that 'many parts were choaked with rubbish and stones which had fallen in the course of years', much of the castle remained intact. The 1732 Buck engraving (Fig. 8.6) shows the castle in essentially the same state as it was at the beginning of the 20th century.

In addition to its role as a fortified dwelling house, during its heyday the castle had also served as court-house, prison and archive depository. After the slighting these functions had to be moved elsewhere. The court-house had already been dealt with; as far back as 1616 it had been moved into the village, the parish house having been refurbished for this purpose at the Earl of Shrewsbury's expense.[2] Courts were also sometimes held in the church at Whitchurch.[3]

The prison was at the castle and there are numerous allusions in the court rolls to those in custody there.[4] After the slighting, and with no one in residence, the prison was no longer secure even though the structure was intact. Accordingly, a lock-up, which features on the map made in 1718/9, was built where Y Crwys now stands; it may form the base for the present house (see Chapter 2). No reference to the construction of this building has been found nor is there any mention of its existence until 1695, when Thomas Fletcher, Joseph Powell and Thomas Lucas were required to:

> … sufficiently repair and amend the way and cutt their overhanginge leading from the Prison belonging to the Mannor Scituate in Crewe [Crwys] to Goodrich passage.[5]

This refers to the right-of-way leading from Y Crwys to the ford and ferry crossing at Goodrich Boat. Ten years later the accounts contain an entry for 2s 4d paid for 'a strong lock for Goodrich prison door'.[6] Archives had also been deposited at the castle, but after the slighting they were apparently placed in the upper floor of the lock-up at Y Crwys.[7] At the beginning of the 18th century there was a move to send these items to the Earl of Kent's chief steward in London: 'In October 1713 A Box with Records of the Mannors of Goodrich and Eccleswall was sent to London to Mr Bellamy in Order to be abstracted'.[8] The following year 60 or so more rolls, from the reigns of Henry VII to Charles II, were dispatched to London by the Hereford carrier, and in 1722 more records were sent.

A letter in September 1722 from Henry Vaughan, the earl's agent at Goodrich, implies that the clearance was nearly complete:

> I am now ready to deliver not only the old records that I formerly mentioned to you that were over the prison but allsoe those of the mannor of Huntley and Leigh those of Longhope and those of Eccleswall all completely done upp in a very nice and exact manner.[9]

At the end of the 17th century the estate records took on a new importance in a long-running legal battle between the Greys and the Halls of Gloucestershire over the ownership of certain fishing rights. This required much searching of the manorial records and those in the Tower and Star Chamber in order to establish title to the property.[10] Such preoccupation with these legal rights underlines the value of the fisheries and the iron works in the manor economy.[11] In the meantime, the River Navigation Act of 1695, which was supported by the Earl of Kent, presented a new set of problems, since weirs which hindered navigation had to be removed.[12]

These disputes led the Earl of Kent to commission a definitive survey of all his estates. The surveyor, Edward Lawrence, travelled the earl's estates, surveying and mapping between 1718 and 1719, at the conclusion of which he wrote to the earl:

> I have surveyed at least 1,000 Acres of Free Land (as appears by ye Mapps) which I could not avoid by reason it lay so intermixt with other of your Graces Lands.
> I have Likewise spent a Considerable part of my time to obtain the Lives in Being to take abstracts of Leases, Coppys and other writings in order to set forth your Graces lands, as well as to make up perfect Rent Rolls with the improved Values from the Same together with the Coppy-holders of Inheritance and freeholders in the Severall Mannors.
> These and the above mentioned Surveys I shall leave intirely to your Graces generousity not Doubting but you will some way or other (as your Grace shall think fit) Encourage me for the Extraordinary trouble I have been at.[13]

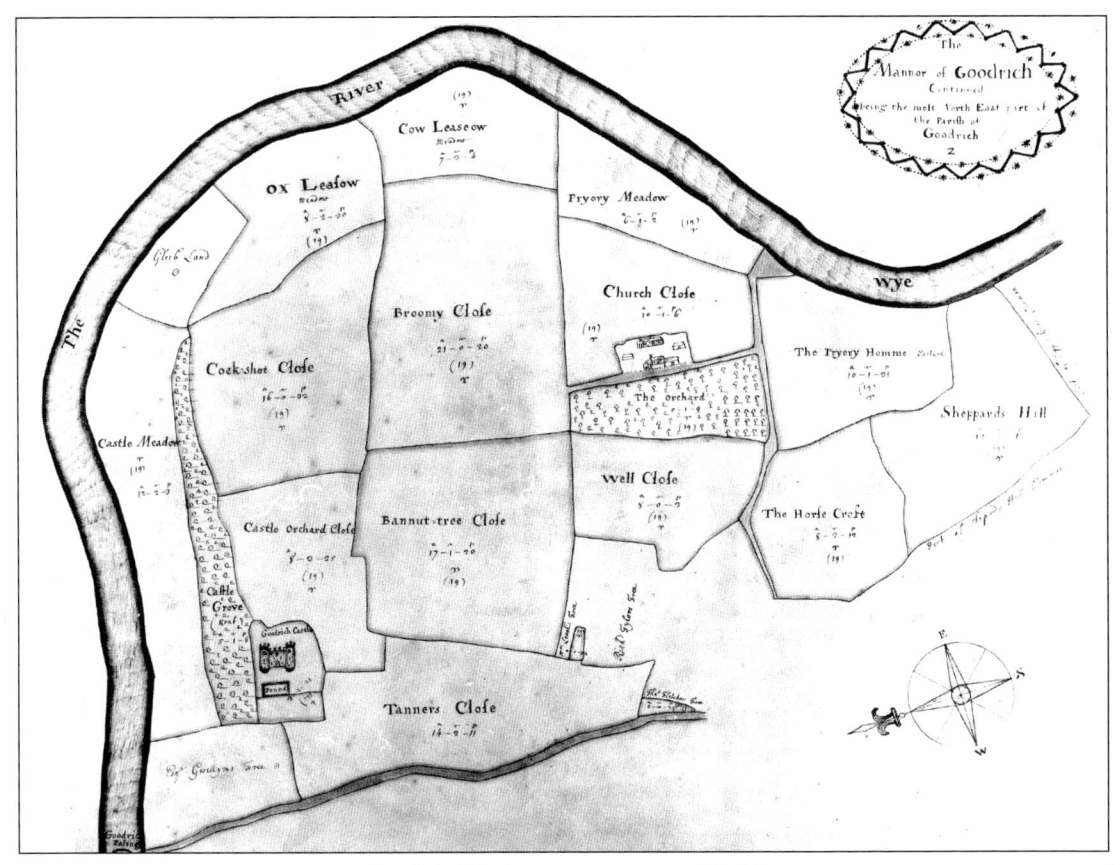

Fig. 9.1 The Lawrence map of 1718

The page from the map book containing Goodrich Castle depicts a stylised castle, with the pound built against the outer courtyard wall on the north-west side, the Boat Lane leading to Goodrich Passage and the buildings of Flanesford Priory, which became the Priory Farm (Fig. 9.1).[14] Lawrence used this map of the environs of the castle as a base for a fictitious map, which he labelled 'A Survey of Dun Boggs Farm in the Manor of Haversham', and distributed it to advertise his skills (Fig. 9.2).[15] In spite of some inadequacies the manor map is of considerable value, both for its large scale and for the information it provides on features that have long since disappeared. These include the Conduit Field, the prison at Y Crwys (see Chapter 2), and the various forges, although the page showing the New Weir is missing.

The various areas of woodland are also marked, emphasizing the continuing importance of timber production as a source of income. The trees were either coppiced, the bark sold to tanners and the wood cut into cordwood, or were sold as standing timber, to be cut and made into charcoal.[16] The general management of the woodlands was the responsibility of the forester, who was supplied with a uniform of green broadcloth and green worsted stockings.[17] His office was no sinecure; in 1716 14s 6d was paid for 'a fortnight's service about the Dowards Wood and Expenses endeavouring to find out the offenders who set it on Fyre'.[18]

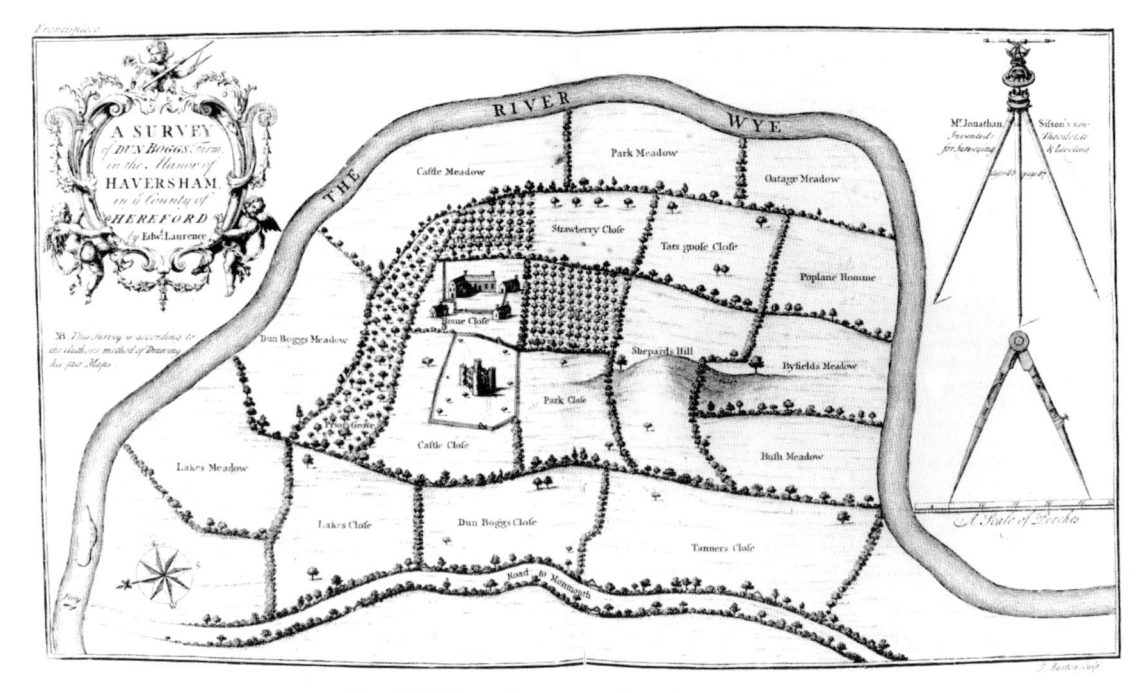

Fig. 9.2 The advertising Dun Boggs map

The early part of the 18th century saw increasing emphasis placed on the profits from the 'Fine Quarry of Stone on Coppid Wood'.[19] The earl was also anxious to get all the lime-kilns in the manor into his own hands so that he could dictate the price of lime.[20]

The earl, by then Duke of Kent, died in 1740 with no male offspring. By his will his trustees were empowered to sell his Goodrich and other Herefordshire estates. The proceeds were to be used to buy land near the family seat at Wrest in Bedfordshire, and this was to be settled on his granddaughter, Jemima Campbell.[21] The particulars of the estate, undated but probably set down soon after the death of the duke, list the most profitable of the assets and emphasise once again the prominent position of the woodlands, iron works and fishery.[22]

For some years the estate continued to be administered by the duke's trustees, and it was not until 1755 that the sale was finalised.[23] The new Lord of the Manor was Thomas Griffin, Admiral of the White Fleet, who lived further down the Wye at Hadnock.

The Tourist Attraction – The Wye Tour (*by* Ron Shoesmith)

It was not until the middle of the 18th century that tourism in the British Isles became an acceptable form of relaxation and a new interest for the gentry, following the growing unrest in Europe. Antiquarians such as William Stukeley not only established a sense of history within the landscape, but also brought a realisation of the potential that buildings and ruins could have in becoming constituent parts of an idealised romantic landscape. Thomas Fosbroke wrote:

> The Romantic in Scenery is characterised by every object being wild, abrupt and fantastic. Endless varieties discover at every turn something new and unexpected; so that we are at once amused and surprised, and curiosity is constantly gratified but never satiated.[24]

The appreciation of such landscapes 'in the raw' led to the 'tours', such as those in the Lake District, the Derbyshire Dales and the Wye Valley, becoming an acceptable alternative to 'taking the waters' at the growing spa towns. The early tourists saw their voyages down the Wye as a sequence of scenic delights that included ruins such as Goodrich Castle and Tintern Abbey. However, they also saw beauty in the industrial developments in the form of the smoking iron furnaces that littered the riverside, the busy scenes of river traffic, and the commercial activities on the banks.

William Gilpin, one of the earlier tourists in the area, recognized the way that ruins in general, and Goodrich Castle in particular, had become integral parts of the scenery. This was the time of the cult of the 'picturesque' and Gilpin wrote of the castle as seen on his boat trip downstream:

> Four miles from Ross, we came to Godrich Castle; where a grand view presented itself; and we rested on our oars to examine it. A reach of the river, forming a noble bay, is spread before the eye. The bank on the right, is steep and covered with wood; beyond which a bold promontory shoots out, crowned with a castle, rising among trees.
>
> This view, which is one of the grandest on the river, I should not scruple to call *correctly picturesque,* which is seldom the character of a purely natural scene.[25]

It is rather disenchanting to have to record that Gilpin then passed on his way downstream without stopping to visit the castle, just because it was raining. However, his written works became a stimulus for what was eventually a well-organised tourist industry and also greatly influenced a whole series of later writers of guide books.

It was in 1749 that the then newly-formed Ross Trust turnpiked the three-mile stretch of road from the town to Goodrich Boat. Most visitors started their tour by finding accommodation in Ross and, to cut costs, some walked, rode or travelled by carriage along the turnpike to the river, crossed by the ferry and then walked up to the castle. Thus the Hon. John Byng, having stayed overnight in Ross, wrote in his diary for the 27th of July 1787:

> [We followed] a bye-course, thro' lanes, by the advice of our host, to the ferry near Goodrich, which our horses cross'd without terror. … Goodrich Castle is in the utmost splendour of a ruin; and our survey was ample and investigatory; tho' situate on a hill top it is most happily skreen'd by wood and soft'ned to the sight.[26]

After leaving the castle he continued his journey to Monmouth and commented that 'A narrow lane of one mile led us [from the ferry] to the turnpike road'. This confirms the fact that although the road from Ross to the ferry had been turnpiked, the road on the opposite bank leading to Goodrich village had remained unturnpiked.

In 1796 Charles Heath visited the Wye Valley and noted that 'Travellers who visit this place by water will meet with a clean room and frugal fare at Mr Davis's, of the Ferry-house, which is situated near the edge of the river' (Fig. 9.3).[27] He noted with disapproval the lack of ivy on the walls:

> If time were permitted to add the ornament of ivy, to some parts of the exterior, so as to cover the harsh feature of the stone, which is of a dingy red colour, it would greatly

Fig. 9.3 The ferry and the Boat House with the castle in the background

contribute to its beauty; but as sheep are kept within its boundary, it is torn down in the winter season, and given to them for fodder.

By this time, tourists wanted to know more about the castle and other historic features on the Wye. Much of the information was provided by T. Bonner, who produced his *Copperplate Perspective Itinerary* or *Pocket Portfolio* consisting of ten views of Goodrich in 1798 (Fig. 9.4). The text includes an outline history of the castle and its successive owners, descriptions of Ross, Flanesford, Coppett Hill etc., and detailed directions for the best and easiest ways to approach the castle. He describes in considerable detail the contents of each of his engravings, even showing on his plan the exact point from which the illustration was made (Fig. 9.5). Bonner's *Perspective Itinerary* was a detailed piece of research, well in advance of its time, and was aimed at the discerning and rich tourist, for it was far from cheap at 7s 6d.

Most visitors approached the castle from the ferry (Fig. 9.3 & Plate 6, p.60) and in 1798 Bonner described the approach as being up a zig zag path through the wood to arrive at the south-west corner of the outer work. From here, the way into the castle involved a scramble up the ditch and through the curtain wall near to the keep, an area subsequently revealed to be the kitchen (Fig. 9.5). As late as 1924, the way up to the castle from the ferry was recognised as a right-of-way.

By the end of the 18th century Ross had become firmly established as the main base for those taking the Wye Tour by river. The visits were so well organized that travellers were escorted from their hotel to their boats by the owners so that 'their ears should not be pained with a coarseness of language, too frequently heard from the navigators of public rivers'.[28] This was when barges were taking coal and household goods upstream to Hereford and beyond, and bringing agricultural produce and cider downstream to Chepstow and thence across the Severn

Fig. 9.4 The Wye and Goodrich Castle (Bonner 1798)

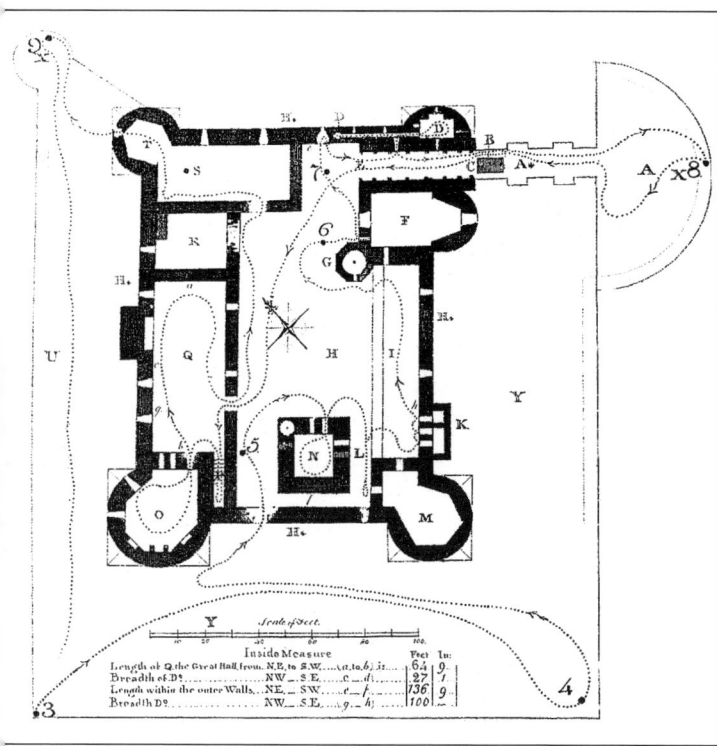

Fig. 9.5 Plan of Goodrich Castle (Bonner, 1798)

Estuary to Bristol.[29] The standard tour on the Wye by boat could be quite expensive – Joseph Farington noted that in 1803 the cost of a boat from Ross to Monmouth was one-and-a-half guineas, with an additional half-guinea for the steersman and the two oarsmen.

By 1804 Edward King had produced the third volume of his impressive work *Monumenta Antiqua or Observations on Ancient Castles*. This contained a section on Goodrich Castle, well illustrated with detailed plans and line drawings but, as with much of his writing, containing several factual mistakes. It is unfortunate that the section on the castle in Brayley & Britton's *Description of the County of Hereford*, published in 1805, is little more than a copy of King, and as a result produces no additional information.

91

Sir Samuel Meyrick's influence on the area has already been noted in Chapter 2. Louisa Anne Twamley, who visited the area in 1838, described her impressions in her book *Autumn Ramble by the Wye*. After visiting the Court, she walked to the castle through a muddy lane hung with blackberries and noted:

> The entrance is very beautiful : you look under a lofty gateway, between towers canopied with ivy, along a gloomy array of portcullises and archways, extending fifty feet; then across the open area, and beyond that through a large lofty arch, which gracefully frames the picture of the distant Court. 'Tis the loveliest reception imaginable! Then you enter, and survey the numerous portcullis grooves, the dark and narrow gallery in the wall, and the other contrivances for defence.

She found a guide at the castle who entertained her with 'parrot-like recitations' and presumably provided the ladder that enabled her to gain access to the spiral staircase leading to the top of the keep, which she described as 'rather a dizzy exploit'. She was particularly attracted to the 'silvery-seeded clematis, or Traveller's Joy' which at that time grew in wild and lavish profusion. She composed a poem *The Traveller's Joy* which included:

> One day, a year ago,–
> Alas! that Time will never stint his wing,
>   I stood within the court
> Of Goodrich Castle, in whose halls now spring
>   Flowers unmolested; and in chimneys cold
> Ferns wave, and nettles cluster; and the growth
>   Of ivy-stems, by freedom long made bold,
> Rivals the oak's gnarled trunk.
> Round about the buttressed tower,
>   And over the Donjon-keep,
> The clematis weaves her dainty bower
>   And decks it bravely with leaf and flower,
> In draperies broad and deep.[30]

By the mid 19th century the castle had been covered by the ivy so valued by Charles Heath. H.T. Timmins, a Birmingham artist, toured Herefordshire in 1891 and of his visit to Goodrich (Fig. 9.6) he observed that:

> Around and within the moat, a luxuriant growth of trees and shrubs veils the old walls in a mantle of delicate green foliage; while the ruined bastions which once frowned upon the drawbridge are now wreathed in masses of dark ivy.[31]

In 1892 a group of four undergraduates from University College, London made a boating and camping trip down the Wye, a journey one of their number recorded in a sketchbook. Arriving at Goodrich Castle:

> a gamekeeper gave us permission to camp. ... The custodian eyed us somewhat askance; he was used to people visiting, but here we were evidently come to stay. We told him we

had permission (without mentioning authority) and he was affability itself. ... This was the best pitch we had, free from coleoptera, diptera etc. ... We dine[d] in the banqueting hall (rather eerie) and though we called on the scullions to clear up, there was no voice, save the bleating of sheep or the restless cry of some bird. ... some visitors arrived and we scaled the walls, were shown the dungeons, and some freehand drawings by King Henry IV.[32]

By the end of the 19th century the castle was becoming reasonably well equipped for visitors. Rather than scramble over the ruined south curtain wall to gain access, visitors were expected to use the ramp from the barbican. The drawbridge pit was left open and was fenced off; the visitor kept to the north of the pit and rather precariously walked on the edging wall to where a gate blocked the passageway (Fig. 9.7). Here was a bell pull, which, by means of wires, attracted the attention of the custodian who had a small, rather attractive, rustic shed set into the window opening to the west of the gate passage (Fig. 9.8).

Fig. 9.6 H.T. Timmins' sketch of the castle in 1891

Fig. 9.7 The heavily overgrown entrance to the castle in 1872

In the early years of The Woolhope Naturalists' Field Club, members' interests were almost exclusively in the field of natural history, and historical sites and antiquities were very much a fringe interest. However, in June 1870, the members, along with their wives, decided to take a section of the Wye Tour including Goodrich Castle:[33]

> The fine woods of Pencraig were soon reached and the turrets of Goodrich Court, which some people admire, gave place to the noble ruins of Goodrich Castle standing well above the trees forming such a beautiful object from the river ....
>
> Here the boats as they successively arrived drew to the shore, and their occupants – with an hour's grace – strolled pleasantly up to the castle and inspected the ruins under the guidance of Dr Bull, the president for the day, who pointed out to them the most remarkable features of the fortress, its square formation, the large round towers at the angles, the square Norman keep on its western side, ...[34]

Whilst at the castle Dr Bull provided a short sketch of the history of the castle and read out the various correspondence of John Birch relating to the siege. The visitors then wandered over the various rooms, and many of them ascended the keep for the extensive views it afforded, gathering wild roses from the very summit as memorials of the day.

> The magnificent Ash tree, which grows in the centre of the ruins, received due admiration. It is indeed a fine tree. Its circumference, at five feet from the ground, being 12ft 1in, and it carries its stem up to a considerable height. The Wych Elms, and especially a small leaved Lime tree, on the Castle hill, also attracted attention.

In the early years of the 20th century the Woolhopians paid two further visits to Goodrich, first in 1901 when they trained to Ross and walked through Walford to the ferry.[35] Guide books had proliferated by then, but the members were so impressed by the one written by Prebendary Seaton, the vicar of Goodrich, that they arranged for most of it to be included in their Club Transactions.[36] The railway from Ross to Monmouth had opened to the public on the 4th of August 1873 and the Woolhopians used the train to Kerne Bridge Station for their visit in 1917, when James G. Wood sent a paper on the early history of the castle[37] to be read to the members on their journey.

Fig. 9.8 The custodian's rustic shed set in a window opening in the courtyard

10 THE ANCIENT MONUMENT

by Ron Shoesmith

The records of the Office of Works (later the Ministry of Works, then the Department of the Environment, and now English Heritage) concerning Goodrich Castle, in the Public Record Office at Kew, are rather disappointing. It is evident that they have been 'weeded', and that the files have become somewhat muddled through time. What has been kept is the legal side (the agreements and access arrangements), some plans and photographs relating to repair work, and an indication of the expenditure. Records associated with the finds are discussed in Chapters 19 and 20. The site foreman's and architect's written records have apparently been lost.

The ownership of the castle had passed from Admiral Thomas Griffin (who bought it in 1755) to one of his granddaughters who married a Major Charles Marriott. Their daughter, Louisa, married Edmund Fletcher Bosanquet in 1876. Louisa styled herself 'Lady of the Manor of Goodrich' and owner of the castle (although this may have only been a life interest). The earliest records relate to the scheduling of the castle as an ancient monument (to afford it some protection) on the 13th of January 1915. Following this, there are several letters from Mrs Bosanquet, who is described in one note as 'this infurious lady!'[1] She was attempting to find a solution that did not involve a state take-over, and at one time wrote 'could a purchaser rebuild and live there?'. In December 1919 the castle was put up for auction but without success.

The attempt to sell may have been partly due to a substantial collapse which was described in a report in June 1919 as:

> a portion of the north-west tower 14ft 6ins long and 48ft in height, and a length of 32ft 6ins of adjoining curtain wall (about 33ft. in height) [which] had fallen into the moat.

It appears that there had been two collapses within a short period of time. The weight of the collapsed material was estimated as upwards of 400 tons. The damage was reported to H.M. Commissioners of Works by George Marshall, secretary of the Woolhope Club, in December 1919. He wrote that 'a stretch of curtain wall [had] ... entirely collapsed, carrying with it a window of the banqueting hall, another in the solar behind, and garderobes and other features above'. This was an area of the castle that was seldom photographed and only one print has been found (Fig. 10.1). Not surprisingly, there are several taken after the collapse (Fig. 10.2).

The castle was taken into guardianship on the 8th of July 1920; a note in the file states that 'when it [Goodrich Castle] was in her [Mrs Bosanquet's] charge she allowed it to get into a shocking decay'. On the 1st of October 1920 the Works Department agreed to keep on the caretaker, Mr Bennett, for the six summer months, increasing his pay from £1 to 30s per week. During the winter a Mrs Treherne held the key at 5s per week.

Since being taken into guardianship the ruins of the castle have been carefully consolidated and all the fallen masonry has been removed. The luxuriant growth of trees and shrubs has disappeared from the moat, the magnificent ash has gone from the courtyard, and the masses of dark ivy have been banished from the walls. The ferns no longer wave from high points on the masonry, and the Traveller's Joy, so much appreciated by Louisa Twamley, no longer weaves its way over the ancient high walls of the 12th-century keep (Figs. 10.3 & 4) (see also Chapter 9).

Although the monument had been put into guardianship, Mrs Bosanquet continued to be concerned about access. In October 1924 she wrote to complain about the road leading to the castle. In reply, it was pointed out that the access was by a lane and right-of-way that was not under the charge or control of the Ministry. However, a report written about that time mentioned that:

> In the first field we laid timber logs which were surplus to our requirements when we cut down a large number of trees in the moats – these formed the foundation of the worst parts of the road, roughly about a 160 yard run. These logs were covered with spare stones and the laying of stones at different periods has extended in all to a distance of about 300 yards.

Fig. 10.1 The northern part of the west wall before the 1919 collapse

Fig. 10.2 The northern part of the west wall after the collapse

Fig. 10.3 Looking south-west across the courtyard in 1822. The central building is the south-west tower with the entry from the stair on the left. The ground-level arched opening led into the great hall.

Fig. 10.4 The view looking westwards from the gatehouse across the north range towards the north-west tower. To the left of the double arch is the lobby with indications of the lost section of the west curtain wall in the background.

Mrs Bosanquet considered that she had every right to visit her castle, and that the condition of the access was such that she could not get her car there, and she was too old and infirm to walk. In addition her son and heir had no legs and would have similar problems when he inherited.

The costs of the work at Goodrich raised some concern for Frank Owen, (M.P. for Hereford, 1929-31) who asked a parliamentary question on the 4th of May 1931. He was given a breakdown of costs per year which provides some indication of the varying extent of the work:

Year	Amount	Unemployment related works included
	£ s d	£ s d
1921	1,422 11 2	
1922	1,700 3 4	172 14 4
1923	3,494 18 11	1,344 9 0
1924	3,020 1 7	1,186 13 2
1925	2,147 12 1	367 10 10
1926	1,272 1 8	
1927	1,354 7 7	
1928	1,020 0 4	
1929	1,318 19 1	
1930	1,292 2 8	105 4 3
Totals	20,002 11 8	3,176 11 7

It is evident that most of the work took place in the mid-1920s, and although there was a core of workers, some of the labour force came from the ranks of the unemployed.

The men working at Goodrich Castle needed a supply of water, and in 1928 an agreement was made with Mrs Dorothy Trafford of Goodrich Court:

> ... to take water from a spring situated in Tanner's Close Wood on the Goodrich Court Estate ... and to construct a storage tank around the said spring; also to fix a pump with necessary delivery and other pipes thereon for the purpose of supplying water to Goodrich Castle at a rent of 5s per annum.[2]

The finds records from November 1920 to February 1926 give some indication of the work carried out (see Chapters 19 & 20). Late in 1920 the work was concentrated in the north-west or Ladies' Tower, where many finds were collected from the basement underneath some 4ft 6ins of debris. The workers then moved southwards where garderobe shafts and the neighbouring external areas were cleared. It is evident that much of this work was concentrated on the Civil War damage and the 1919 collapse. By 1921 the courtyard was being cleared, initially by the keep and then, to a depth of some 2ft, on the east side. By October the clearance had extended towards the entrance and the south-west corner, followed by the dungeon.

The kitchen and oven areas were cleared at the beginning of 1922, followed by the basement of the south-west tower. Next, debris was removed from the great hall, the lower levels of the keep, and the basement underneath the chapel. By May, work had extended to the outer wards where the stables area, the north ward, and the area underneath the drawbridge were all dealt with. In early 1923 the workers had moved to the stone-cut ditches where work continued for several months – cannonballs, bullets and horse furniture being found in quantity.

Late in 1922 it was decided to excavate the well, which had presumably been discovered during the clearance operations as it does not show on earlier plans. By the end of the year they were some 50ft down with few finds, but in 1923 many carved stones were found about 140ft down. From there to the bottom at 166ft finds turned up in profusion. These included the remains of the windlass and chains together with cannonballs and the broken parts of an 'exploding shell' that may well have been fired from Roaring Meg and presumably scored a direct hit on the well head, taking it down the shaft.

Fig. 10.5 The long crack in the south-west tower that caused great problems

Later in 1923 and early in 1924 the clearance extended to the woodland side of the outer wall of the west ward and the extreme south-western corner. By the end of 1924 the main clearance had been completed and consolidation work could begin.

The great south-west tower was scaffolded in March 1925, following evidence of movement (Figs. 10.5 & 6). The foreman, Mr Roberts, and his men worked throughout the night and for the following two weekends to ensure the tower was safe, using wire banding and shoring the weaker parts. Plans were proposed to insert a concrete ring beam and to carry out remedial work to the external faces. A report in April assured the Ministry that:

> The scheme will not involve any alteration to the appearance of the building with the exception that the masonry at the base of the tower, where the ashlar has been robbed or destroyed, must be treated by replacing the facing with old ashlar masonry selected from the site ... A small circular staircase on the westerly section of the tower had been partially destroyed and built up in order to give additional strength to the wall.

Many of the drawings (plans at various levels, cross-sections and elevations, the extent of shores and hawsers) associated with this emergency work have survived.[3] They indicate an excavation between the foundations of the present tower and those of the earlier, smaller one to insert a large concrete block acting as a support. It is assumed that this block was removed when the tower had been made safe. The work on the great tower was to take several years and photographs show the top parts emerging from a veritable forest of scaffolding and shores (Fig. 10.6). (The Royal Commission on Historic Monuments organised a comprehensive photographic survey of the castle in 1927 and 1928.)[4]

Members of the Bristol and Gloucester Antiquarian Society were impressed when they visited the castle in 1931:

> They [H.M. Office of Works] have treated the subject [restoration] in a skilful and sympathetic way, and the long hidden features, including the great rock-cut moat, have been revealed and restored in a manner which should constitute a model of the methods to be employed in conducting such restorations.[5]

Fig. 10.6 Scaffolding surrounding the south-west tower (RCHM)

The tourist potential of the castle was considered in 1933, and a series of Ministry of Works postcards were prepared (such as Fig. 10.7). Discussion took place about erecting a new museum, the existing one being in the masons' hut on the barbican. The Ministry was trying 'to free the barbican … from any modern structure which, it is felt, is a disfigurement which should not be allowed permanently to remain'. A proposal to put a hut in the woodland near where the present drive turns eastwards around the ditch was eventually abandoned.

In 1939 the Commissioners agreed to take an additional area into guardianship. The deed, which includes: 'the ditch and moat and a rectangular area' around the barbican, is dated May 1940. The 'rectangular area' was planned as the site for a small hut. However, by the end of the Second World War the whole scheme had been forgotten, and only recently has the barbican been freed of the 'disfigurement' (Plate 11, p.62) and a new reception area built adjoining the car park (Plate 12, p.63).

Fig. 10.7 One of a series of H.M. Office of Works postcards showing the eastern side of the castle

There are some indications of further works that took place during the two or three years preceding the war. In 1937 repairs to the keep were estimated at £800 of which £150 was for consolidation work. This included 'an oak staircase and gangway' that gave access to the spiral stair in the north-west corner and from there to the flat roof, probably installed at the same time. During 1938-9 £1,700 was earmarked for taking down part of the bastion on the north-east corner, taking out all the trees and vegetation, rebuilding and pointing. It is assumed that all works came to an end late in 1939 or early 1940.

It is evident that there are large gaps in the record during which consolidation works to make the castle safe for visitors continued. Pre-war postcards show the new stone steps that replaced the ramp leading to the entrance and the bridge across the drawbridge pit (Fig. 10.7).

After the war, the next stage of repair/improvement, for which there is firm information, followed the preparation of a comprehensive photogrammetric survey and ground plan in 1981.[6] Survey work was carried out by staff of the City of Hereford Archaeology Unit. The first area to be dealt with was the interior of the south-east tower. The sections under scaffolding were surveyed in detail and two faces were drawn from photographs. A drawn elevation of the external west face of the tower indicated the work that had been carried out.[7]

A detailed survey of the south-west tower in advance of general repair work took place in 1983. A photographic survey from a free-standing central scaffold was followed by drawn internal elevations and plans. In 1984 the elevation facing the great hall was drawn (Fig. 17.8) and plans were made of the wall passage and the western wall walk.

The chapel and gatehouse were surveyed in 1984, with details added to the chapel records after the 1930s first floor had been removed. Detailed elevations were drawn and first-floor plans produced. The survey was extended to the ground floor and basement elevations in the chapel when the timber ground floor was replaced. The internal elevations of the gatehouse passage followed in early 1986 and the area between the gatehouse and the north range was examined to establish details of the building that once filled this area[8] (see Chapters 13, 14 & 16).

When the arcade screen in the north range was scaffolded on both sides, the opportunity was taken to produce detailed elevations (e.g. Fig. 18.2). In 1990, survey work was carried out in the keep,[9] and in the Great Hall[10] (see Chapters 11 & 17).

Limited excavations took place in the mid 1980s. These were mainly in advance of paving the over-walked areas and gravel being laid to indicate areas that once were internal to buildings. The excavations associated with the west and south pentices were recorded.[11] In 1987/8 a trench for an electricity supply was dug from the car park to a junction box adjacent to the castle ditch. The trench was then extended along the footpath to the barbican and round the barbican ditch to provide an entry for electricity cables to the castle via the gate-passage garderobe shaft. Skeletons were exposed along the path leading to the barbican (see pages 29-32).[12] A shallow trench for a telephone cable followed a similar course, but did not expose any archaeological levels.[13] In 2004 and 2008 further work took place on the solar arch.[14]

In the chapel, the 15th-century west window of three trefoiled lights has modern stained glass commemorating the Second World War Radar Research Squadron. The window, completed in June 1992, also serves as a memorial to the 11-man crew of a Halifax bomber, containing the prototype of a ground-mapping radar bombing aid, that crashed near Goodrich Castle (Plate 9, p.62). The modern stained-glass in the 15th-century east window is the Millennium Window. Designed by local Herefordshire artist, Nichola Hopwood, and donated by the parishes of Goodrich, Marstow and Welsh Bicknor, its central motif represents the meandering course of the River Wye (Plate 10, p.63).

Finally, as mentioned above, between 2006 and 2008 the barbican was cleared of the custodian's hut (Plate 11, p.62) and the area was surveyed and minor excavations took place.[15] A brand new visitor centre was built on the edge of the car park several hundred yards from the castle (Plate 12, p.63).

Part Three

The Buildings

Chapters 11 – 18

11 Earthworks & the First Stone Castle
by Ron Shoesmith

The Site Before the First Stone Castle

Mention has already been made of the traces of possible ditches and other features apparent as crop marks on some aerial photographs (Fig. 1.6). They are no longer visible on the ground, but Octavius Morgan, during the visit of the Monmouthshire & Caerleon Antiquarian Association in 1877, commented 'It is not improbable that the castle was erected on some earthworks which were plainly traceable'.[1]

The site, overlooking a ford that was certainly a recognized crossing of the River Wye as early as the Roman period, is protected on two sides by steep slopes and could well have been a possibility for an Iron Age promontory camp. A similar example of this type of fortification in Herefordshire is Eaton Camp, on the south bank of the Wye some 6 miles west of Hereford. The situation is very similar to Goodrich with a deep dingle on one side and the river on the other. Only the base of the promontory required a rampart defence to enclose the 7.3ha site.[2] The reasonably flat area that would have been within the ditch shown on the Goodrich aerial photograph would have been just under 1ha. However, there have been no finds of Iron Age date recorded from any of the excavations within and around the castle, so this proposition remains unverified. The ditches could perhaps have been associated with an early church and burial ground (see p.32).

Another possibility is that the crop marks represent a ditch or ditches associated with an early castle, in use before the present rock-cut ditch was dug. Such ditches could well have been associated with a timber palisade enclosing the end of the promontory, very similar to the situation at Ludlow.[3] The western and northern sides of the promontory are likely to have been much steeper than at present due to later castle earthworks to form the outer wards. The likelihood of a timber and earthwork castle – possibly a ring work – with all the buildings constructed of timber, cannot be disproved. If this is accepted, then the position of the stone keep almost central to the earthwork may be significant. The later works, and especially the excavation of the rock-cut ditches, are of such a monumental nature that any earlier earthworks would have been completely obliterated and only apparent as crop marks from the air. A castle such as this could well have been built by Godric Mapson soon after he received it from William FitzOsbern *c.*1070 (see Chapter 3).

However, it should be appreciated that some crop marks further away from the castle could well be associated with the siege during the Civil War. Some aerial photographs show a diffuse shaded area approaching the castle from the south-south-east that may well represent an approach from the ford at Kerne Bridge – a track that could be seen on the ground until quite recently (Fig. 1.6).[4] The photographs also have slight indications of features which apparently cross the two suggested ditch lines. In addition, two possible building outlines have been noted. One large and apparently two-celled, well to the south-east of the castle, would seem to be too large for a building so may represent some form of cattle pen, and the other, just within the ditch line and to the east of the existing rock-cut ditch, is a building that appears to be of similar dimensions to the keep.

The First Stone Castle

It was probably Baderon of Monmouth who built the first stone defences of the castle either towards the end of the reign of Henry I or during the early years of King Stephen (see Chapter 3). The stonework included the keep and the original curtain wall. Thurlby gives reasons for supposing that the carved decoration of the keep is allied to the work of the 'Herefordshire School of Romanesque Sculpture' active in Herefordshire and neighbouring counties and suggests that the keep should be dated c.1120-40, which fits with this hypothesis (Plate 13, p.64).[5] Other internal buildings were probably of timber.

The Early Curtain Walls

Introduction

Part of the east curtain wall is earlier than the rock-cut ditch and the circular corner towers. There are also indications that parts of the south wall may also be early. They are likely to have been associated with a ditch of some description, widened and deepened at a later date. The original entrance into the castle is uncertain, but it is most likely to be in a similar position to the present entrance because of the ridge of ground at this point.

The main parts of the curtain wall, the round corner towers, the gatehouse and chapel towers and the barbican are considered to be part of the grand Edwardian castle (see Chapters 12 to 15). Later alterations and replacements, including the great hall and the large south-west tower, were probably part of the 14th-century improvements (see Chapters 16 & 17), whilst the extension to the gatehouse and the construction of the garderobe or latrine tower followed later as the castle gradually became a house and the defences were of little importance (see Chapter 18).

Fig. 11.1 Part of the east curtain wall showing the three constructional phases

The east curtain wall
Even a relatively cursory inspection of the external face of the section of the eastern curtain wall between the garderobe and chapel towers reveals that it is not a simple structure, being banded into at least three constructional phases (Fig. 11.1). The most obvious early features are two small loops (narrow openings – effectively arrow slits) set into the wall directly underneath two of the later and wider window openings. This band pre-dates the rock-cut ditch for it was underpinned when the ditch was cut. The loops are no longer visible internally, being below the present ground level in the courtyard. Assuming that the wall containing the loops was of a similar thickness to the present wall – about 2.2m – then to be effective for lighting and for defence, they would have had to have had splayed jambs through the whole thickness of the wall. The pre-castle surface contours are very uncertain, but the original internal ground level adjacent to this stretch of wall must have been well below the present surface.

In the chapel basement a small loop is in line with the outer face of the eastern curtain wall and there is a distinct construction break in the south wall, some 2.4m to the west of this loop, that aligns with the inside face of the curtain wall. This section of wall is on the same level as the earliest part of the curtain wall described above, and could represent a refacing of the core of that wall when it was cut away to insert the chapel tower. It may be that the original floor level in the eastern part of the courtyard was at a similar level to the chapel basement floor.

The south curtain wall
The earliest parts of the south curtain wall consist of two short sections adjacent to the south-east and south-west corner towers, both sections being parallel to the south wall of the keep. Had these two originally been joined in a straight line, which seems likely, and had the wall been the typical 2.2m thick, then there would only have been a narrow passage between the wall and the keep. Unfortunately, the junctions between the corner towers and the sections of curtain wall are heavily mortared, obscuring any indications of constructional breaks that may be present. However, there are distinct changes in the character of the masonry between both towers and wall sections and it is suggested that the straight sections of this curtain wall pre-date the corner towers and the rock-cut ditch. The central part comprises a V-shaped extension to the wall which was apparently built to provide additional space between the keep and the curtain wall (see Chapter 16).

The north curtain wall
The entrance passage, the gatehouse passage and the adjoining section of the courtyard are some 8m higher than the flat, outer area or ward, but the basement of the north hall is only some 3m above the outside level. As with the eastern area, it is now impossible to establish the contours of the original ground surface, but accepting that a sudden change in ground level is unlikely, either the outer ward has been cut away or the gate passage and courtyard area are substantially built up. A mixture of the two is an obvious third possibility. It is noteworthy that the long gate passage is formed on a ridge of ground – to the south there is the cellar underneath the chapel with a floor at a similar level to that of the basement underneath the north hall.

It may be that slight evidence for the ground on each side of the gate passage being cut away can be gained from the short section of wall separating the gate passage from the wall passage on the north which leads to the guardroom. This wall contains two loops now facing onto the gate passage, but there are indications in the sills that they were originally built to point in the opposite direction. If so, the only obvious deduction is that this was at one time an outside curtain wall. The sills are level, rather than sloping downwards externally, and as defensive features would have been totally useless unless the ground level outside was substantially higher than it is now. Unfortunately, apart from the loops, this section of wall has been almost totally rebuilt and there is no other evidence to demonstrate an early date. However, if the interpretation is correct, this section of wall could also be of the second quarter of the 12th century.

The west curtain wall
The whole of the present west curtain wall is associated with the later great hall and south-west tower and is on a different orientation from the early curtain wall (see Chapter 17). Assuming that this early stretch of curtain wall was reused when the circular corner towers were added towards the end of the 13th century (see Chapter 12), careful measurement has shown that it probably ran at right angles to the present north curtain wall and across the present great hall.

The Early Entrance
The surviving parts of the gate passage are usually considered to be of one constructional period (see Chapter 13), but there are slight signs that it may be of two quite distinct builds. The gate passage has a constructional break just to the west of the inner portcullis slot next to the main central arch. From this point the passage to the east is on a slightly different alignment to the remainder to the west. This change is also reflected in the varying thicknesses of the side walls of the passage. It could well be that the inner half of the passage reflects the 12th-century entrance built directly into the face of the curtain wall without any part being set forward. Such a simple entry could still have included a room above the passage for a drawbridge mechanism, such as occurred at Richard's Castle,[6] or it could have been a simple defended opening such as the one at Chepstow Castle, where William Marshal's gateway of *c.*1200 now forms the entrance to the middle bailey.[7] Refacing and the construction of the wall passage and gate-keeper's room would have concealed most of this earlier work, leaving the varying alignments and wall thicknesses to point to an earlier, simpler structure.

Early Internal Buildings
Apart from the keep, the two loops in the east wall may well have been associated with an internal building, but if so, almost all traces are probably well buried underneath the raised courtyard level. Any other buildings within the curtain wall may well have been of timber, but no traces have been found.

The Keep
External Description
The architectural features of the keep, which stands towards the southern side of the courtyard, suggest that it was built in the second quarter of the 12th century.[8] When the decision was made to build a stone castle, a well-defensible tower or keep would have been of prime importance. It would not have been built on top of any earlier motte, should one have existed, for the made-up ground of the mound would not have been sufficiently compacted to take the weight

of a stone tower. A new approach had to be taken. In the first instance the chosen area was cleared down to the bedrock, which is very close to the surface.

Although the top of the keep is ruined and there are only traces of the parapets, it still stands some 16m high above the present courtyard level. The keep is quite small; it is 8.8m square externally but, as the walls are all between 2.1 and 2.3m thick, the inner rooms are only some 4.4m square. It has three stages – basement or undercroft, first, and second floors.

The lower walls were almost certainly designed to be hidden by an earthen mound, as is clearly indicated by the rough external stonework which extends to about 2m above the present courtyard level. There are slight indications of a rough opening in the west wall, which shows both internally and externally (Fig. 11.2 & 5). This may well have been for ease of construction, for to build the thick walls of the undercroft just from the outside with no direct access to the interior would have been laborious. The edges of the rough opening are irregular so that the masonry sealing it could be properly tied in. The opening would have been sealed off when the first-floor level was reached, and before the surrounding mound was put in place.

The upper parts of the keep are faced with well-coursed grey conglomerate sandstone with shallow buttresses that clasp around each corner starting, in the main, some 2m above the courtyard level (Fig. 11.3). There is a slight variation at the north-west corner, where there are two offsets on the west face associated with the spiral stair built in the thickness of the wall at that corner. The wider one continues across a decorated string course to the top of the wall. Its lower parts were broken away when a crude opening was inserted in the wall, but below

Fig. 11.2 The lower part of the west wall of the keep with traces of a crude opening with a later opening above

Fig. 11.3 The keep from the north-east

that repairs in red sandstone continue the alignment down to the ground. The north-eastern buttress is also slightly different due to a later replacement of a damaged section.

Buttresses of a similar depth to the corner ones are present in the middle of each face except the western one, effectively forming two bays on each face. The one on the south wall continues for the full height of the keep; the north wall one stops just below the string course; and the one on the east wall continues a little higher and has a sloping top. The string course continues all the way round the keep and buttresses with continuous Romanesque chevron (zig-zag) decoration, apart from on the east face, where it is plain.

The north face (Figs. 11.3 & 4) contains the original first-floor entrance doorway (later converted to a window when the mound was removed and a doorway inserted into the basement) (see Chapter 16). The sill has been removed, but the bases of the jambs indicate that it was about 4m above the present courtyard level. It was presumably approached by a ramp laid on the surrounding mound together with some timber stairs. Also on the north face are two narrow loops, adjoining the western clasping buttress, that illuminate the spiral stair between the first and second floors. At second-floor level above the central buttress there is an original window of two lights (the central stone mullion is missing). The round arch is enclosed within a moulding that is partly chamfered and partly carved with 'rope' ornament. The shafts have scalloped capitals, the inner jambs being carved with chevron ornament. They support a single piece of stone which incorporates the round heads of the two original lights. There is a similar window, complete with its central mullion, centrally placed in the west wall at the same level (Fig. 11.5 and Plate 13).

Fig. 11.4 The north face of the keep

Fig. 11.5 The west face of the keep

The lower part of the east wall of the keep is beneath the platform and within the later dungeon (Fig. 11.6). The west wall of the dungeon is therefore the east wall of the keep. However, the face has been lost in the northern bay where there was an opening that was blocked with core work set back from the face during the 1920s (see Chapters 10 & 16). Just above the platform is the only original opening in this face. It is in the north bay and comprises the lower part of a narrow loop with splayed sides and a steeply sloping sill allowing maximum light to the undercroft. The top has been cut away by a later opening, but the maximum loop height, allowing for the first floor within the keep, is only 0.6m. The loop is positioned high in the wall of the basement so as to be above the mound.

At the south-eastern corner of the keep a later passage leads through an arched opening joining the platform to the paved area to the south. There are no openings on the south face of the keep (Fig. 11.7).

Internal Description (Fig. 11.8)
The keep's internal arrangements have remained relatively unchanged throughout its life, at least as far as the floor levels are concerned. The present basement floor is now some 0.65m below the level of the courtyard, but, as it has been laid in concrete, the position of the original floor is uncertain. The slight offsets in the east and north walls, just above the concrete, have no apparent purpose and may represent laying-out problems. The internal faces are of random rubble to between 1 and 2m above the concrete floor; above this level the masonry is better coursed. The tops of the corbels in the north and south walls indicate the level of the first

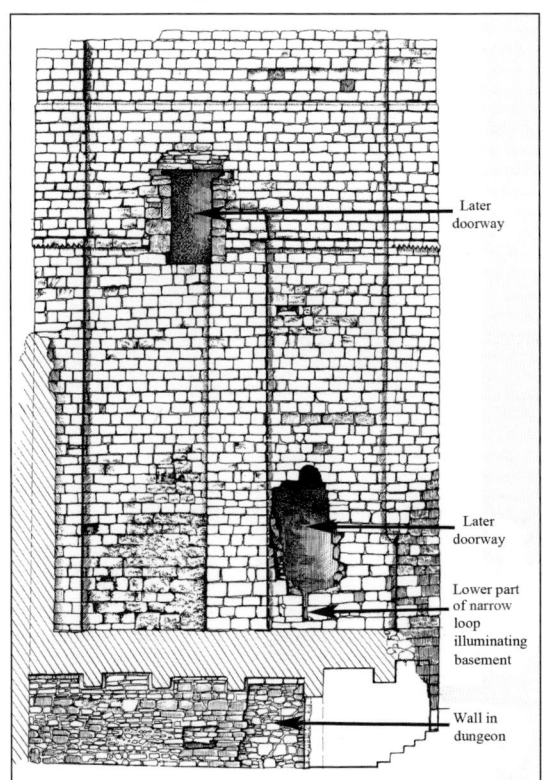

Fig. 11.6 The east face of the keep

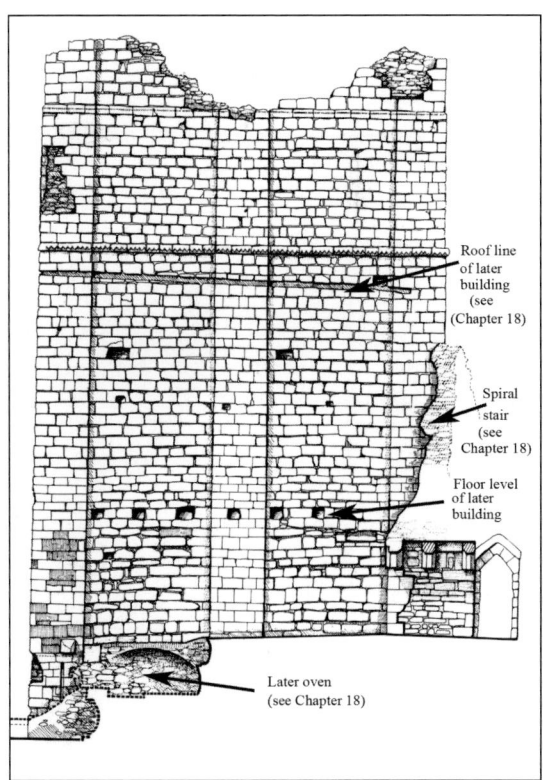

Fig. 11.7 The south face of the keep

Fig. 11.8 A reconstruction drawing of the keep from the south-east

floor. The basement room had been plastered – traces survive on the south and west walls – but originally it could only have been reached by an internal ladder from the first floor. It was lit by the single, high-level loop in the east wall. Modern timber steps lead up to a gallery at first-floor level.

The first floor was the main room of the keep, with the elaborate entrance doorway in the north face. It was a very high chamber in relation to its size – although only 4.4m square, the total height to the second floor was 6.2m. There is now no trace of any windows, but there could have been small ones in the east and west walls where there are later openings. Even so, it would have been a very dark room due to the thickness of the walls. Throughout the keep there is no trace of any heating system, a point which is rather surprising as fireplaces and a hearth, apparently adjoining the first-floor west wall, are mentioned in two early descriptions.[9]

The first floor includes a doorway in the west wall leading into a short north-south vaulted passage constructed within the thickness of the wall. On the west side of the passage there is a square-headed recess with an arch above it. The remains of rectangular splays to this recess indicate that it may originally have been a small window providing some light to the first floor and the bottom of the spiral stair. The spiral stair or vice leading to the upper floor and the roof starts at the north end of the passage. The two narrow slits illuminating it have the west sides splayed so as to allow the maximum amount of light within the stair. As the sills are almost horizontal it is unlikely that these slits were designed to have any defensive purpose.

At the second-floor level the vice leads into a short east-west passage in the north wall, from which a doorway led into the upper chamber. Allowing for joists and floorboards, this second floor would have been at least 3.5m high. It was well illuminated by two, two-light windows, both with window seats – this must have been by far the most pleasant room in the building.

The vice continues to the top of the keep which has a modern roof. A short, narrow passage originally led along the north wall and up three steps to the wall walk. A few stones, set on top of the keep wall, provide the only indication of what would have been a parapet.

The design of the original roof is uncertain – some of the evidence being concealed by the modern flat roof. Even so, built into the tops of the walls are indications of two early roof lines. In the north and south walls traces of the earlier roof consist of stones laid at an angle that would originally have acted as a weathering, but are now cut back to the wall face. This roof would have had its apex running north-south.

> **The Geology of the Keep** (*by* Thomas Richards)
> No evidence of the use of limestone was found in the external walls of the keep – certainly not in the courses that could be physically accessed, or in those inspected through binoculars.
>
> *North Elevation* (Plates 13 & 14, p.64)
> The stone of the lower 12 to 14 courses is a mixture of red and grey sandstones, with a few blocks of green-yellow. The rest of the elevation is predominantly composed of the grey stone with rare blocks of red and green-yellow.

West Elevation (Plate 14, p.64)
The lower courses are constructed of rubble, with probably a 40%:40% split in usage of the red and grey varieties of sandstone/conglomerate. The remaining 20% or so is composed of a pale green-yellow sandstone which is interpreted as being blocks of the red sandstone that have been reduced (due to the iron being leached out – a process that took place whilst the rock was still in the ground), blocks that have been repaired using a red-brown cement with fragments of brick, and a rarer orange-grey variety of sandstone (with an orange weathered surface, but appearing grey/green underneath). The majority of the upper part of the wall appears to be constructed of the grey sandstone with occasional use of the red and green-yellow varieties.

East and South Elevations
These are mostly of grey sandstone, with small areas of red sandstone and very sporadic use of the green-yellow stone.

General comments
The majority of the well-dressed / coursed areas of the keep (*c.*2m upwards) are predominantly built of the grey sandstone, with red blocks used sporadically throughout – sometimes isolated, sometimes with two to three blocks together, and sometimes half a dozen or so blocks in one course. The red stone is also used for quoins in places, most notably on the lower north-east corner, where around a dozen courses are finished off with this stone.

Interestingly, the decorative upper northern and western windows may have been built in such a way that red, grey, and green stones were deliberately used to create a colour contrast between the elaborately dressed stones.

It is notable that stones which have significant amounts of quartz pebbles (pebbles appear in all colour varieties) seem to have been used for the central portion of each elevation. The blocks with fewer visible pebbles (at least from ground level), or with no pebbles at all, seem to have been predominantly used for the corners and central buttresses of the south, north and east elevations.

Parts of the north and east elevations are badly weathered or covered with a red / grey patina, making identification of the true stone colour difficult.

Interpretation
It is considered that the keep is constructed entirely of sandstone with the vast majority, if not all, being sourced from the outcrop on which the castle stands. There is evidence that the grey stone was sourced from the rock exposures visible in the ditch. The conglomerate that is found on Coppett Hill, suggested as a possible source for the stone of the keep, is in fact a red conglomerate and not grey at all.

It would make sense if the castle builders found and exploited the bands of grey sandstone /conglomerate for the construction of the keep. As the supply of this superior stone became exhausted, they probably used the red sandstone for repairs to the keep and the rest of the castle. The suggestion that the keep originally had a mound, which was subsequently removed on three sides, seems reasonable, if only for the apparent random use of both the grey and red stone in the lower two metres of the external north and west walls.

The Well
The well, in the northern part of the courtyard next to the north range, is 1.7m square, the stone sides starting from the present ground surface. It was built at a slight angle to the later north range being slightly cut into the line of its south wall, making it very probable that it pre-dates that range. It aligns almost exactly with the keep and the early east curtain wall. The well is not mentioned by any of the 19th- and early 20th-century writers; there was apparently no knowledge of it before the 1920s clearance (see Chapter 10).

Summary
The Curtain Walls
Attempts at designing fortifications that included a positive defensive role started during Henry II's reign and became more successful towards the end of the 12th century. The main change was from a fortified dwelling with poor perimeter defences to a fortified perimeter with residential buildings inside. The new design of these early castles is totally different to the ring works and motte and bailey castles that proliferated along the Welsh border during the 11th century. With the introduction of straight sides, the defenders on the tops of the walls could see along the whole length – it was impossible for the attackers to hide around the curve of the perimeter defence. Thus the castle could be efficiently defended by a smaller number of men firing from arrow slits within the walls and from behind a parapet along the top. The changes at Goodrich were more radical than at other castles in the area. In many cases the new stone curtain walls merely replaced the palisades, perhaps with corner towers and intermediate towers added at a later date so as to enfilade the curving walls such as at White Castle.[10] The straight-sided form for a stone defence is well shown in the design of the extensive outer bailey of Ludlow Castle, which was probably completed by 1177. Originally such perimeter walls may have been built without towers, but several early examples include one or two projecting rectangular towers, including corner towers such as those on the inner bailey wall at Ludlow.[11] Here also, the original outer bailey gatehouse was mainly within the line of the curtain wall, although like Goodrich it may have had extensive external additions at a later date.[12] Circular or semi-circular corner and wall towers did not make an appearance until the 13th century (Chapter 12).

The central band of the east curtain wall represents a small part of this initial effort to create a rectilinear castle. The same may be the case with the two short lengths of curtain wall on the south side, built parallel to the south wall of the keep and, with a degree less certainty, with the inner wall of the northern guard passage.

The Keep
The keep would have looked vastly different when built with an artificial motte. There are several excavated examples such as at Ascot Doilly (Oxfordshire) where the base of a tower was found within what appeared to be a small motte. The keep, which was slightly larger than that at Goodrich, was probably built between 1129 and 1150.[13] Sometimes the mound was apparently an afterthought – the square keep at Tote Copse (Aldingbourne, Sussex) had a chamfered ashlar base hidden by a later mound,[14] and the larger keep at Wareham (Dorset) may have been built free-standing and the ground around it raised later.[15] Similarly, at Lydford

(Devon) the mound totally covered the slits which had lit the lower room. Creating artificial mottes in this fashion continued for some considerable time – the circular 13th-century keep at Skenfrith in neighbouring Monmouthshire is still mounded, but has been shown to have been built free-standing.[16] Mounding around the base of the tower would improve the defensive capability of the keep by making it more difficult for any attackers to get sufficiently close to the building to erect scaling ladders. At Goodrich the mound was at least 2.2m high and the first-floor entry would then have needed a short ladder or wooden steps.

Although the Goodrich keep was a quality building with clasping and central buttresses, decorative string courses, and well-designed windows and doorway, it is one of the smallest keeps in the country. Such keeps are defined as 'solar-keeps' as distinct to the larger 'hall-keeps'. Throughout the country there are some 24 solar-keeps.[17] Even so, there are few that approach Goodrich in smallness – Farnham (Surrey) is internally 5m square; Oxford is 5m by 5.5m; Totnes (Devon) is a minute 5m by 4m, but the record is held by the keep at the nearby White Castle (Monmouthshire) which, if square, had rooms with sides only 4m long.[18]

Perhaps the earliest keep on which Goodrich could have been based is St Leonard's Tower at West Malling (Kent), which was built towards the end of the 11th century.[19] The rooms are just under 5m square, only slightly larger than those at Goodrich and it has similar corner buttresses and central buttresses on two sides, whilst the corner enclosing the vice has a larger clasping buttress. Although of similar plan size, the rooms at West Malling were considerably taller than those at Goodrich, the main chamber being over 9m high.[20]

At Goodrich there were spacious two-light windows with seats; dry, wooden floor levels well above the ground. Heating could well have been by braziers burning charcoal. By 12th-century standards it would have been considered to be a perfectly adequate suite of rooms, fit for a lord and his lady. The only feature that was really lacking was a fore-building to accommodate a permanent stair-well.

Apart from being residential, Goodrich keep was built for passive defence – there was no indication that it could be a base for returning the fire of attackers. Thus, although there are one or two loops in the walls, they are not designed for use with bows and arrows as they do not have outwardly sloping sills. In addition, the keep had a pitched roof which would have limited the use of this area for machinery for attacking any enemy. It is evident that it was intended as a residential building – not just a place of last resort to be used in an emergency. Had it been designed for emergency use during a siege, one would have thought that it would have needed a source of water – a well or a cistern. However, it has been shown that a large proportion of keeps and keep-gatehouses do not have internal water supplies and their capability for independent defence should therefore be questioned.

12 The late 13th-century Castle – The Ditch, Curtain Walls & Corner Towers

by Ron Shoesmith

The grand Edwardian castle of the late 13th century, probably built by William de Valence (1261-96), had an emphasis on defence but also included several new internal buildings. The castle was almost totally rebuilt as a rectangular fortification some 40m by 45m with three round corner towers. The gatehouse and its guardroom, at the north-east corner, was protected by a semi-circular barbican or outer defence and approached by a ramp. The whole was surrounded by a rock-cut ditch on the south and east sides and by steep slopes on the other two sides.

The Rock-Cut Ditch

The rock-cut ditch surrounds the main part of the castle on the south and east, where there are prominent exposures of the bedrock, whilst a lesser ditch partially surrounds the barbican (see Chapter 15). The base of the ditch is grass-covered at a level chosen during the restoration works in the early 1920s. It is assumed that the vertical profile of the ditch is roughly the same as it was when in use, but this has not been confirmed on all sides. However, the rock faces nearest the castle were smoothed out and strengthened with concrete during the 1920s. On the whole of the east side the ditch is broad and deep – averaging some 28m wide, and up to 9m deep (Fig. 12.1 & Plate 3, p.58). Immediately in front of the gatehouse, a spur of rock was used as a base for the stone-built ramp (now steps) leading into the castle. On the north side of the ramp the line of the ditch continues at a higher level – a level that carries on around the north side of the castle as an outer flat area or ward (see Chapter 18).

On the south side of the castle, the ditch is over 30m wide in places. The original ground surface on the outside of the southern ditch now

Fig. 12.1 The rock-cut ditch

includes the access path. Further to the west, opposite the great south-west tower, the ground falls away rapidly and the ditch becomes shallower until it is finally lost in the slope of the ground. Along the southern side of the castle the shallow V-shaped part of the curtain wall is based on a high exposure of the bedrock.

The East Curtain Wall

About 1.4m below the bottom of the loops (see Chapter 11 and Fig. 11.1), the nature of the east wall changes. Initially there is a band of poorly-coursed masonry, but, towards the exposed bedrock, there is a well-coursed, slightly-battered plinth. When the rock-cut ditch was originally dug, the earlier curtain wall had to be underpinned on a slight batter to prevent it collapsing.

Just above the tops of the loops the character of the wall changes to a rubble build which includes windows associated with an internal building (see Chapters 16 & 18), and above them a parapet and internal wall walk. The parapet, of a white stone, contained four widely-spaced openings (embrasures) separated by cruciform arrow slits. Three of the arrow slits are complete and there are traces of the fourth. They were well constructed with circular openings (oilets) top and bottom and at the ends of the cross member. The sill has a steep slope down to the outside, the defender being protected by a thin wall that originally stood well above waist height. There is much less left of the embrasures than of the arrow slits, but the positions of all four are evident, each being about 0.8m wide and at least 1.6m high. They each contained a single horizontal iron bar (Fig. 12.2).

The section of curtain wall between the northernmost loop and the chapel tower is built of poorly-coursed masonry for the full height, apart from the battered plinth. The southern part of the wall was demolished to make way for the garderobe (latrine) tower, which was inserted through the wall line at a later date (see Chapter 18). The short section of wall between the garderobe tower and the south-eastern tower is evidently part of the build of this corner tower. Much of the interior of the wall has been totally refaced, the southern part being widened by about 0.4m probably when the garderobe tower was inserted.

Fig. 12.2 The inside face of the east curtain wall showing the windows and parapet. The later garderobe openings (see chapter 18) are on the right.

The North Curtain Wall

The north curtain wall, which runs from the gatehouse tower to the north-west or Ladies' Tower, is of considerable height (Fig. 12.3). It appears to have been built in two main parts – the eastern section (on the left of the photograph), which is associated with the gatehouse, and a later section which mainly comprises the outside wall of the north hall and includes a postern door (see Chapter 14). Around the eastern side of the square base of the Ladies' Tower and extending into the curved section is a triple chamfer. The two lower chamfers continue along the north wall underneath the postern gate steps as far as the beginning of the gatehouse wall.

There are traces of a construction break in the lower part of the wall directly in line with the west face of the gatehouse building. At higher levels there is no specific variation in the size of the stones or the coursing, but the eastern (gatehouse) part has an eroded surface with deep weathering, whilst there is relatively little erosion to the west. This suggested construction break is associated internally with an increase in the thickness of the wall to accommodate the guard passage, reinforcing the suggestion that it is of a different build to the curtain wall to the west (see Chapter 12). However, the gatehouse and chapel complex are aligned with the north wall and north hall, so the variation may be little more than the joining together of two separate constructional elements of this phase.

The South and West Curtain Walls

It is suggested that changes to these two walls took place during the 14th century when space was needed around the keep and the west hall and great tower were built (see Chapters 16 & 17). The late 13th-century curtain walls were probably on the same alignment as the earlier curtain wall (see Chapter 11).

Fig. 12.3 The north curtain wall from the north-east. The variations in construction are apparent, the postern door being in the east end of the north hall undercroft.

Fig. 12.4 The circular south-east (prison) tower with its tall spurs rising from a square base set on the sloping bedrock

The South-east (Prison) Tower
External

The tower appears to be mainly of one period of construction and consists of a basement, ground floor and first floor with some surviving upper works associated with the roof and a later bridge access to the keep (see Chapter 16).

The tower is round externally with a diameter of 10.2m, but it is built on an almost square base with sides approximately 11m long. It is built on a platform incorporating several sloping levels of the bedrock, but is well above the lowest level of the ditch (Fig. 12.4). The change from square to round is achieved by three tall corner spurs that continue up to mid first-floor level. The tower is built of well-shaped and coursed sandstone. The junction of the tower and the southern curtain wall is heavily mortared, but there are distinct changes in the character of the masonry and it is suggested that this section of the curtain wall pre-dates the tower.

On the outside of the tower above the east-facing basement loop there are three holes in the masonry (Fig. 12.4). They are slightly off centre to the opening and may well be associated with a line of white stones inserted three courses below the holes (not readily seen on a black-and-white photograph and probably much later in date, see Chapter 18). It would appear that the holes were designed to hold timbers, but they are not putlog holes (for repair scaffolding), as they are too close together and do not appear to have any defensive purpose.

Internal

The interior of the south-east tower was scaffolded in 1982-3 to enable work to be done and most internal elevations were drawn at that time enabling a reconstruction drawing to be produced (Fig. 12.5).

From the courtyard, the tower is completed by two walls set at right angles. The east-west wall is some 2.4m thick and contains two ground-floor

Fig. 12.5 Reconstruction drawing of the south-east tower looking from the west

openings (Fig. 12.6). The western (higher) opening led through a passage in the thick wall directly into the ground floor. The eastern one still provides the approach to the basement by means of a straight stone stair. The upper nine steps are outside the tower and, where they enter into the wall, the opening has a draw-bar hole which would have allowed the basement to be locked from the inside. It is usually suggested that basements were used for storage, but the internal draw bar perhaps indicates an alternative, possibly residential use. A doorway and passage led from the eastern wall walk to the first-floor room in the tower (Fig. 12.7). The thinner north-south wall has a flight of steps attached to its outside that led up to the first floor of the tower. There was no internal communication between the various floors apart from a stair that led from the first floor to the roof.

Internally the tower is an almost regular polygon with a gorge or lobby set at 45 degrees to the courtyard. Each of the octagonal rooms are about 6m long and 5m wide (Fig. 12.7). The internal sandstone walls have ashlar quoins and are reasonably squared and coursed, being of similar quality to that in the north-west tower.

The present basement floor is some 3m below the level of the adjoining section of the courtyard and in part consists of the natural bedrock. This room, which is well above the bottom of the rock-cut ditch, is lit by two identical small loops in the south and east walls. They are both set into square-headed external recesses and the splays, through the *c.*2.6m thick walls, open to become 1m wide internally. Both openings contained four horizontal bars and a vertical one.

The surviving pattern of joist holes is sufficient to generate the original lay-out of the ground floor (Fig. 12.7). In the main, octagonal, part of the tower, the joists sat on ledges with only slight depressions into the wall. However, towards the gorge the joist holes become more obvious and there are no ledges. The joists were arranged symmetrically across the tower, angling very slightly to accommodate the entrance.

The two ground-floor windows are set in the north and west faces and thus adjoin the east and south curtain walls. Each opening has a square-headed recess similar to those in the basement. Internally, the openings

Fig. 12.6 The covered stair that led from the courtyard to the first floor of the south-eastern tower

are slightly larger with stone seats on each side. The windows were designed to be defensive for each is set at a slight angle so as to enfilade the curtain wall, but the view from the northern one was blocked when the garderobe tower was built. The sides of both openings once possessed a series of carvings in low relief, but these have almost totally disappeared (see pages 126-27). Each opening originally contained ten horizontal iron bars and one vertical one.

A fireplace is set symmetrically between the two windows (Fig. 12.8). Corbels and jambs support the remains of the hood which was repaired in 1983 using some new stone. The chimney breast protrudes slightly into the room and continues up through the ceiling into the first-floor chamber where it disappears in the thickness of the wall.

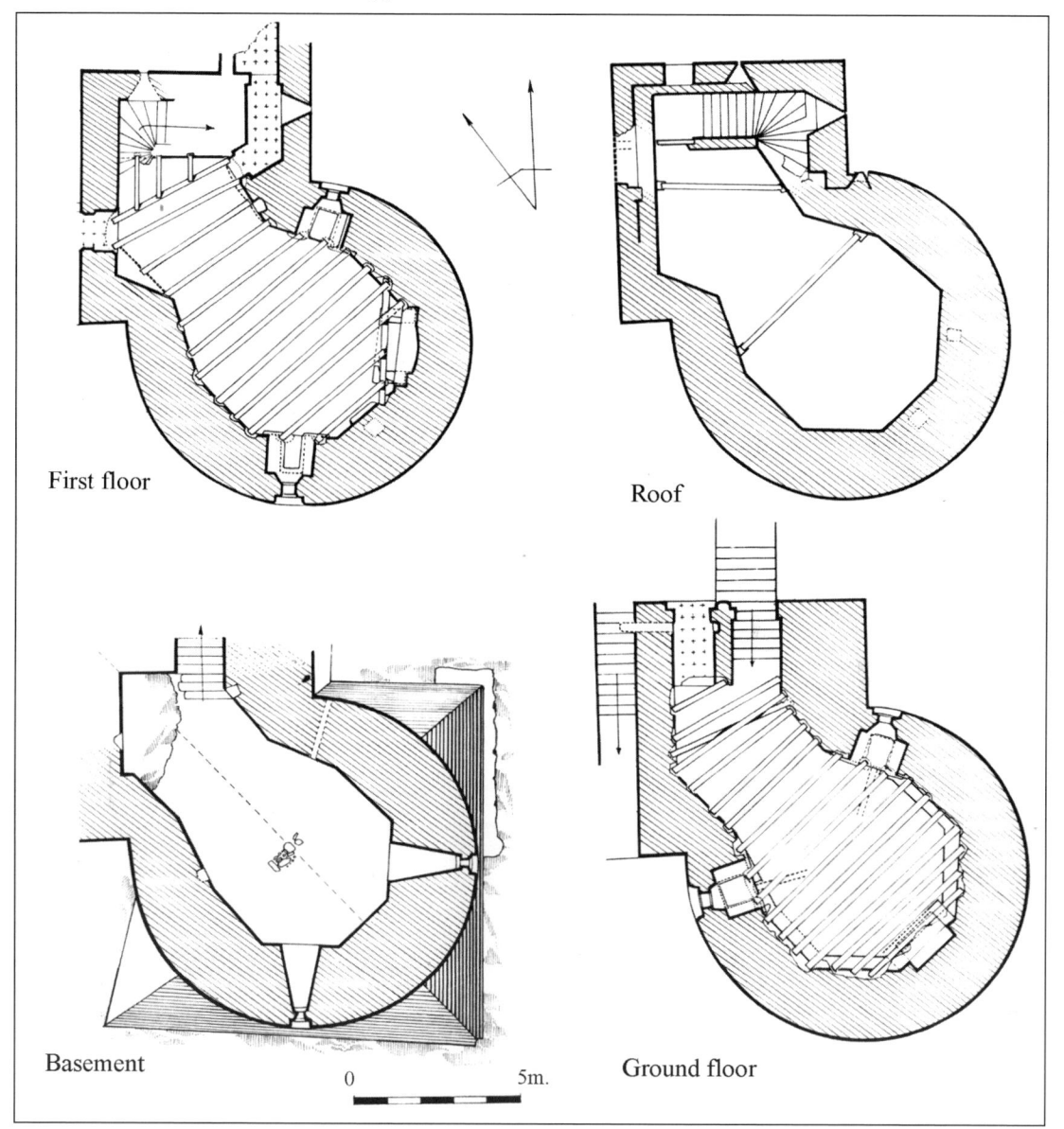

Fig. 12.7 South-west tower reconstruction plans showing the position of floor joists

In the wall on the west side of the gorge is a recess containing a bowl. There is a similar bowl on the same face on the floor above – both appear to be original features and the drains are visible on the outside of the curtain wall.

The entrance to the ground floor room was through a 2.6m long passage in the thickness of the north wall. The left-hand side and roof of the passage have recently been rendered as a protection against erosion. It is partially blocked by a modern wall. The entrance is of similar design to the adjoining basement opening and is rebated on the inside with slots for a draw bar. Stone footings and a socket suggest a 1m high timber wall between the basement steps and the ground-floor passage, presumably for safety reasons.

The sockets for joists belonging to the first floor are apparent throughout the octagonal chamber, but the positions are somewhat conjectural in the entrance passage where the joists were supported on ledges (Fig. 12.7). The basic pattern is almost identical to that of the floor below, but there were only 12 joists compared with the 15 of the ground floor. Three short cross-joists joined the main pattern to the north wall and a secondary joist was inserted at a slightly lower level in front of the fireplace to carry the ends of the main joists and take the weight of the hearth stone.

Access to the first floor was from a covered flight of steps on the western flank of the tower (Fig. 12.6), which also led to the southern wall walk, and also from the eastern wall walk. This eastern entry led into a passage within the thickness of the north wall that was lit by a narrow loop that widened internally. Beyond the window the passage turned through 45 degrees to an inner doorway that led into the rectangular part of the tower. The two opposing doorways are now joined together with a modern timber bridge. This part of the through passage would have been separated from the octagonal chamber by a timber partition. The passage could be locked off both from the wall walk and the stairs. There is a recess with a bowl and drain in the western wall identical to the one on the ground floor.

The first-floor chamber had two windows similar to those on the ground floor with a fireplace set between them. The northern

Fig. 12.8 The interior of the south-east tower

window is next to the junction of the circular tower and the east curtain wall. The other one faces south, but the design is uncertain as the head is broken away. They were both barred and contained window seats.

The fireplace is not above the one on the ground floor, being central to the next face to the east (Fig. 12.8). It is of similar design to the ground-floor one, but has a slightly taller hood and is somewhat better preserved. The surviving part of the hearth is supported on shaped corbelling. The two holes in the fireplace back, common to all the tower fireplaces at Goodrich, may have been for some form of metal fire-back or for a bar to support objects over the fire.

In the north-western corner of the passageway an opening leads to a stone stair, contrived in the thickness of the wall, that led to the roof (Fig. 12.9). The steps were illuminated by two loops, one in the north face and the other facing east. The lower one faced the entry to the stair whilst the other illuminated the second bend. It is positioned in the section of curtain wall between the corner tower and the later garderobe tower. The stairs were completely under cover and there was room for a full-height doorway at the top which led to a flat timber walkway, that returned eastwards on the south side of the stairs wall. The corbels for the beams that supported this walkway still survive. Apart from providing access to the tower roof, this walkway led to a later opening in the west parapet of the tower, directly opposite a similar-sized opening in the east wall of the keep. They were presumably joined by a covered timber 'bridge' (see Chapter 16). A decorative string course, around the rectangular and circular parts of the tower, separated the main tower wall from the parapet.

There would have been an access from the walkway, presumably by means of a few wooden steps, to the flat section of the roof above the stairs. This flat roof served two openings in the north parapet wall – here complete up to and including the coping stones (Fig. 12.6). To the east is a half-cruciform arrow slit, angled to overlook the entrance to the barbican. The other arm of the cross was

Fig. 12.9 Reconstruction of the upper part of the south-east tower showing the steps within the north wall and an indication of the timber bridge that joined the roof to the keep (see Chapter 16)

obviously not considered necessary as it would have pointed downwards into the courtyard. Apart from the missing arm, it is identical in design to the cruciform slits in the east curtain wall. To the west of the slit is a rectangular embrasure that appears to be original. It is straight-sided and again similar in design to those on the east curtain wall.

There would have been an access from the walkway to the wall walk around the corner tower. Much of this wall walk and all of the parapet has been lost and the design of the tower roof is uncertain, but was presumably conical.

The late 14th-century carvings in the South-east or Prison Tower

Although most prisoners were doubtless incarcerated in the dungeon adjoining the keep basement, the ground-floor room of the south-east tower is considered by some to have been the room where prisoners of higher degree were interned, hence the alternative name – Prison Tower. Tradition asserts that the figures carved on the jambs of the two window embrasures were the work of the prisoners during their confinement. The illustrations shown here were made over 100 years ago – the figures have now totally disappeared. Some were carved in relief rather than being indented and were therefore the production of someone skilled in stone carving. Seaton in his *Guide* to the castle[1] was therefore of the opinion that the figures and inscriptions were carved before the stones were placed in position and were executed by masons with proper tools.

On one of the blocks there were the figures of a hart couchant and a swan close to each other. There was also a figure of a man with a hawk or falcon on his fist. He is dressed as a falconer of the time of Richard II, and is belted with a pouch suspended on his left side; beneath his feet is the figure of a dog (Fig. 12.10). Other carvings included a lady holding a baby; rabbits at play; a hawk or falcon standing on the back of a partridge; and a peacock (Fig. 12.12). There was an inscription that read:

MASTRE
ADUM
ADAM
HASTYNS

Seaton, following Fosbrooke,[2] considered that the figures were carved to commemorate the visit of the Earl of Derby (later Henry IV) in 1386 at the time that his son (later to be Henry V) was born at Monmouth. He noted that the hart was the badge of Richard II and the swan that of Henry IV. If correct the figure could represent Henry, Earl of Derby, and the lady and child his wife and son.

Fortunately, photographs and drawings of the figures and inscription survive and are included in this section.

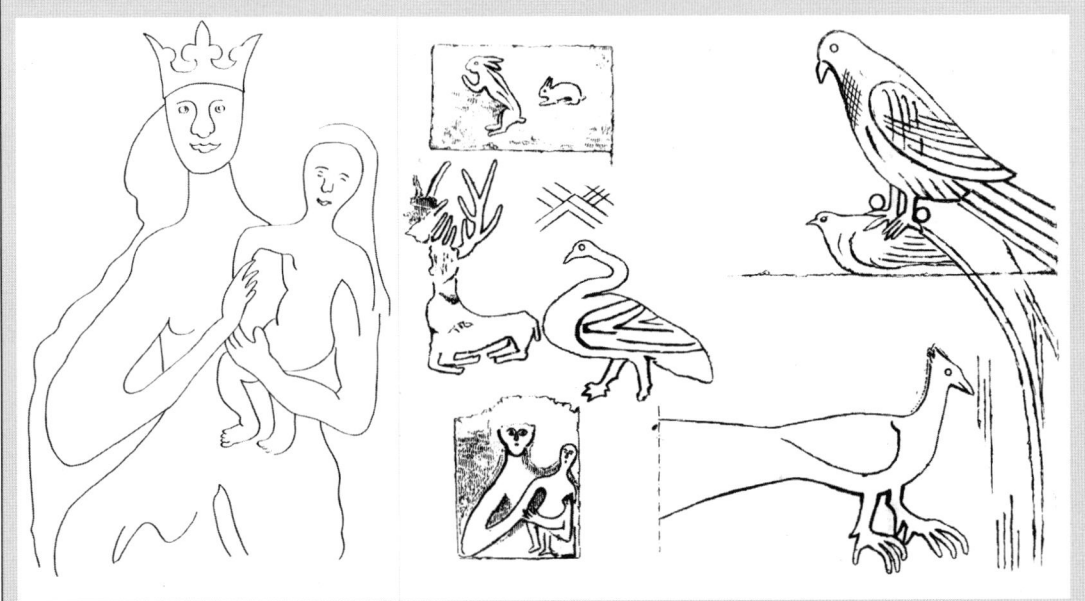

OPPOSITE: Fig. 12.10 The figure of a man with a hawk on his hand and dog at his feet
ABOVE TOP: Fig. 12.11 Copy of the inscription as it was carved
ABOVE: Fig. 12.12 Drawings made of some of the carvings that have since disappeared

The North-west (Ladies') Tower

External

This tower suffered severely in the Civil War and the greater part of the north-western part was lost, possibly due to mining (see Chapter 8). The ground around the square base of the tower is now relatively flat, but when the tower was built as a defensive strong point, the ground may well have fallen away rapidly both to the west and the north. The original ground level may be better indicated by the level of the basements within the tower and the north hall. These basements were presumably excavated as a 'shelf' on the end of the spur on which the castle was built. Although there is no exposure of bedrock in the two basements, this may be due to later works. It would be surprising if the area that now forms the two outer wards was not originally quarried down, as occurred on the west and south sides of the castle, to improve the defensive capabilities.

The north-west tower was of similar size to the south-east one and consisted of basement, ground and first floors with a vestibule, but the loss of much of the north and west faces means that there is little evidence for the upper floor, the roof, and any associated features. However, the east wall, that separates the vestibule from the north range, survives for almost its full height. The south wall, which separates the vestibule from the lobby, also survives for most of its original height. These two walls are set at right-angles to one another. Although the curved wall that formed the west and north sides of the tower survives only part way up the basement level, the short sections adjoining the east and south walls give some indication of some of the window openings. The circular part of the tower had spurs from the square base which are lower than those in the south-east tower. This may be due to the different lie of the land from relatively flat ground at the north-west to the deep ditch at the south-east corner.

Internal

The only direct access into the basement of the tower is from the undercroft of the north hall; there is no indication of a separate flight of steps as was the case in the south-eastern corner tower. The 14th-century construction of the grand western hall and lobby may well have obliterated all traces (see Chapter 17).

At ground-floor level there was a direct access to the tower from the north hall through the double arch, and through a doorway from the south. There is now no indication whatsoever of the original access to the upper floor and roof, apart from the doorways leading to the west and north wall walks.

Although this tower is of similar size to the south-east one, the internal design and use are different as all the floors probably had a residential use. The basement room in the tower is some 5m below the level of the courtyard and over 3m above the present ground level in the outer ward. The internal shape is slightly different to that of the south-eastern tower, due to the gorge or vestibule being narrower presumably originally to accommodate stairs. The absence of stairs means that there is a small vestibule, some 5m wide and 3.8m deep. At basement and ground-floor levels these spaces were simply extensions of the two floors in the north range, with only the pillar supporting the double arch providing a break. There was no window in the rectangular vestibule at basement level – whatever light was needed was presumably obtained from the adjoining basement.

At basement level the rectangular vestibule led directly into the octagonal room in the tower proper. There is no sign of any partition – the room may just have been separated from the main basement by screens. Apart from some slight repair work, the whole of the internal stonework is well coursed and appears to be of one period. As with the south-east tower, the two basement windows enfilade the west and north walls. The west window is substantially complete and sufficient remains of the north window to indicate that it was of similar form. They have rectangular internal recesses with window seats on all three sides. The base of the west window is inconveniently high from the basement floor, suggesting that the original floor of the tower was some 0.2m above the present floor level. The residential function of this octagonal basement room is confirmed by the presence of a small fireplace in the east wall. It was an original feature with the chimney built in the thickness of the wall, and again the hearth is too high above the present floor level.

Above the basement the south and east walls of the vestibule survive almost to full height, but the southern part of the west wall was lost in the 1919 collapse (Figs. 10.1 & 2). In the adjoining part of the tower only fragments of the north-east and south-west faces survive. The ground-floor room was slightly larger than the basement room with ledges on which the ends of the floor joists were laid. It was designed to be residential and although only one side of each window opening survives, it is apparent that they had rectangular recesses with seats and barred openings. One window pointed to the south-west and the other to the north-east – they were not angled to enfilade the curtain walls as was the case in the basement. As the room was obviously residential, it is suggested that there would have been a fireplace in the wall facing the gorge. The surviving joist sockets indicate that the main floor timbers ran parallel to the postulated fireplace wall.

There were two entries to the ground-floor room – directly from the north hall through one of the two arched openings, and by a triangular-headed doorway leading through the thick wall from the south. The draw-bar hole indicates that the door could be locked from the tower side.

At first-floor level the east wall of the rectangular vestibule above the double arch survives to its full height, as do short stretches of the north and south walls. When the western part fell in the 1919 collapse it left behind the east side of the doorway that originally provided access from the tower to the western wall walk. A second doorway, in the east wall, originally led directly onto the almost flat roof of the north hall and from there to the northern wall walk (Fig. 14.2). Holes in the north and south walls indicate that the joists ran from south to north in the rectangular room.

Although the west wall of the vestibule was partly lost during the 1919 collapse, sufficient remains to be certain that there were windows at both ground and first-floor levels. The ground-floor window was of double height with splayed reveals but was not designed with a window seat. Both parts had horizontal bars – two in the bottom part and nine in the upper. The first-floor window was smaller, again with splayed sides but no seat.

The south and east faces of the corner tower contain holes at first-floor level indicating that the joists ran in the same direction as those on the floor below. There is no trace of any window or fireplace at this level and there are no indications of the nature and design of the roof.

The South-west Tower and West Curtain Wall

Until recently the outer curve of the foundations of a small south-west tower could be seen in the floor of its larger replacement. These stones have since been buried, but are shown on a plan (Fig. 17.14). From the traces it appears that this earlier tower was of a similar size to the north-west and south-east towers.

It only became apparent when the surviving curve was extended on paper to meet the adjacent sections of curtain wall (Fig. 12.13) that the junction with the southern wall was, as expected, almost at right angles, but that the one with the present west curtain – the wall of

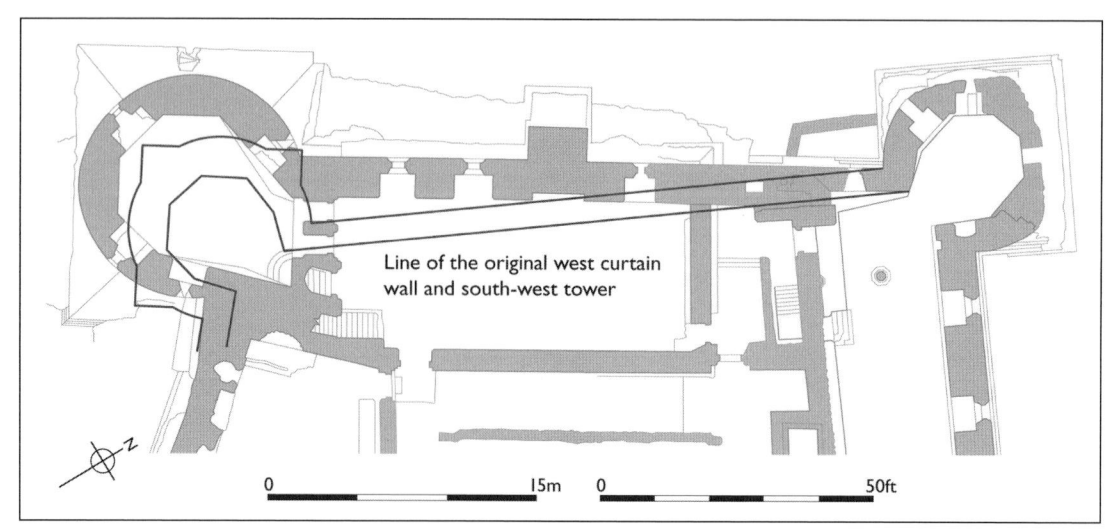

Fig. 12.13 Plan showing the position of the original west curtain wall

the great hall – was almost tangential. Such a junction would have been a very weak defensive feature so, if the small south-west corner tower was designed to the same standard as the other towers, then the western curtain wall would have left it at right angles, from a point well within the line of the present wall. To join up with the north-western tower it would have had to take a course diagonally across the present great hall. Footings seen underneath the east wall of the present hall when the courtyard area was relaid suggest that there was a previous building on that site.[3] If so, it was demolished in the 14th century when a larger tower was built along with the great hall (see Chapter 17).

13 The late 13th-century Castle – The Gatehouse, North-east Tower & Chapel

by Ron Shoesmith

The gatehouse and chapel are at the north-eastern corner of the castle and take the place of a corner tower. The entrance is between two semi-circular spurred towers – one, the larger, contains the chapel, whilst the other houses the guard chamber. The entrance passage has had many alterations during its life (see Chapters 11 & 18), but the remainder is now mainly of one design, although the inner part may well be earlier (see Chapter 11). This area suffered considerable damage during the Civil War and afterwards as a result of the slighting.

The gatehouse is a remarkable survival of late 13th-century military architecture with a long and complex passage incorporating a drawbridge, massive doors, two portcullises, and other defensive features. Construction of the gatehouse, north-east tower and chapel followed the excavation of the rock-cut ditch. With the exception of the adjoining east and north curtain wall and the possible inner gatehouse, this building complex was effectively free-standing.

Fig. 13.1 The entrance to the castle about 1900

The chapel tower includes a basement, ground-floor chapel and first-floor chamber. The chapel has a modern floor and ceiling.

The Gatehouse and North-east Tower

The gatehouse consists of a long passage flanked by the chapel on the south, the corner guard-tower to the north-east and the curtain wall including a wall passage on the north. In front of the passage is a drawbridge pit and a flight of steps (a 1920s addition to what was originally a sloping ramp) leading downwards into the barbican.

Externally, the small semi-circular north-east tower had high spurs and is well-constructed of large blocks of stone set on a square base, standing on the flat ground that is now part of the northern outer ward. There are slight traces of what was probably an original south-east spur, cut away by later alterations. This later work has also obscured the original relationship between the tower and the gate passage. There are traces of a construction break in the north curtain wall in line with the west face of the gatehouse building (see Chapter 12).

Most of the mechanism associated with the drawbridge has been lost, but several features can be seen within the pit. Two surviving large sockets in the west wall would have held the roller-bearings of the drawbridge, which had three thick and heavy counterbalancing arms that rested in slots in the base of the passageway (Fig. 13.2). When the drawbridge was raised on the bearings these arms also rotated, ending up in the vertical parts of the slots. With efficient counterbalancing, perhaps with the use of lead weights, only a small effort would have been needed to raise or lower the drawbridge (Plate 15, p.193).

With an average width of some 3m and a length of about 16m, the gate passage would have presented a daunting prospect to any attacker. Starting from the eastern end of the surviving section, the main archway is rebated on the inside to take

Fig. 13.2 The counterweight slots for the drawbridge

Fig. 13.3 The backward facing arrow slits above the passageway

double doors that could be locked by means of a 3.5m long draw bar contained in a square hole that continues through the south wall into the chapel. In front of this there was originally an additional vaulted passage, of which only traces survive. It supported a first-floor room from which the drawbridge was operated. In the surviving west wall of that room are two arrow slits that point inwards and downwards through a void so as to catch the unwary attacker from the rear when he was well inside the gate passage (Fig. 13.3).

The gate passage contains two portcullis slots – when both were down they would have formed a 'cage' just over 2m wide (Plate 16, p.194). The vaulted roof between the two portcullis slots contains two so-called 'murder holes', but they may well have been slots for counter-weights associated with the inner portcullis. Included in this 2m wide 'cage' are two narrow windows: one from the northern wall passage and the other from the chapel. About 5m along the existing passage there is a central arch that did not contain a door. However, the large holes in the walls on the inside of the arch were apparently designed to take great baulks of timber that could act as a semi-permanent blocking, especially if mounded up with soil on the inside. They are of possible Civil War date. The passage has a slight bend centrally, which suggests that it is of two different constructional periods – the western part, internal to the curtain wall, being the earlier (see Chapter 11).

The gate passage contains a flagstone floor which is now quite eroded. Such a floor is unlikely to have survived in its entirety from the time of the Civil War – it was probably laid by the Ministry of Works in the 1920s, together with the steps up the ramp.

An arched opening in the north wall of the gate passage leads into the wall passage that heads eastwards to the guard room and westwards to a garderobe. The narrow passage, some 11m long, has a barrel-vaulted roof. There are two splayed openings in the outside passage wall and a single one in the inside, all with steeply sloping bases. The inside one overlooked the space between the two portcullis slots.

The guard room in the north-east turret is small and heated by a small fireplace in the west wall. The north wall contains a large window that presumably indicates the difficulty of attacking the castle from this side. It contains two original iron cross-bars with spaces for three others; the vertical member is missing. The comparatively wide opening provides an excellent view for several miles across the river. In contrast, the east wall has a narrow and very deep slit, slightly angled to overlook the ramp leading up from the barbican. The thickness of wall is such that the defender would have had to lie down in between the narrow splays to fire an arrow through the slit, presumably using a crossbow. There is a third slit on the south side of the room that provided a view of the platform just within the drawbridge. The lower part of the opening has an internal blocking, presumably to help protect the guard from possible attack. The lower parts of the two openings into the gate passage have slight indications that they may once have operated in the opposite direction (see Chapter 11). At the western end of the passage, the vertical lavatory chute joins the one from the first-floor to an arched opening in the curtain wall in the outer ward. The chute now serves a modern purpose – it provides an access route for the electricity supply within the castle.

The first-floor room above the gate passage is some 4.6m wide, extending partly over the south and east walls of the ground-floor passage. The walls are 'squared-off' and thus do not reflect the angling and variable thicknesses of the gate passage walls. The room has a stone floor that may well be original; the walls are all tied together and appear to be of one constructional

Fig. 13.4 The first-floor room above the entrance passage from the south-west with the portcullis slots and the doorway leading to the room that contained the drawbridge machinery

build. This is an excellent example of a room designed for multiple use. The presence of a fireplace in the south wall, complete with a hearth, indicates that the main part of the room would certainly have had a residential function. A timber partition probably separated this room from a passageway that was part of the throughway joining the northern and the eastern wall walks.

However, the east wall includes two rectangular openings that contain the remains of the arrangements for raising and lowering the outer portcullis. A circular bearing for some form of windlass crosses both of the openings. In the floor in front of the wall is the slot for the inner portcullis and the two so-called 'murder holes' that may be for counter-weights as there is no indication whatsoever of the mechanism that operated this one (Plate 16, p.194 & Fig. 13.4).

Centrally placed in the north wall was a window that originally contained a narrow light and window seats. Only the sides survive – the whole of the window including the seats was broken out down to floor level probably it was were converted to take a large wooden window frame at a late period (see Chapter 18). A single light in the west wall opened into the courtyard and contained window seats.

Six corbels on the north and south walls presumably held wall plates as they are not opposite each other. There are also single, centrally-placed sockets in both the east and west walls that would have held a longitudinal timber. These timbers would have formed a framework on which either a flat or ridged roof would have been set (Plate 16, p.194). There are three smaller sockets in the east and west walls set below the corbels that may have taken some form of up-braces.

A small doorway in the north-western corner leads through a short passage and down three steps to the northern wall walk. Contrived within the thickness of the wall is a small garderobe with a narrow window in the north wall. The latrine had a door, but with a draw bar on the outside presumably to keep the door shut when it was *not* in use. Had the door been shut when the seat was *in* use, the user would have been very cramped – the whole chamber is less that 1m wide and 0.6m deep! The wall had to be corbelled out between the gatehouse and the north curtain wall to accommodate the diagonal passage and garderobe and could therefore have been added later.

The north-eastern doorway led into a passage set above the eastern part of the ground-floor wall passage. It contains a single light in the north wall, set in a splayed opening. On the opposite side of the passage there is a well-constructed alcove. Although it has no apparent purpose, it has ashlar jambs and appears to be an original feature. The passage led to the small first-floor room in the north-east turret. The fragments that survive indicate that it was slightly larger than the ground-floor guard room. It had one slit on the north-western side and probably another on the east side overlooking the entrance. In the south wall is the western jamb of a doorway that would have led from the passage to the drawbridge control room above the outer part of the gatehouse. It is almost certain that this room was part of the late 13th-

Fig. 13.5 The chapel tower and gatehouse

century gatehouse construction, although it apparently had some later rebuilding. The door jamb includes a rebate for a door and a draw-bar hole that would have locked this room from the passage side. As there was no other entry, this would have sealed any occupant within the room. It is this small chamber that contained the backward and downward-pointing arrow slits in its western wall overlooking the portcullis 'cage' (Fig. 13.3).

The Chapel Tower

The rectangular base of the chapel tower is set on the sloping edge of the bedrock as it descends down into the ditch and extends out from the line of the east curtain wall by some 5m (Fig. 13.5). The tower, on the south side of the gate passage, contains a basement, a ground-floor chapel, and a residential room on the first floor. Until the 1920s it was open to the elements (Fig. 13.6) but subsequent restoration has added a modern floor and ceiling and stained-glass windows.

There is a high spur at the south-eastern corner that breaks into two small spurs at first-floor level. There are indications of a similar spur at the north-east corner, but it did not enclose as much of the curve as the south-eastern one and was probably designed to be more upright so as to present a vertical side to the gate passage. The tower is constructed of large, well-coursed blocks similar to those used in the north-east tower. The large 15th-century chapel window is an evident insertion in the main face of the tower, whilst above it, on the angle overlooking the barbican, are traces of a large first-floor window.

The basement is approached by a wide flight of steps that starts well outside the south wall of the building and ends with only three steps inside the room. Within the room the eastern end of the south wall contains a narrow slit with deep splays that enfilades the east curtain wall. The single light in the central facet of the east wall is of similar design and, with its sloping sill and deeply splayed jambs, clearly had a defensive function. The west wall, set

Fig. 13.6 The chapel and rooms above and below about 1900 looking east

slightly forward from the wall of the chapel above, appears to be tied into both north and south walls.

Sockets in the north and south walls were presumably designed to carry the joists for the ground floor. However, this was apparently not satisfactory for all four walls include inserted corbels, designed to take a full ring of wall plates. Some of the corbels were evidently replaced in the 1920s when the new floor was first inserted (this floor was replaced in 1986). The basement was about 4m high and originally would have had a flagged floor – there was a drain in the south-east corner.

The chapel has evidently had many alterations during its life (see Chapters 10 & 16). The room is separated from the gate passage by a thick wall that tapers slightly from east to west. The south wall is also very thick, the main part being almost 3m wide. The doorway that leads into the chapel from the courtyard is in the extreme southern end of the west wall and its operation is dependent on a set-back in the south wall. The frame is rebated for a door that hinged on the south and was fastened by a draw bar that slotted into the northern jamb. The opening now contains a modern door.

Fig. 13.7 To the right of the altar are a sink for washing the holy vessels (piscina) and a trefoil-headed niche containing a seat for the priest (sedile)

The east end, effectively an apse with three facets, was separated from the main body of the chapel by an arch, but only the lower parts remain. It contains the remains of an altar that almost filled the width of the recess. The facet to the north-east contains an aumbry (a recessed cupboard that contained the sacred vessels). The one to the south-east includes a piscina (a shallow basin used for washing the communion vessels), and a sedile (a recessed seat for the clergy) (Fig. 13.7).

The eastern end of the south wall contains a narrow light similar to the one in the basement. It is set in an embrasure (a wide opening with rectangular sides) that has a seat on the eastern side. A short distance to the west is a similar-shaped embrasure with seats on three sides, but here the resemblance ceases. From the south-eastern corner of the embrasure, a skewed passageway, some 2.5m long, leads to a window which is angled to the passageway in such a way that it is set in the east curtain wall, matching the windows that illuminated the ground floor of the east range (see Chapter 16). A large cupboard or locker was inserted into the west side of the embrasure. It is constructed of a white stone and there is a possible external hinge position on the east, but no signs of any fastening. The whole could have been used as a small vestry by the priest, with the locker forming an aumbry.

The original west window was much narrower than the present one – part of its relieving arch survives above the present opening. All other openings are later (see Chapter 18).

The only original feature associated with the north wall of the chapel was a wide rectangular window embrasure containing a narrow splayed light that opened from the gate passage within the portcullis 'cage'. Although it was presumably constructed with defence in mind and could not have generated much light, it originally contained window seats on both sides. It was altered later when a stair was inserted into the wall (see Chapter 16).

Three sockets aligned vertically were cut in the north wall of the chapel directly to the west of the large window embrasure. The top one is matched by a single socket in the relieving arch above the eastern window embrasure in the south wall. This could well represent the position of the rood, which is discussed, together with the associated piscinae, when dealing with the 14th-century alterations in Chapter 16. As with the basement, there is a narrow shelf and sockets in the north and south walls to support the joists for the first floor and, underneath them, inserted corbels for the additional wall plates. The apse had a curving roof of stones set on edge, but the floor above rested on joists.

The first-floor chamber above the chapel could be approached from three different directions – from the north curtain wall, from the east curtain wall along a passage built in the thickness of the south wall of the chapel tower, and from the courtyard up the spiral staircase in the octagonal turret. The chamber, which is approximately the same size as the chapel, has a floor of modern concrete slabs that forms the flat 'roof' to the chapel. It was inserted in 1986. The room was at least 4.5m high.

There is a fireplace in the north wall, similar to the one in the adjoining room but larger in size. The east end of the room has three facets similar to those in the room below, but the central facet does not have an opening – instead, advantage was taken of the defensive potential of the north-east facet. Here is a skewed, but almost rectangular embrasure, which had seats on all three sides. Although only the lower part survives, it is evident that alterations have taken place. The original opening, doubtless a narrow slit, was designed to overlook the ramp leading up to the drawbridge.

The window at the east end of the south wall was also constructed with defence in mind, for it is directly in line with the east curtain wall. The rectangular embrasure contains window seats on all three sides, but there is nothing left of the window opening. The west wall contains a window identical in shape and design to the one in the west wall of the adjoining chamber. There are two holes for shutter hinges on each side, and a hole for a shutter bar on the left.

The south-western corner of the room is set at an angle and a short passage leads to the spiral stair, and, through a wall passage, to the east curtain walk (Fig. 13.8). The walls in the passage are corbelled in at the top to take a series of flat slabs that form the roof. The doorway leading onto the wall walk had a draw bar allowing the passage to be sealed off from the wall walk. The two lights in the south wall were eventually obscured when the east range was rebuilt (see Chapter 16). The entry to the spiral stair had a door that could be locked from within the room.

Gatehouse and chapel roofs

The spiral staircase continued upwards to provide access onto the wall walks around the chapel and gatehouse and to a still higher level in the spiral turret itself (Fig. 13.8). A small doorway on the diagonal flank of the tower led onto the wall walks. With the exception of the two lost window heads on the east, the wall walk survives around the whole of the room above the

Fig. 13.8 The octagonal stair tower from the south with later openings and fireplace associated with the final east range (see Chapter 18)

gate passage and around the western half of the room above the chapel. There are substantial indications of a parapet, about 1m high, on the courtyard side but 2m high to the south, where the wall walk rose above the east curtain wall. The south parapet contained at least one arrow slit. To the north, and above the first-floor gatehouse chamber, there is a trough and a drain that connects into the first-floor latrine shaft. The wall between the two rooms contained the two chimneys and was not part of the wall walk.

The roof of the room above the chapel was originally supported on eight corbels set into the north and south walls slightly below the wall walk in a similar fashion to those in the adjoining room. The design of the roofs above this room and the adjoining one are somewhat uncertain, but the evidence suggest a hipped roof over each chamber (Plate 16, p.194). There would have been a central gully resting on the spine wall between the two rooms to drain the inside slopes of the two roofs.

The octagonal stair tower must be integral with the chapel tower, for it is difficult to see how the latter could have functioned without the tower (Fig. 13.8). It has an entrance on the south side facing the east hall. The lower steps have been replaced in stone and replacement timber treads complete the stair as far as the first floor. The latter are not quite in the position of the original stone treads.

All the original window openings in the stair tower were simple square-headed slits. The lowest one survives and faces to the north-west. The second was converted to a doorway leading to the first floor of the east range (see Chapter 18), but the original window faced south. The next window faced west; it was protected by a single horizontal bar and had an internal shutter There is a later opening leading to the second floor of the east range (see Chapter 18). There is an upper window in the north-west facet and above that the doorway that led out to the wall walk.

14 The late 13th-century Castle – The Internal Buildings

by Ron Shoesmith

Apart from the rooms in the corner towers (see Chapter 12), there were several new internal buildings. The most important was probably the north range with a vestibule joining it to the north-west tower. The replacement building on the eastern side of the courtyard was also of this date. There may have been a building on the west side of the courtyard, replaced in the 14th-century, but no trace has been found. The keep was retained, apparently with minimal alteration.

Fig. 14.1 1798 engraving of the north hall range.
In the background to the right are parts of the curtain wall that collapsed in 1919.

Fig. 14.2 A general view of the north range from the east. The original gently sloping roof level cuts across the later features in the wall.

The North Range and the Vestibule

The north range and the vestibule between it and the north-west tower is separated by the two-storey pillar with its double arch, which is the subject of many engravings and photographs (Fig. 14.1). The north range started its life as a single-storey hall with an undercroft or basement and was converted, in the 15th or 16th century, to include an upper floor (see Chapter 18). Several early writers incorrectly describe the undercroft as being the kitchen for the castle whilst later ones simply called the whole block the solar range (Plate 1, p.57). However, as it is earlier than the great west hall, it may well have started its life as the main hall of the castle, with a change in use when the great hall was built (Plate 17, p.195) (see Chapter 17).

The north wall of the hall is also part of the curtain wall and survives in places almost to wall-walk level (Fig. 14.2). The west wall, with its double arch, is structurally the east wall of the rectangular vestibule to the north-west tower and continues to a higher level than the north wall. The south and east walls are only present within the basement, and do not rise above the courtyard level. Within the basement many of the facing stones of the walls are missing.

To the west of the arcade the north-western tower and its vestibule were open at basement and ground-floor levels to the undercroft and north hall. Above this the first-floor room in the vestibule had a doorway leading onto the almost flat hall roof and from there to the northern wall walk (Fig. 18.2).

The north range basement is now approached by a dog-leg flight of steps in the southern lobby to the north-west tower, initially leading eastwards before turning north to descend into the undercroft through a triangular-headed arch in the south wall, just to the east of the octagonal column (Fig. 14.2). The opening had a door which could be locked from the basement side. This access may well have replaced an earlier stair when the west range was built in the 14th century (see Chapter 17).

The only other feature in the south wall is at the extreme eastern end where there is a basin with a central pillar cut from a single piece of stone and set into the wall (Fig. 14.3). It would appear that the basin had some form of water supply from above, probably associated with the well, although it is difficult to see how this could have functioned. It had a drain, but this is now blocked. There are no indications that this basin was inserted, and it appears to be an original feature.

The north wall of the basement contained a window set slightly to the east of centre, and a postern doorway in the eastern corner. Both are considered to be primary features. The sides of the window are chamfered to a rather narrow light set into an external, square-

Fig. 14.3 The basin in the south wall of the basement

headed recess. However, the window is high and is approached from the undercroft by a flight of six steps. There is a short seat on the left-hand side which extends in front of the opening. The window was well protected – it had six horizontal bars and two vertical ones in addition to what appears to be a draw-bar hole on the west side that would have held a shutter, hinged on the east.

The postern doorway was well defended, containing two massive doors and a portcullis (Fig. 14.4). The 2.3m long passage through the wall includes steps leading down to the present outer ward. Internally there is a rebate for a door which could be locked by a draw bar set in a slot in the eastern wall and connected with a pair of iron staples set in the opposite wall. The external door was set behind a second rebate with a draw bar housed in a square hole on the west and a return on the east. The portcullis slots on each side of the passage have been partially blocked in antiquity.

The east wall contains no features of importance at basement level and much of the face is lost. There are two sockets in the north and south walls that may represent the position of a timber partition separating the main undercroft from a narrow (and rather dark) area to the east.

Fig. 14.4 The postern door leading from the basement of the north range to the outer ward

The undercroft floor was probably of stone, perhaps some 5cm above the present level as the steps are uneven. Although the room was of reasonably high quality, with a 4m high ceiling and connecting directly to what appears to have been a residential chamber in the basement of the north-west tower, it was poorly lit with only the single window in the north wall. There was no apparent means of heating apart from braziers and the lack of ventilation would probably have made such a method positively lethal. Although the window provides a seat and apparently had drapes, it would seem that the room's primary purpose was for storage.

In the eastern half of the north wall the positions of the joists that supported the timber ground floor are quite distinct with many of the individual holes surviving. The slight shelf was probably repeated on the southern side, allowing the joists to be supported on the solid wall. The 20 or so beams that supported the ground-floor of the hall were each about 0.4m square in cross-section.

The ground-floor hall was some 12.4m long and 6.7m wide. It was approached both from the north-west tower vestibule and by a small doorway in the north-eastern corner, associated with the postern doorway portcullis. There may well have been another doorway in the south wall, but the present difference in levels would have meant going down several steps. However, there are indications that the courtyard surface may have been 0.5m or more lower than it is now when the north range was first built, thus avoiding the need for steps.

The hall had two windows in the north wall and there would doubtless have been others in the south and east walls. The westernmost window survives reasonably complete, but has lost its inner arch. It included a rectangular internal recess complete with window seats. Only the square recess survives of the eastern window, but it appears to have been similar to the western one. Externally each window was set in a square-headed recess, similar to the basement window. The ground-floor vestibule was some 5m wide and had a large double-height window in its western wall that would have added considerably to the illumination of the hall itself. It would be surprising if the hall had to depend on braziers for heating, especially as it did not have the standard pitched roof into which a smoke bay could be inserted. It is possible that there was a fireplace within the south wall, but no trace survives.

The portcullis that guarded the postern door, when raised, was entirely within the thickness of the curtain wall. It was operated from the north-eastern corner of the ground floor of the north hall where a half arch contained the mechanism (Plate 17, p.195). The device was serviced through a narrow doorway in the thickness of the east wall of the hall. Only slight traces of the opening remain, but it is apparent that it had a door, hinged on the north, so that it opened into the thickness of the wall. Accepting that the postern doorway was part of the original north range construction, it follows that this doorway was also of that period. A circular hole in the western side of the alcove indicates where the portcullis shaft was seated. There is no indication of counter-weights of any description, so presumably the portcullis had to be cranked up by hand. The portcullis works were presumably screened off from the main part of the ground-floor hall, and a slot towards the top of the arch probably indicates this partition.

The creasing in the east face of the arcade wall, although slight, provides the sole evidence for the roof (Figs. 14.3 & 18.2). It apparently had a very slight slope down to the south, and one to the north towards the level of the wall walk. There would have been drains through the parapet wall to remove the considerable amount of water when it rained, and something similar on the courtyard side. A doorway from the first floor of the north-west tower vestibule led onto the roof and from there to the wall walk (the doorway was lengthened at a later date to provide an entry to the inserted first-floor room in the north range – see Chapter 18). To the left of the doorway a rectangular window provided light to the first-floor vestibule.

The design of the hall roof is difficult to establish. Presumably timbers would have been laid across the hall from corbels or seatings in the north wall just below the level of the wall walk to similar positions in the south wall. The timbers had to span a gap between north and south walls of some 6.7m. The whole would then have to be boarded over and leaded, and would have been very heavy. Surprisingly, there is no trace of a socket for a longitudinal timber to provide additional support.

In this first phase of use, the north hall was probably one big open space that continued through the arcade wall to the vestibule. On the basement and ground floors there were probably screens separating the vestibules from what appear to have been private chambers within the north-west tower.

The East Range
Sufficient survives of the east range of buildings, which filled the gap between the chapel tower and the south-east tower, to indicate that this part of the castle was the subject of more rebuilding work that any other. There is evidence of three distinct building phases, not including any building that may have been associated with the earliest section of the east wall (see Chapter 11 & Fig. 16.7).

The first phase was apparently a simple lean-to building that occupied the northern three-quarters of the area; the second was a large hall, with windows and a fireplace inserted into the curtain wall and providing a roof for the wall walk (see Chapter 16); whilst the third involved an almost total rebuild to provide a three-storey galleried building with a series of chambers on the first and second floors (see Chapter 18).

The earliest indication of a building associated with the rebuilt curtain wall is represented by the projecting plinth and cut-back chase immediately below the wall walk (Fig. 12.2). They are present along the northern three-quarters of the curtain wall including the widened part of the wall, but stop before the line of the doorway that led into a single ground-floor latrine. The plinth and chase were apparently associated with a horizontal wall plate that would have taken the ends of the rafters for the sloping roof of a low single-storey building – in effect a lean-to built against the curtain wall. At that time the ground level in the courtyard was still some 0.5m to 1m below the present level. As a relatively low-status building, still utilising the simple arrow slots in the outer wall, such a building could well have been simply stabling or storage. It is apparent that the room would have included the entrance into the basement underneath the chapel (Fig. 16.7). As the building did not extend as far as the south-east tower it would have had a separate south wall. The indications are that this building would have been made mainly of timber.

Other Internal Buildings
There would doubtless have been other buildings within the castle, particularly on the western side, but no traces have been found. Any buildings in that area would have been totally demolished when the great hall was built (see Chapter 17). It would appear that there were no alterations to the keep until the 14th century (see Chapter 16).

15 THE BARBICAN & ACCESS TO THE CASTLE
by Ron Shoesmith

A barbican is a fortified outer defence to the gate leading into a castle – often a small castle in itself. The present Goodrich barbican is a roughly D-shaped structure built immediately to the east of the stepped ramp leading up to the gatehouse (Fig. 15.1), and is evidently of more than one constructional period. As it is separate from the main castle, the various constructional phases are discussed in this chapter. Including the walls, it is about 25m across and 12m wide. To the south of the ramp leading up to the castle gatehouse, the western, flat side of the barbican sits on the side of the main ditch, and to the north of the ramp it faces the eastern end of the northern ward. The curtain wall that surrounds the northern outer ward is an

Fig. 15.1 The barbican from the top of the keep in the mid-1990s with the custodian's old hut

extension from the north wall of the barbican. The barbican ditch is very shallow to the north-east, but gradually deepens as it continues round to the south where it is rock cut and eventually joins into the side of the main castle ditch. The present wooden bridge crosses this ditch where there was once a drawbridge and here the ditch is some 4m deep and about 4.5m wide.

Much of the barbican has been demolished, probably during the Civil War and the slighting that followed. The existing masonry extends upwards from the ditch to a little above the internal ground level around most of the perimeter, apart from on the east where it survives to the level of a wall walk.

Fig. 15.2 Detail of the lower courses on the east side of the barbican showing one side of a possible entry

Initial construction

Although only fragments survive, it would seem that the original barbican was a totally different shape to the present one. On the north-east the masonry is partially hidden by a later garderobe extension but from a slight curve it takes up a straight line to the south-east. This alignment continues for about 3m as a foundation, before being lost in the shallow side of the ditch. The face of the wall includes a carved stone that could represent one side of an entrance (Fig. 15.2). The ground level is such that a track could have approached the castle from that general direction, possibly as a result of bringing stone from the nearby quarry (Fig. 15.3). The stonework behind the face, which appears as a triangular platform, acts as a foundation for the later barbican wall which takes a southerly course before curving round to the present entrance. All the evidence suggests that the barbican was originally built without a ditch.

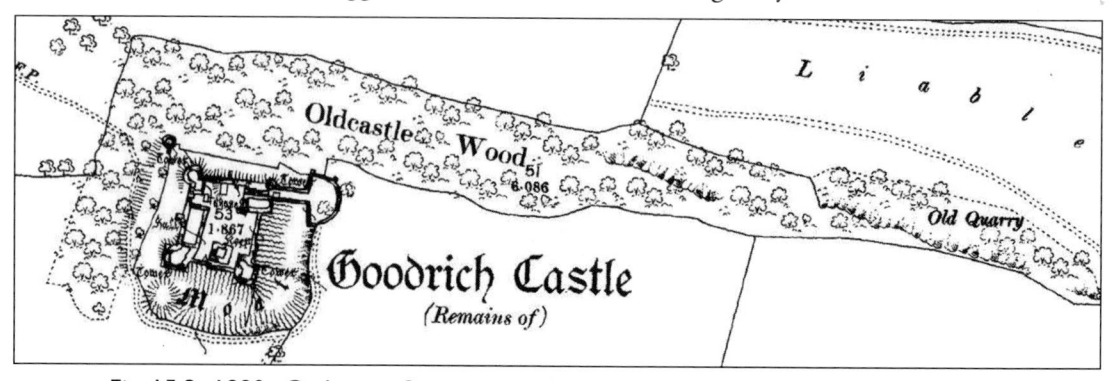

Fig. 15.3 1880s Ordnance Survey map showing a quarry to the east of the castle

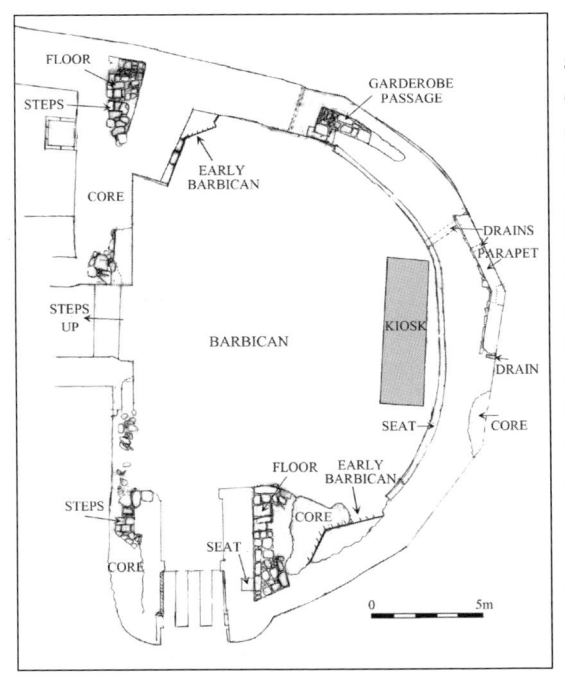

Fig. 15.4 A recent plan showing traces of the earlier barbican

Fig. 15.5 Facing stones of the earlier barbican underneath the later guardhouse floor – the remains of the floor are at the extreme top of the photograph

There is further evidence for this early structure from within the barbican. At the extreme north-western corner, the foundation of an inner face of a diagonal wall is exposed for a couple of courses (Fig. 15.4). This is probably part of the inner face of the original barbican, and if so indicates that it was built before the northern ward was constructed and walled. Additional evidence for the early barbican is apparent within the south-eastern corner, where an area was excavated in the past to a level well below the floor of the later guard chamber (Fig. 15.5). The top and external faces of two walls are visible in this trench. One apparently represents a facet of the original perimeter wall whilst the other could have been the south-eastern side of a wall leading to an entrance in the same position as the present one. A further early angled wall is shown centrally in the barbican on a 1925 plan (Fig. 15.6). It has presumably been reburied as there is now no trace on the surface.

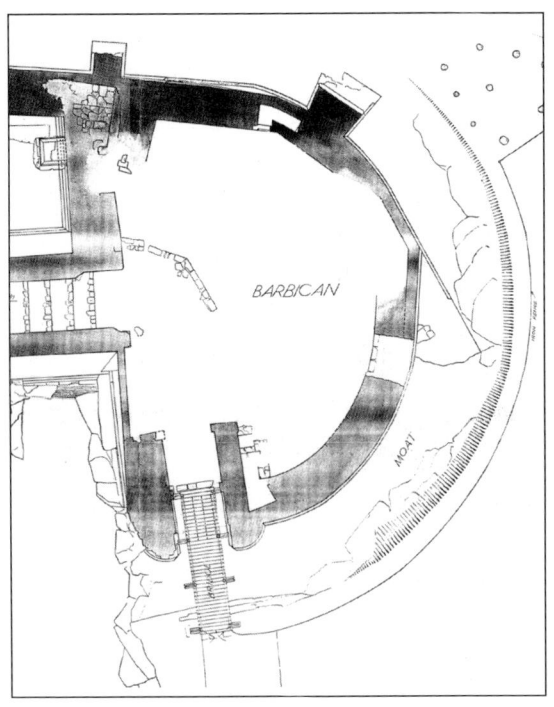

Fig. 15.6 1925 plan of the barbican showing early masonry now buried

Development of the Barbican

The alterations to the barbican probably took place in several stages. To improve the defensive capability a drawbridge and its accompanying ditch was needed, and the whole of the southern part of the barbican was reconstructed with a smooth curve where it could be seen by anyone approaching the castle. Joining this wall to the existing masonry on the eastern side must have created problems with the sudden change in direction. As a result much of the face on this joint has since collapsed.

The approach to the barbican is now over a fixed bridge that replaced the drawbridge (Fig. 15.7). On the south of the barbican, the two turrets and the associated drawbridge pit wall are almost complete below what would have been the level of the drawbridge. Underneath are the three slots that originally contained the counter-weights and, in the east wall, the socket for the drawbridge pivot (Fig. 15.8).

Traces of the remaining parts of the defensive works are slight, but it appears that, having crossed the drawbridge, the visitor entered a 6m long gate passage. Just within this are the rebates for a doorway. There is no indication that the gate passage ever included a portcullis.

Fig. 15.7 The timber bridge that replaced the drawbridge; looking westwards

Fig. 15.8 Underneath the timber bridge are the slots for the drawbridge counter-weights

Fig. 15.9 The guard chamber

The eastern passage wall formed the side of the guard chamber, whilst on the west the thick wall includes traces of steps that would have led to the room above the gate passage containing the machinery for operating the drawbridge. There is little indication of how the small upper room functioned, but it would doubtless have included a door on the east side leading onto the wall walk.

There are only slight traces of the guard chamber which had to fit into the triangular area between the barbican curtain wall and the gate passage wall (Fig. 15.9). Three steps led up from the internal ground level to the flagged floor of which traces remain. The room included a seat built into the gate passage wall which would doubtless have also included a window. The northern limit of the guard chamber is set by the steps, whilst the eastern end of the room probably relates to the beginning of the seat that continues around the eastern curve of the barbican. This would mean that the guard chamber had maximum internal dimensions of about 2.5m and 1.5m, not too dissimilar from those in the main gatehouse guardroom. There could well have been a fireplace in the northern or eastern wall.

A later alteration to the barbican suggests that it was being used as a meeting place, for an 8m long seat was built inside the eastern curve. It may have been then that a garderobe was constructed on the northern side of the barbican. It was built into the thickness of the curtain wall and consisted of a narrow entry with an equally narrow wall passage leading to the latrine (Fig. 15.10). There is now no

Fig. 15.10 The passage leading to the garderobe in the thickness of the wall

Fig. 15.11 The garderobe chamber was added to the outside wall of the barbican

indication of the shaft or of the seating arrangement. Although the passage is slightly higher than the present level within the barbican, the height of the wall walk is such that it could have continued above the passage, still leaving sufficient headroom below. Construction of this garderobe involved rebuilding the north-eastern section of the barbican wall to incorporate the latrine chamber in a specially designed extension that is properly tied into the adjoining sections of wall. It is about 3m wide and extends from the wall by 1.8m with a low-level extension at the foot that contains the hole for cleaning the chamber. It stands just over 2m high to a sloping stone capping (Fig. 15.11).

The north-western part of the barbican was rebuilt at a late period in its history when the flat north ward and its encircling wall was being constructed. On the west side, the surviving fragments of the wall between the barbican and the north ward indicate that it was some 2.5m thick and included the remains of an internal paved area forming a narrow wall passage (Fig. 15.4). This passage was only slightly above the barbican ground level and minimal traces of a doorway survive. The wall passage led in a northerly direction through a second doorway and down four steps into a stone-flagged room of which minimal traces remain. This formed a vestibule at the top of a long flight of steps set against the inner face of the outer curtain wall leading down into the north ward (see Chapter 18). Only the bottom courses of the walls that formed the vestibule survive, but as it included doorways it was almost certainly roofed. The construction of this vestibule created a weak structural point at the junction of the outer curtain wall and the barbican which had to be supported by a buttress.

The curtain wall that surrounded the semicircular part of the barbican stands at its highest for a short distance between the guard chamber and the garderobe and varies in thickness from 2 to 2.5m. The flagged wall walk is just over 2m above the present internal level and includes traces of a parapet wall. There is nothing to indicate that the whole of the barbican was ever

Fig. 15.12 The eastern side of the castle in the 1920s showing the new steps leading from the barbican to the timber bridge and gate passage

Fig. 15.13 The arches that supported the ramp to the castle from the north

roofed and it is considered unlikely. However, individual elements including the two-storey gatehouse, the guard chamber and the vestibule would each have had a separate roof. There may also have been a pentice type of roof over the stone seating. The main part of the barbican was almost certainly an open area with the encircling walls being sufficiently high with a strong parapet to provide a practical defence to the area at the bottom of the ramp, and thus to the main gatehouse. Indeed, the open area was well overlooked from the main castle and would only have had a low parapet on the castle side so that, should it be taken, the open area within would become an enclosed killing ground with little possibility of shelter apart from the barbican gatehouse.

From the Barbican to the Castle

The access from the barbican to the castle was described in the late 1920s as 'a sloping causeway and a bridge of two spans'.[1] It is now up a flight of shallow steps which were presumably constructed as a safety measure to replace the ramp (Fig. 15.12). There were evidently walls on each side of the ramp, although they were probably no more than waist high.

The ramp sits on a rocky outcrop and two stone arches (Figs. 15.13 & 14) – there was probably some means of access in this position to the earliest stone castle. At the top of the ramp was the drawbridge pit – only the outer walls continued across. They are supported on two half-arches that butt against the main gatehouse building. The three slots for the drawbridge counterweights, similar to those in the barbican gatehouse, were filled in at a time

Fig. 15.14 The ramp entry to the castle from the barbican and the arches from the south. The barbican ditch and bridge are on the right.

when a new, more fashionable entrance was constructed. The slots were replaced by corbelling designed to support a permanent wooden bridge and the entrance gateway was moved further forward.

Summary

The slight indications of the first barbican are insufficient to provide a design or even to give any indication of a constructional date. It may well have been associated with the first stone castle. However, the drawbridge and its associated guard chamber, built of well-cut stone on a smooth curve, which is of a similar design to the main castle entry, was most likely constructed in the latter part of the 13th century.

Barbicans, or external defences to town or castle gates, were in use from *c.*1200 and gained in sophistication throughout the century.[2] At Dover the encircling wall with its square towers was built about 1180 with an outer enclosure with round towers built in the early 13th century. At the Tower of London, the Lion Tower is part of a barbican of a similar design and date to Goodrich. The D-shaped barbican at Sandal (a suburb of Wakefield in West Yorkshire) is part of a motte and bailey castle, being within the bailey and tower-shaped. Excavation has shown that this barbican also had a garderobe.[3]

16 The 14th-century Alterations
by Ron Shoesmith

It was during the 14th century that efforts were made to improve the general accommodation in castles and to provide suitable retiring rooms for the lord and his family. At Goodrich this included the complete redesign of the western part of the castle with a new perimeter wall forming one side of the new great hall, and a larger replacement for the south-west tower (see Chapter 17). In addition, the east hall was rebuilt and extended southwards. The mound around the keep was partially removed to provide space for the kitchen and prison and was probably spread over the courtyard raising the level by perhaps 0.5 to 1m. This was probably the time when the V-shaped extension to the south curtain wall was built. In addition, in 1338, the first steps were taken to found a priory at Goodrich. In the first instance the canons or chaplains were given the castle chapel – this was probably when alterations were made to provide them with accommodation in a room above the internally extended gatehouse (see Chapter 6). Much of this work was commissioned by Richard, 2nd Lord Talbot (1327-56) and Elizabeth, his wife (1356-72).

Alterations to the Chapel
It was probably when the canons arrived that the eastern side of the window opening in the north wall was cut back in a curve, and the western side was altered to allow a flight of 12 steps (including one that was originally the window seat) to be inserted into the thickness of the wall. The steps curve round to a high-level opening in the north wall that was associated with a timber balcony joining this doorway to one in the west wall (Fig. 16.1 & Plate 18, p.196). This doorway, which is now blocked by a timber door, led to an external building above the lengthened gate passage (see below).

A socket, at the bottom of the ashlar, was blocked during the early repair works, and directly below it is a corbel matching one in the south wall. Immediately underneath the northern doorway is a piscina, again similar to one in the south wall.

The two decorative corbels (Figs. 16.2 & 3) and the sockets above them may relate to the timber balcony or possibly a gallery. It is suggested that a single beam joined the two sockets with supports curving upwards from the corbels. Although the beam went across the chapel, there is no indication that the gallery ever filled the whole width – it probably just ran from the supporting beam along the north side of the chapel to the doorway in the west wall. The sockets adjacent to that doorway tend to confirm this interpretation (Fig. 16.1).

LEFT: Fig. 16.1 The north-west corner of the chapel showing the two high-level doorways and the entry to the stair

Doorway to room above extended gatehouse

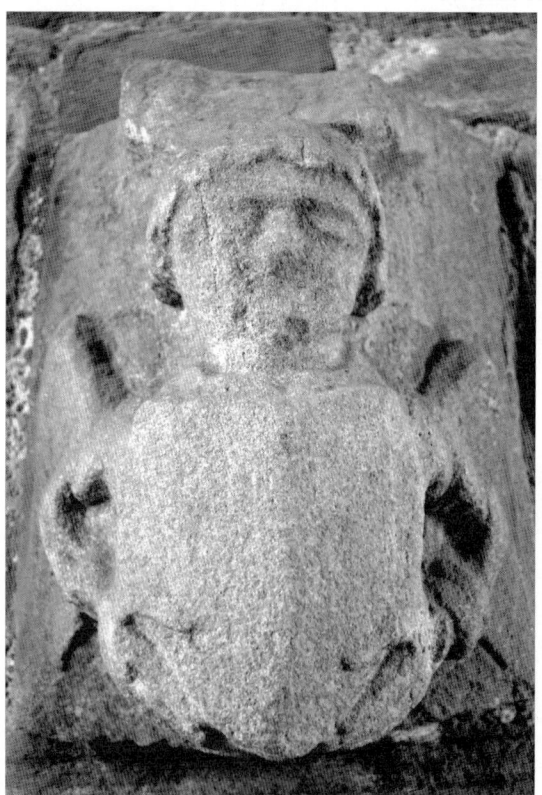

Doorway from stairs within thickness of wall

Bottom of wall stair in window embrasure

Fig. 16.2 One of the decorative corbels in the chapel

Fig. 16.3 One of the decorative corbels in the chapel

Fig. 16.4 The north wall between the north range and the gatehouse

Three sockets aligned vertically were cut in the north wall of the chapel directly to the west of the large window embrasure. The top one, at just over 4m high, is matched by a single socket cut into the relieving arch above the central window embrasure in the south wall. This could well represent a one-time position of the rood, with a rood screen underneath. In such a position it would have allowed the central embrasure in the south wall to have been used as a small vestry, with access from both sides. If this was the case then the piscinæ in the north and south walls would have served side altars positioned to the west of the screen. There are several other small sockets that may well have been associated with wall hangings. Until recently the plastered section of wall had traces of red paint, but there is now no trace of colour.[1]

The Building inside the Gatehouse
Entering the courtyard from the gatehouse passage there is an area of open ground once bounded on the west by the east wall of the north range, on the north by the curtain wall with a large window (Fig. 16.4) and on the east by the chapel. It was probably during the first half of the 14th century that this space was filled with a new two-storey building. This would have been mainly of timber and inserted between the three stone walls. Two corbels in the north curtain wall and a blocked doorway in the chapel wall (constructed of the white stone typical of late features throughout the castle) indicate the first-floor level. This floor could also be reached from the northern wall walk by several steps that led down close to the doorway leading into the first floor of the gatehouse.

In the courtyard, two five-sided half-bases stand close to the west and east walls. In the west wall of the gatehouse and chapel the scars of this lost building provide the final clues (Fig. 16.5). Above the stone base at $c.$2m high there are the remains of what appears to have been a deliberate stone tie consisting of two white stones and, at the base of the doorway leading into the chapel, a further socket, that would have held the first-floor girding beam of the proposed timber frame. Higher still and well above the doorway is the socket for the timber supporting the south side of the roof. From this point the scar on the wall indicates

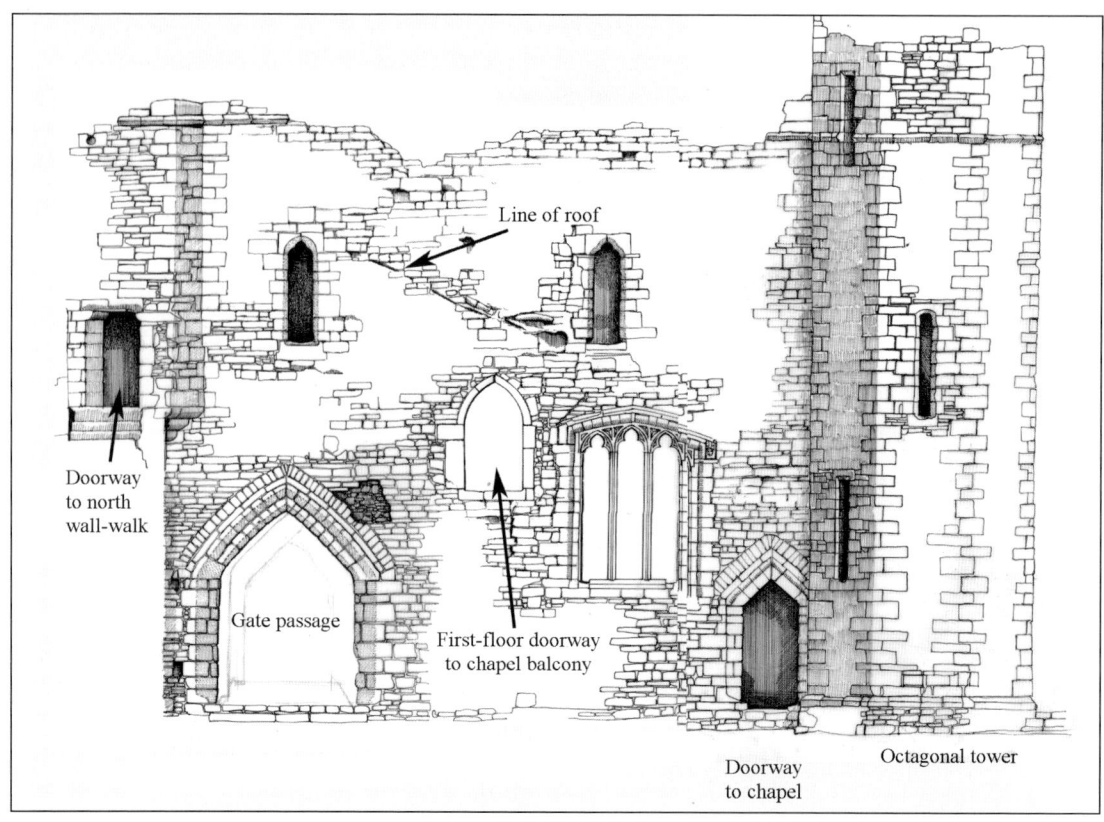

Fig. 16.5 The courtyard side of the west wall of the gatehouse and chapel showing the various features mentioned in the text

that the roof of this lost building sloped up at some thirty degrees to an apex that included the window belonging to the first-floor room above the gate passage. The evidence indicates that the building inside the gatehouse was two storeys high with a ridge running east-west. The remaining part of the roof to the north was almost flat and ran above the northern wall walk.

On the ground floor there was direct access from the gatehouse passage and, in the west wall, there was a doorway that led down a few steps to the ground floor of the north range (Fig. 16.4). The two large half-bases suggest that there were columns on each side for an opening, some 4.8m wide, leading from the courtyard to the extended gate passage. The position of joist holes indicates that there would have been a flattened arch above the opening, probably made out of the white stone used in this period (Fig. 7.3). The ground floor between this arch and the curtain wall probably remained open – it was some 6.5m wide from west to east and about 7m deep. The large window with seats on all three sides, which was inserted into the curtain wall, provided some additional light into what would otherwise have been a rather dark passage.

The corbels indicate that the first floor was about 1m below the level of the wall walk, there being at least six steps leading down. The first floor was supported on three beams running east-west. One rested on the corbels along the north wall; the position of the central one is indicated by a mortice hole to the right and above the arch to the gate passage, and the third was above the flattened arch. These joists were about 3.7m apart – too wide to support floorboards – so they would have had to support a series of north-south joists on which the floorboards were laid. This inserted floor would have cut across the top of the arch of the gatehouse passage entry.

The south wall of this large first-floor room or rooms would almost certainly have contained windows and may have included a gallery. To the north it is suggested that a timber partition separated the room(s) from the wall walk. The wall-walk parapet would have had to be raised to the new flat roof line. There is no trace of any access to this flat roof above the wall walk.

The New Eastern Range

The replacement building on the eastern side of the courtyard involved a downgrading in the defensive function of the castle. The project involved the total demolition of the earlier lean-to and the construction of a new hall block with several windows inserted into the thick curtain wall (Figs. 11.1 & 12.2). Two of these windows were associated with the new east hall whilst a third, at the northern end of the wall, led through a contrived diagonal tunnel to what appears to be a minute vestry associated with the chapel (see Chapter 13). The large breach in the curtain wall may also have contained a window – an engraving of 1732 shows a small, almost square window in this position, with a sill on a level with the others (Fig. 8.6). The windows are widely-splayed single lights, that include rectangular internal recesses with window seats on all three sides. The windows are directly above the earlier loops and it is apparent from the levels of the window seats that the internal ground level must have been raised by between 0.5m and 1m to its present level by the time that this new building was constructed.

The insertion of the windows would have involved the replacement of much of the internal face of the wall below the wall-walk level. Externally, it is almost impossible to identify the construction breaks associated with these insertions due to the considerable amount of erosion that has taken place. Indeed, the extent of masonry replaced during this work could well be represented by the eroded sections.

Associated with this massive reconstruction was probably the large fireplace built into the curtain wall, although this could be of 15th-century date. Only the lower parts survive, including a chamfered back to the hearth. The flue appears to have risen on the courtyard side of the wall walk with a protruding chimney breast.

Fig. 16.6 The outer north face of the south-east tower contains traces of both the 14th-century and the 16th-century buildings that stood on the eastern side of the courtyard

The basic elements of this 14th-century building are still apparent on the external faces of the south wall of the chapel and the north wall of the south-east tower which formed the two ends of the range (Figs. 16.6 & 7). The inserted diagonal stone string courses in both walls are associated with the sloping roof of this single-storey building. The new roof was considerably higher than the earlier one and continued over the top of the wall walk to connect with the parapet wall. Here, a series of corbels held a wall plate to take the rafters, with the roof protected by a projecting plinth. The steeply-sloping roof would have consisted of a series of common rafters running from that plate to one set on top of the courtyard wall (Plate 19, p.197).

The front, courtyard wall was mainly of stone, but only the stub remains in the angle between the polygonal stair tower and the south wall of the chapel (Figs. 16.7 & 8). The wall continued parallel to the east curtain wall, on a similar line to the later low foundation wall with its prominent chamfer. However, there is no scar to show that the wall joined the south-east tower wall and it may be that part of the front wall was built of timber rather than stone or that it was substantially altered when the east range was again rebuilt in the 16th century (see Chapter 18). Although the east range would have been illuminated by the inserted windows in the curtain wall, there would doubtless have been windows in the west wall as well, perhaps similar to those in the great hall opposite.

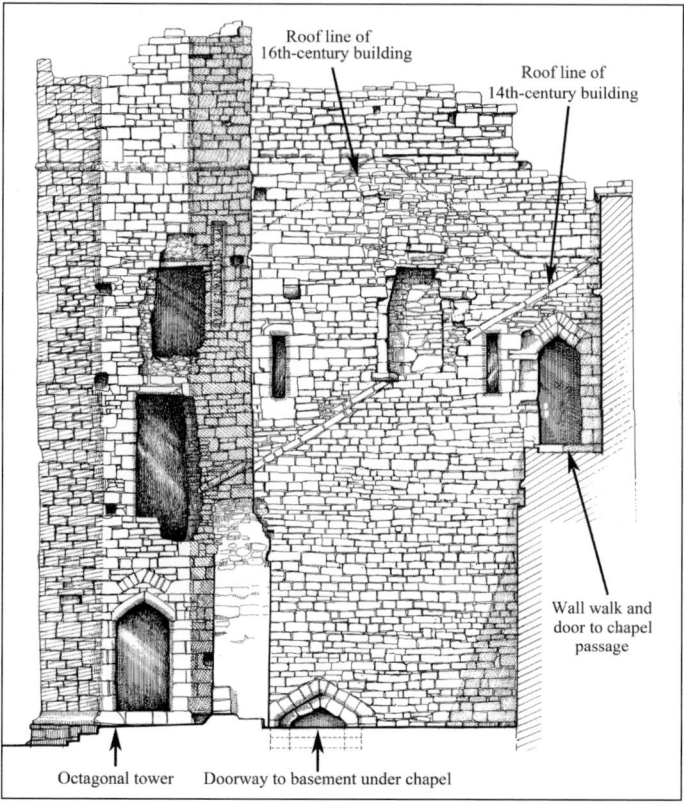

Fig. 16.7 The external south face of the chapel tower showing the two periods of construction of the building on the eastern side of the courtyard

Fig. 16.8 The 'stub' of the west wall of the 14th-century eastern range is apparent between the polygonal tower and the external south wall of the chapel

The building so described would have been 4.7m wide and 22.3m long and, assuming it had an inserted flat ceiling under the sloping roof, would have been some 4.5m high. The stone front wall to the courtyard, the windows inserted in the east wall, and the large fireplace, are all features that one would expect to be associated with a large hall, and although the sloping roof is perhaps a little unusual, it had the advantage of forming a roof over the wall walk – the first-floor access from the chapel and guardhouse area to the south-east tower and beyond. The 'high end' was probably to the south and the services, making use of the basement underneath the chapel, to the north. Behind the 'high end' would have been an ante-room that led into the various rooms in the south-west tower. The southern part of the curtain wall was widened to accommodate two latrines; one at ground-floor level, constructed within the thickness of the wall and a second positioned in a small room on the widened wall walk. The shaft for the latter is still apparent on the wall walk, where it is covered by a grille. Traces of the ground floor one are slight, as it was comprehensively altered when the later garderobe tower and its accompanying latrines were built (see Chapter 18). However, the southern of the three latrine openings is markedly different to the other two, having rounded jambs as compared to chamfered ones and a lower head. Its position, adjoining the top three steps to the basement of the south-east tower, is very inconvenient. The low head provides some direct evidence that the internal ground level was lower by between 0.5m and 1m when the south-east tower and the doorway for the garderobe was constructed, suggesting that they may both have been earlier features.

The new east building was evidently built some time later than the chapel tower for the string course of the sloping roof cuts across the top of one of the windows associated with the first-floor wall passage in the chapel wall, thus blocking it completely.

Alterations to the South Curtain Wall
When the castle was redesigned in the 14th century, a decision must have been made to retain the Norman keep, a dominant and strong feature in the southern part of the courtyard. It has been suggested that the original south curtain wall ran parallel to the keep and was immediately adjacent to its south wall (see Chapter 11). This section of wall was eventually demolished and rebuilt with a shallow V-shaped extension, thus providing a narrow space between the keep and the curtain wall – a space that had a variety of uses during the life of the castle.

However, there was never a ground floor passage on the south side of the keep. Presumably the ground on that side was kept at the height of the mound that once surrounded the keep. The relatively narrow space provided a link some 2.5m above the courtyard level. It was this area that was eventually cut away to take ovens (Fig. 11.7) associated with the kitchen that filled the space between the keep and the great south-west tower.

Buildings to the east of the keep
Set against the east wall of the keep, and between that building and the staircase leading up to the first floor of the south-east tower, was a building that was initially of two storeys, but in its final stages stood three storeys high (Fig. 16.9) (see also Chapter 18).

The lower storey – the dungeon – has a floor some 1.2m below the level of the courtyard and about half a metre below the present level of the basement in the keep. It is approached by a narrow passage over 2m long that includes six steps down and incorporates two door frames.

Fig. 16.9 Detail from a late 18th-century engraving showing the curtain wall between the keep and the south-east tower at the top of the steps leading into the first-floor of the tower. The long opening in the curtain wall appears to have been windows at two levels: one on the level with the platform above the dungeon and the other a floor above.

Fig. 16.10 The entrance to the dungeon

The opening from the courtyard shown half buried in Fig. 16.9 has ashlar jambs, but a poorly constructed head (Fig. 16.10) with a half arch set back some 0.8m into the passage, perhaps suggesting that at one time there was a wider opening. The first doorway was inconveniently positioned on the steps. It had a door that was hinged on the west with a draw-bar hole set into the eastern side. The second doorway was at the bottom of the steps and again had a draw-bar hole on the east. The passage varied in width, the first part with the steps being only 0.56m wide with the remainder 0.8m.

The dungeon is some 6m long and about 2.45m wide. It has a vaulted roof with cross ribs forming four bays. The maximum ceiling height above the present floor is 2.7m. The walls are of rubble stone with little attempt at coursing. The internal face of the west wall is part of the east wall of the keep, but has a set-back section at the northern end. This is apparently a modern infill, for before the castle was taken over by the Ministry of Works it was possible to enter the dungeon from the basement of the keep, the courtyard doorway being almost blocked (Fig. 16.9). Indeed, all 19th-century writers describe entering the dungeon in that way, inferring that it was impossible to get in through the present north doorway and passage. Thus, King, writing in 1804, noted that 'This den [the basement of the keep] has not even one loop hole for light and air – But [there] is a very narrow passage to a still smaller dungeon, strongly secured under the platform belonging to the steps; and to this second dungeon is a very small air hole, but such as cannot deserve the name of a loop'.[2] In fact there was one small loop in the east wall of the keep, almost totally cut away by a later opening.

The flagstone floor above the dungeon (now a platform) is 2.5m above the courtyard level. On the east the floor is separated from the steps leading to the first floor of the south-east tower by the stone footings for a wall that would initially have supported the roof over the stairs, but eventually also carried the pent roof belonging to the room over the dungeon. The south wall of this room survives and contains a doorway leading to what was a small room or platform on the south side of the keep. This wall also includes indications of the pent roof. The east wall of the keep formed the west side of the room above the dungeon where there is an irregular opening that has been cut through the wall. There is also a damaged corbel in the wall, and indications of a possible second one above the irregular opening, both related to the lean-to roof.

The original approach to this room above the dungeon, apart from the doorway from the keep, is somewhat uncertain. If there had been a doorway providing an access from the south-west tower stairs, it would have been rather awkward as there is no landing at this level. The alternative could have been a flight of stairs, probably mainly of timber, erected against the north walls of the dungeon and keep, thus replacing the original stairs leading to the keep first-floor doorway (see Chapter 11 and Figs. 11.4 & 6). Such a flight may be reflected by the low stone wall that runs across the two faces at this point – a wall that could have acted as a base for a rather narrow flight of steps. King described the entry to the new first floor of the keep as being up the south-east tower steps and onto the platform above the dungeon.[3] In effect he was suggesting that the platform was an entrance hall providing a direct and possibly reasonably grandiose entry to the suite of rooms within the keep. It is quite possible that the front, courtyard wall of this entrance hall was of timber.

The rear wall of this postulated entrance room contains a doorway with a pointed head which opened to a short passageway with three ribs and an inner doorway before turning to the west. The passageway leads through a now-destroyed higher arch onto a platform formed in the V-shaped space between the keep and the curtain wall. The ground below this platform is solid. Although very oddly shaped, this room was some 4m long and up to 1.8m wide, with a window inserted through the 2.5m thick curtain wall. Only the lower parts of the window survive, but the rectangular opening was 1.7m wide with window seats on three sides. The room may originally have continued above the space later occupied by the kitchen ovens to the west. There would seem to be little doubt that this room was intended for residential purposes and that it was built at the same time as the dungeon and the room above it. Its roof line is somewhat uncertain as additional floors were inserted to the east and south of the keep at a later date (see Chapter 18).

Buildings to the west of the keep

The area between the keep and the stairs leading up to the first floor in the great south-west tower was evidently the kitchen in the final phase of occupation of the castle and may well have been used for that purpose previously. There are no indications of any features that might be of an early period, although the footings of two north walls may indicate two separate periods of construction. Because of this, the kitchen area is discussed in Chapter 18.

Changes to the keep

The various alterations to the keep would not all have taken place at the same time. The main changes were designed to make practical use of the rooms. When the keep was surrounded by a mound, the ground level in the courtyard was lower than at present. After most of the mound was removed, possibly using the material to raise the courtyard to its present level, a doorway was inserted in the eastern bay of the north wall allowing direct access to the basement (Fig. 11.4). There are two modern steps leading up to the sill, and wooden steps lead down to the concrete floor. When this new opening was inserted is rather uncertain, but the low, triangular, chamfered head and chamfered jambs suggest a 14th-century date. The original first-floor doorway was then converted to a window of two lights in a square chamfered head.

It is unlikely that the basement doorway was ever the main entry to the keep (as it is now), for this would have involved replacing the basement ladder with an internal flight of stairs similar to the modern staircase which would have made the first floor room virtually useless. To resolve the problem, a new doorway was broken through the east wall from the platform above the dungeon (Figs. 11.3 & 5). This opening, which almost totally replaced an original small loop that lit the basement, is very irregular, but would doubtless have contained an ornamental wooden door-frame. Traces of plaster on the south jamb indicate how the gaps would have been filled. The door and frame would have been a useful item for sale or use elsewhere during the post-Civil War slighting, and removing it forcibly would also have had the benefit of leaving an irregular and less defensible opening. The main floor in the keep is about 1m above the flagstone floor and there must have been several steps presumably of wood which would have allowed some light and air into the keep basement through the damaged slit.

There is also an opening at the same level in the west wall at the bottom of the vice where there may originally have been a window (Fig. 11.6). The opening may simply be a collapse of what was a particularly thin section of the keep wall, but it could equally have contained a doorway that led into a first-floor room above the kitchen (see Chapter 18).

The second floor also gained a new doorway which was cut through the east wall of the keep with its sill just below the string course (see Chapter 18). When the original roof of the keep was replaced, the upper parts of the walls were rebuilt and the new roof was constructed with the ridge running in the opposite direction to the earlier one. The eroded sandstone corbels in the east and west walls indicate the position and height of the ridge. The date of this new roof is uncertain.

17 The 14th century – The New Western Range & South-west Tower

by Ron Shoesmith

The small south-west tower and its associated curtain wall and perhaps a small hall, built in the later 13th century (Fig. 12.13), were all dismantled and replaced to a totally different design after a relatively short time. The most likely reason was the growing need for grand chambers – the old keep was rather primitive and apparently without even a fireplace, and whilst the corner towers and north hall had reasonable facilities there was a lack of retiring rooms. The new build provided a magnificent great hall with its associated larger south-west tower complete with a splendid first-floor chamber which, together with the chambers in the north-west tower, would have provided accommodation fit for the lord and his family. This part of the castle survived the slighting to a reasonable extent (Fig. 17.1).

Fig. 17.1 The southern end of the great hall about 1900, before any restoration work

The West Curtain Wall

The new west curtain wall was designed to be the external wall for the new great hall and its lobby. The lobby section to the north is fragmentary following the collapse of 1919 and, unfortunately, this is the one side of the castle that early photographers tended to avoid – only one illustration has been found (Fig. 10.1). This area was further confused when additional stonework was added to the original core during the 1920s repair, creating a totally amorphous appearance which is very misleading (Fig. 17.2).

Apart from the collapsed section, the remainder of the curtain wall, including two of the hall windows and a substantial rectangular tower, survives up to wall-walk level. The base of the 2.4m thick curtain wall sits on the bedrock, which is exposed above the level of the present flat outer ward. The wall, rectangular and south-west corner towers all have a common string course and, below this, the walls have a slight batter. The wall and towers, including the three windows of the great hall, are evidently of one constructional period (Figs. 17.3 & 4). The wall walk and rectangular tower had internal and external parapet walls, the walkway being paved. The inner parapet wall also supported the roof of the great hall. Although the outer parapet is mainly lost, there are traces of both drains (for the hall roof as well as the wall walk) and three arrow slots. The wall walk continues southwards to where steps led downwards to a doorway leading into the south-west corner tower.

The rectangular tower on the curtain wall, some 3.5m long and 2m deep, is an unusual feature that does not occur anywhere else in the castle (Fig. 17.4). Although it is directly in

Fig. 17.2 The northern end of the west curtain wall – the area that collapsed in 1919

Fig. 17.3 The west curtain wall – the outside of the great hall

front of the hall fireplace and chimney stack it is not associated with them in any way and does not contain the flue. Within the hall the face of the flue has been totally lost, but it is apparent that it rose within the thickness of the curtain wall and exited on the inside of the wall walk. The reason for the tower is uncertain, but it could have been defensive in nature. However, it may not be as strong as it appears for, according to tradition, there was a secret chamber built into the tower and the adjoining section of curtain wall above the fireplace.[1]

Fig. 17.4 The west curtain wall and south-west tower from the north-west, with the rectangular tower centrally placed

The Great Hall

The great hall was a large single-storey building set against the west curtain wall. It is almost 20m long and 8.4m wide (not all that different to the common ratio for ground floor great halls of 2:1^2). The north wall of the south-west tower acts as its south wall, whilst the east wall also supported a pentice, or covered walk, along the courtyard side. The north wall separates the great hall from the lobby – the stair well that contained entries into the north-west tower and the north range.

The surviving corbels providing stone supports for timbers indicate that the hall was divided into four almost equal bays (Figs. 17.5 & 6). The enormous fireplace, set in the west wall

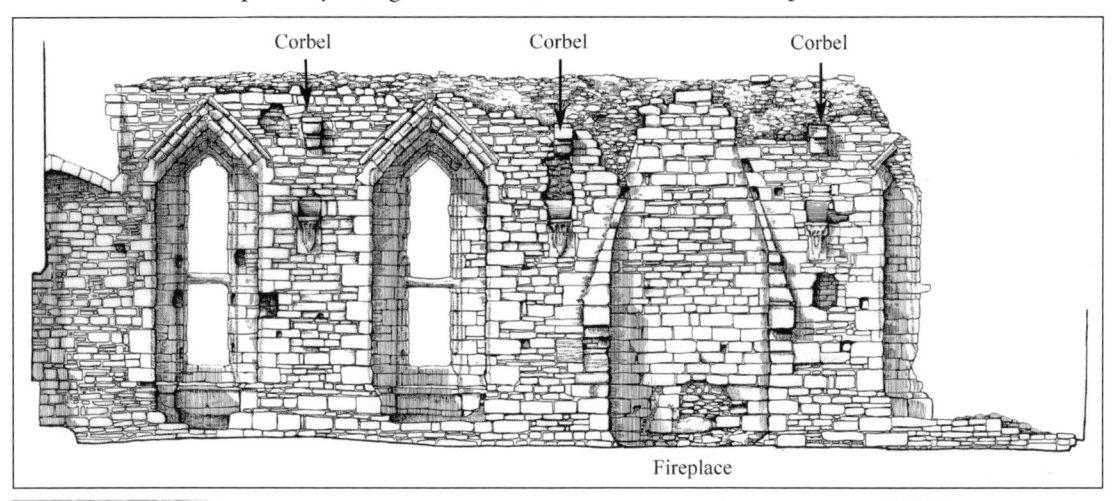

Top: Fig. 17.5 The west wall of the great hall showing the corbels separating the four bays
Lower: Fig 17.6 The west wall of the great hall with the grand fireplace to right of centre

in the bay to the north of centre, is 3m wide. The back is set only 0.4m into the curtain wall and the hood, of which fragments survive, was supported at each side by corbels. The flue was slightly chased into the curtain wall, the chimney being set within the inner parapet wall. Two stones remain of the chamfered curb which ran around the hearth, demonstrating that it extended over 1m into the room.

The two bays to the left of the fireplace each contain a complete window, but in the bay to the right only the southern side of the window survives. All three windows were high and wide with holes for horizontal iron bars. There is no indication that the windows were ever glazed, but they have holes for hinges which would have taken shutters on both sides. Internally, the rectangular embrasures had stone seats on both sides underneath the windows.

The east, courtyard wall is just over 1m thick (Figs. 17.7 & 8). Along most of the hall side there is a long seat made of stone slabs. The northern three bays of the east wall each

Fig. 17.7 The southern part of the east wall of the great hall.
The keep is in the background

Fig. 17.8 The east wall and part of the north wall of the great hall, with the doorway leading to the courtyard on the right

contained a window, but only the central one survives in a reasonably complete condition. Although the windows were in a safe position they are much smaller than those in the curtain wall as they had to have high external sills to be above the roof of the pentice. Both the southern doorway and the adjoining window are in a rebuilt section of the wall. To the south of the doorway the internal face is set forward and forms the eastern wall of the stairs leading up to the first floor of the south-west tower.

The 1m thick north wall separates the great hall from the lobby (Fig. 17.9). Throughout much of its early life this lobby was related more to the north-west tower and north range than to the great hall. The lack of any firm relationship between the great hall and the lobby is emphasised when it is realised that the doorway in the eastern end of the north wall is a later insertion.

The northern part was doubtless the 'upper end' of the hall. The low ledge along this wall may well have originally provided a base for a timber dias, appropriate to the status of the lord. It is probable that at a later date a high-level doorway, leading from a landing in the lobby, was inserted into the north wall leading to a gallery. Large sockets in the west and east walls, some 5m from the northern end of the hall, indicate that the gallery was wide – almost a first-floor room – overlooking the floor of the hall and designed to respect the windows in the west and east walls (Fig.17.9). There may well have been a central stair leading up from the hall to the gallery, which would have provided greater seclusion for the lord and his guests than a simple dais, whilst still giving them a view of the events below.

Fig. 17.9 The north wall of the great hall with the doorway leading into the lobby. Traces of the 'high end' balcony can be seen

The north wall of the south-west tower is also the south wall of the great hall (Figs. 17.10 & 11). At its eastern end steps lead upwards to the first floor of the tower. The steps start close to the courtyard doorway in the east wall, the first eight treads being within the hall itself. Adjoining this high doorway is the opening for steps leading down to the basement of the tower. To the west again are a matching pair of doorways that led through short wall-passages into the ground floor of the tower. They are set in a large recess now broken away on the east. The floor level of these doorways and that of the ground floor of the tower is approximately 1m above the present floor level in the great hall – a change in level that is assumed to be roughly the same as when the buildings were in use. There is a narrow platform in front of the two doorways, and a flight of perhaps four steps, probably made of wood, would have been needed. These two doorways would have led to the buttery and pantry in the ground floor of the tower, where wine and bread was stored.

Above the western of the two doorways is a rather odd diagonal section of walling supported on corbelling which contains a passage leading from the south-west tower to the western wall walk. Although it looks rather awkward, it is probably a primary feature, for the string course

Fig. 17.10 The south wall of the hall with the stairs going up to the first floor in the tower on the left. Next to the stairs is the basement entry and, on the right, the doorways to buttery and pantry

which marks the position of the roof of the great hall continues across both planes of this passage wall.

There is considerable evidence for the almost flat roof of the great hall which apparently survived throughout the whole life of the building with no obvious alterations (Figs. 17.10 & 11). The creasing in the south wall, and the fragment in the north wall, indicate that the roof had a very shallow slope down towards the west, where it sat on the inner wall-walk parapet. With such a shallow pitch, the roof must have been planked and leaded.

The three sets of paired corbels in the west wall, symmetrically arranged with respect to the windows and fireplace, are evidently primary (Fig. 17.5). In the east wall only two of the lower corbels survive, but it is assumed that the design was the same as the west wall. The upper corbels are doubled to bring them further out from the wall and are some 6m above the assumed level of the internal floor – the lower ones are at

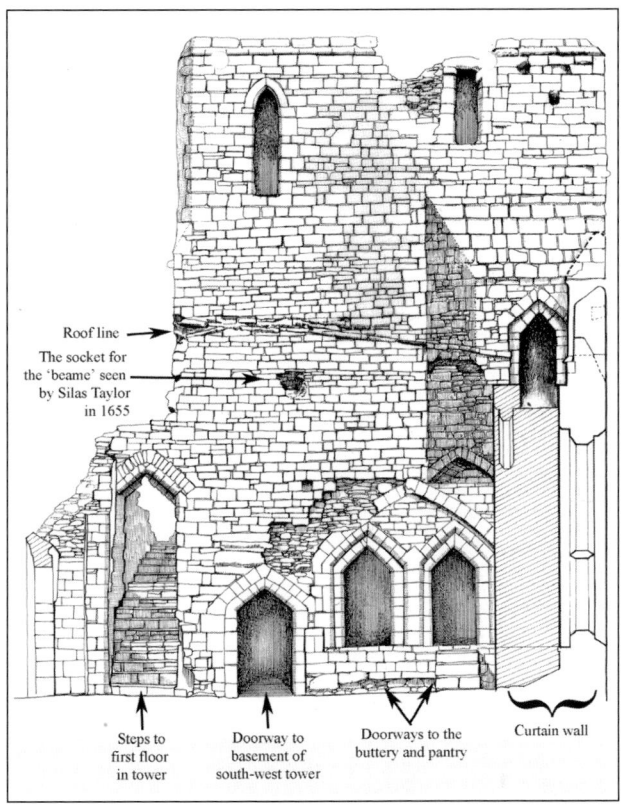

Fig. 17.11 The south wall of the hall showing the various features mentioned in the text

4.2m. It is evident that the lower corbels supported up-braces, the masonry immediately above them being cut back on a slant to take their feet. The upper corbels did not hold wall plates, but supported the ends of cross-beams that were supported by the up-braces. There is a further piece of evidence for the design of the roof, which comes from an account written in 1655 by Silas Taylor (see Chapter 8). He observed 'a beame of oake intire without knott or knarle of 66 feet long, and held 20 inches or 2 feet square the whole length'. The 'beame' – central to the hall – presumably sat in the square socket that survives in the south wall (Figs. 17.10 & 11). The opposing socket would have been above the gallery doorway in the north wall. Taylor's 'beame' would have been supported by the three cross-beams that rested on the upper corbels. In turn the cross beams would have been strengthened by the up-braces rising from the lower corbels. Above this was the roof proper, which probably comprised a series of joists laid across the hall, possibly supported by a series of short posts rising from Taylor's 'beame', the top of which was some 0.8m below the roof. There may also have been additional supports rising from the cross-beams. It is almost certain that the spaces between the cross-beams were ceiled with some form of boarding, so as to present a flat 'ceiling' consisting either of four pairs of almost square panels or four long panels stretching the width of the hall. The exposed timbers were doubtless chamfered and stopped and would have been carved to match the undoubted magnificence of the remainder of the great hall.

From the wall walk it would have been relatively simple to climb three or four wooden steps to gain access to the slightly sloping leaded roof – a reasonably private outdoor area with excellent views to the west and similar to the roof of the north hall. Such reasonably flat roofs may well have been designed as summer 'living platforms' – probably much more salubrious than the dark confines of the castle, or the malodorous courtyard where the slaughtering of animals would have been a regular event. Indeed, the view from the roof, and the chance of watching the hunt in progress, may well have made its use a pleasant part of the social scene for the womenfolk. Evidence for very shallow roofs of this nature in the 13th and early 14th centuries are few, but there are traces of similar designs at both Clun and Ludlow.

The floor of the great hall was presumably of stone pavers which would have had a good commercial value and would have been removed when the castle was slighted. Assuming such a floor and the boarded ceiling as described above, the internal height of the hall to the infill panels would have been just over 6m.

The Lobby

The lobby is to the north of the great hall and separates it from the north-west tower. The west wall collapsed in 1919 (Figs. 10.1 & 2), but the south wall between the lobby and the hall survives in part (Fig. 17.12). The lobby contains the upper part of the steps that lead down to the basement of the north hall (see Chapter 14). There are traces of a first floor, but this may have been inserted when the north range was reconstructed with a first floor (see Chapter 18).

The Pentices

When the great hall was built, the windows in the courtyard wall were designed with high sills, not as a defensive feature, but to allow for a pentice or open-fronted cloister along the length of the building. The foundation of the courtyard wall remains – the upper part would have been open, and probably of timber. The weathering associated with the pentice roof cuts across the base of the hall windows.

It is suggested that there was a matching pentice along the front of the single-storey east hall, but that when the east range was redesigned the pentice became the ground floor of the three-storey gallery (see Chapter 18).

Fig. 17.12 The wall separating the lobby from the hall from the north-east

The presence of the well may have been a deciding factor in not constructing a similar pentice along the north side of the courtyard – there is certainly no trace of any such structure. The south side of the courtyard comprises the area in front of the keep and the kitchen. The area in front of the junction between the keep and the kitchen was examined archaeologically in 1984[3] and the foundation of a stone wall indicates that there was probably a pentice along at least part of this frontage similar to the ones on the east and west sides of the courtyard. However, this section was apparently demolished whilst the castle was still in use.

The South-west (Great) Tower
External
The tower is round externally with a diameter of almost 13m (as compared with the south-east tower which is 10.2m) (Fig. 17.13). The almost square base is built on the natural bedrock but, as the plane of the rock slopes down to the east, some underpinning was needed to achieve a flat platform. The tower contrasts with the others in having short, stubby spurs rather than tall ones. They only rise to just below the lowest string course – effectively to the internal basement level. Much of the lower curved face between the spurs and up to the string course was refaced with a smooth red sandstone during the 1920s work. Above the string course the masonry is roughly coursed with a mixture of red and white sandstone.

Internal
Internally, the tower is much more irregular in shape than the smaller

Fig. 17.13 The south-west tower from the south-east

Fig. 17.14 South-west tower – the basement and ground floor from the south-west with the double doorways leading to the great hall on the left

corner towers, possibly because parts of the earlier, smaller tower were re-used. The rooms average some 7.5m across.

The entry into the basement is down a flight of steps set alongside the east wall. The steps open out at the bottom with three semi-circular treads (Figs. 17.14 & 15). The ground-floor opening has a rebate for a door that could be bolted from the inside. There is now no sign of bedrock or of the smaller tower in the floor of the basement, although stones from the latter were visible some years ago. The room, which has six main facets, was illuminated by two small windows, facing outwards to the south and west. The southern one is now set in a square-

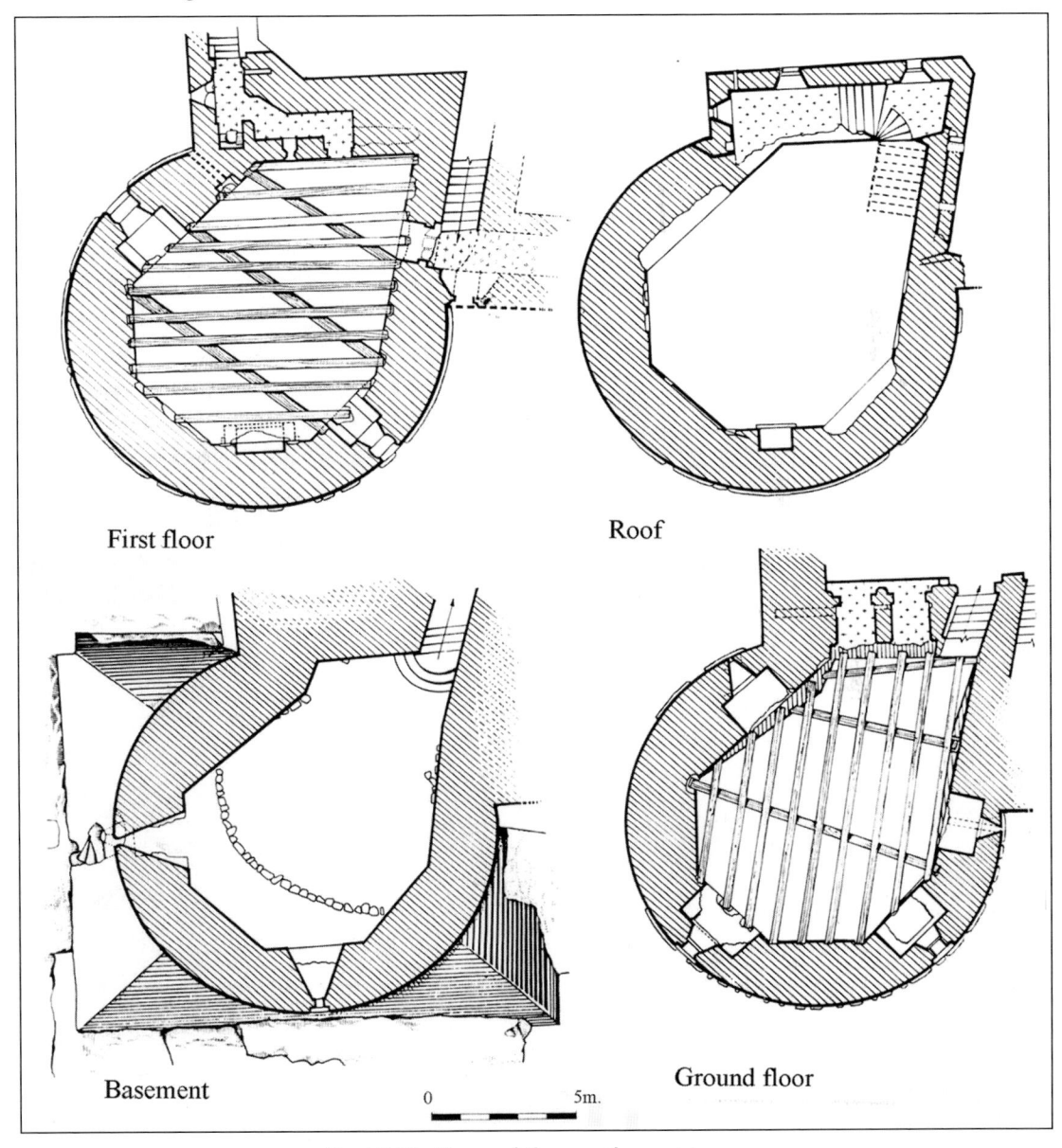

Fig. 17.15 Plans of the south-west tower.
The basement plan shows the line of the earlier tower

Fig. 17.16 South-west tower – all three floors from the north, with the first-floor fireplace on the right

headed external recess that was part of the 1925 refacing – the original shape is uncertain. The western one was altered at a later date to provide an exit to the outer west ward (see Chapter 18). Internally, the deeply-splayed openings are almost 2m wide.

The ground-floor joists, which were arranged lengthwise across the tower and parallel to the great hall, consisted of timbers some 10m long. Three cross members, that provided additional support, may have been part of the original design or a later addition. The narrow stone shelves on the north-west and south sides of the tower are too high to have supported joists – they could only have been used to support the ends of floor boards.

At ground-floor level the wall separating the tower from the great hall includes the entry from the basement and the two doorways that led into the buttery and pantry. There is no apparent reason for the difference in floor levels between the hall and the ground floor of the tower. It may be that the tower was built first, the floor level in the hall being fixed by the courtyard and lobby levels.

On the tower side the two doorways are set in a shallow recess. Both openings were rebated to take doors that opened within the thickness of the wall passages. The western doorway has a long draw-bar slot allowing the room to be locked from the inside. There is no indication of any fastening for the eastern door. The 4.6m high ground floor of the great tower, being designed as buttery and pantry, did not require a fireplace. There would doubtless have been some sort of partition between the two parts, but no trace survives.

The ground floor was well served with four windows – two look outwards in the south-west and south-east and are set in external square-headed recesses. Internally, the splays open out into rectangular embrasures containing the eroded remains of window seats (Fig. 17.16). Whilst these two windows have a distinctly domestic feel, the other two openings are much more of a military nature, being designed to enfilade the south and west curtain walls. Both are uniform with the outside face of the wall and contain cruciform arrow slits with oilets and steeply-sloping sills. Behind the slits there is a low wall to protect the defender. Each opening widens out to a rectangular embrasure, some 2m wide, but without window seats. The bases of the embrasures are at the same level as the wooden floor, allowing the defender to walk into the openings.

Fig. 17.17 The outside face of the east wall of the tower with the steps rising to a first-floor landing. The weathering above indicates that the steps were under cover. This wall was also the west wall of the kitchen with the stone base of the sink in front of it and a hole for a cupboard on the far right.

The first floor had a more traditional system of joists – they run parallel to the north wall and thus cross the space by the shortest distance (Fig. 17.15). Even so, the floor needed the support of three cross joists at a lower level. It was approached by a flight of some 30 steps, that started within the south-east corner of the great hall. As the hall was wider than the tower gorge, the steps rose against the outside face of the east wall of the tower. They were under cover for the whole height; the weathering and parts of the arched roof still survive (Fig. 17.17). The two side walls were not parallel, so that the treads widened with height. The stairs stopped at a landing on the same level as the first floor of the tower and the southern wall walk. A window at the top of the stairs was set into the 4m high parapet to the curtain wall. It is now mainly broken away, but the splayed opening widened out to a rectangular embrasure. The doorway from the landing into the tower has a rebate for a door which opened inwards. The short draw-bar hole indicates that the chamber could be locked from the inside.

In the north wall of the first-floor chamber a doorway led to a wall passage providing access, first to a latrine contrived in the thickness of the southern end of the curtain wall, and then through a shorter passage and up three steps to the western wall walk. The doorway leading from the tower into the passage could be locked from the inside. The latrine chamber is well-preserved with two stone sides still supporting traces of the wooden seat. The passage was lit by a small splayed opening in the west wall. The doorway that led onto the wall walk had a draw-bar slot that allowed the passage to be secured from the wall walk.

The grand first-floor chamber contained two windows and a fireplace, the latter set in the face opposite to the north wall (Fig. 17.16). The windows were of a similar general design to the principal ones in the ground floor, but had larger openings. Both had window seats. The fireplace was very similar to those in the south-east tower, with a head supported on moulded corbels. The hood had originally been supported on an iron bar set into the stonework above the corbels with lead. The bar had been broken and all the central parts of the hood are missing.

The first-floor chamber was certainly the largest and probably the grandest private chamber in the castle, being some 8m across and standing over 4m high. As with the other tower rooms, there is only slight evidence for the partition that presumably separated this chamber from the general passageway joining the south and west wall walks.

The upper works of the great tower are very fragmentary, but sufficient survives on the northern side to provide an indication of the overall design. Access to the roof was by a flight of wooden steps set against the east wall leading to an opening high in the north wall, but well below the ceiling. The opening led to stone steps that curved round to the west and continued up in the thickness of the north wall to a platform above the first-floor passageway and latrine (Fig. 17.15). This platform would originally have provided access to a wall walk around the tower. One small section of the wall walk and part of the parapet, which survives adjacent to the south curtain wall, includes three drainage gullies that presumably sent the roof water cascading down onto the roof above the first-floor stairs. The platform includes a parapet complete with coping stones on the hall side and on the short west and east sides. The parapet contains holes indicating that both platform and stairs leading up from the first floor were covered with a flat roof.

18 THE GRADUAL CONVERSION TO HOUSES FROM THE 15TH TO THE EARLY 17TH CENTURY

by Ron Shoesmith

There is little trace of any specific work being done during the 15th century, but changes were probably gradual over a reasonably long period of time. Throughout the period the main work included the insertion of a first floor in the north hall, the construction of a three-storey eastern range, the addition of the garderobe or latrine tower and other latrines around the castle, the improvements to the kitchen, and much minor work to add to the comforts of the residents. The flat north and west wards were laid out with relatively low external walls and corner towers and an extension was put on the front of the gatehouse. Much of the work was probably undertaken during the time of George, 6th Earl of Shrewsbury (1560-90), but it is also evident that extensive repair work was undertaken by the tenant, Richard Tyler (1631-45) (see Chapter 7).

Rebuilding the North Hall
Radical alterations were made to the north range, probably in the 16th century. The slightly-sloping roof was removed and the north, east and south walls of the hall were raised to allow for the insertion of a first floor, probably containing a series of chambers. To the west, the first-floor connection with the north-west tower and its vestibule was altered.

The new first floor was inserted just below the tops of the twin arcade arches and 1.7m below the level of the wall walk. It was supported on joists mortised into a wall beam laid on a series of corbels set into the north wall, of which two survive, and presumably a similar series in the south wall. This meant that the doorway with the triangular head in the arcade wall, that had previously led from the first floor of the vestibule of the north-west tower to the roof of the north hall and from there to the north wall walk, was high up above the new first-floor level. To resolve this, the threshold was lowered on the hall side and a short flight of steps was built in the thickness of the wall to reach the higher first-floor room above the vestibule. Additional steps would have been required on the hall side both to drop to the new floor level and to rise up to the wall walk. There are slight traces that the latter was built partly within the thickness of the curtain wall. When the opening was enlarged, the triangular head was blocked off with a lower lintel to provide a rectangular shape to take the door frame. Unfortunately, this upper blocking, visible on all early illustrations of this wall (Fig. 18.1), was removed as part of the 1920s restoration work. The line of the first floor was apparent in the moulding associated with the twin arcade – it was broken back to allow for floorboards at exactly the level at which the new floor would have been inserted (Fig. 18.2). Unfortunately, once again, these deliberate breaks were removed during the most recent restoration.

The western corner of the south wall was substantially remodelled and a new doorway was inserted at first-floor level to provide access from the lobby, which had by then been converted to become the principal staircase (Plate 17, p.195). The side of the doorway, in the white stone characteristic of this phase of construction, survives together with traces of some three or four steps leading upwards from the new floor in the lobby to the first floor in the north range. The extended socket at the top of the existing jamb doubtless contained a lost part of the doorway head, indicating a door opening some 2.4m high.

Apart from the changes described above, the addition of an upper storey to the north hall would have had little effect on the existing west wall, for there was already a first-floor level on the opposite side. With the alteration to the

Fig. 18.1 A postcard of about 1900 showing the partially-blocked upper doorway

Fig. 18.2 The upper part of the arcade arches showing the features described in the text

door, only the light from the one small window would have been lost. A high level moulding probably represents the new roof line (Fig. 18.2). A large socket, just below the string course, matched by one low down against the northern jamb of the doorway, (almost completely filled in during consolidation work), are probably associated with a timber rear wall to the first-floor chambers, separating them from what had become a covered wall walk.

The new, flat roof would have been about 2.6m above the wall walk. The core work in the arcade wall indicates that the original south wall was of stone and that it was raised by some 2m when the first floor was added. However, to provide reasonable access to the rooms on the first floor, this wall would have had to be the front of an open gallery, with a timber wall separating the passageway from the rooms, similar to that in the east hall (Fig. 7.3). The east wall would also have had to be heightened, but apart from the scar in the curtain wall, which only extends to wall-walk level (Fig. 16.4), there is no evidence for this wall at all.

The western side of the first floor in the north range must have caused the designers some problems. The doorway from the lobby would have led into the end of the south-facing gallery, but there would presumably have had to be a passage leading northwards to a short flight of steps and a landing outside the doorway leading into the north-west tower. Continuing northwards, a further three or four more steps would have led upwards to a lost doorway that gave access onto the wall walk. There was a similar feature towards the eastern end of the hall, where a series of curving stone steps built into the inside edge of the wall walk led down to the eastern end of the first floor.

It would seem likely that the changes to the north hall were designed to provide a series of private rooms at first-floor level and possibly to allow the ground-floor hall to be split into separate rooms. The latter is perhaps likely as the reduction in the level of the ceiling from about 7.5m to 5m could have otherwise made this large room feel rather oppressive. The new first floor would have been ceiled at a height of about 4m. The proposed gallery along the courtyard side would have allowed individual access to the first-floor chambers and each chamber would have had a window providing light from the open gallery. On the north side, a series of window openings in the timber wall could have provided some borrowed light from the crenellations in the parapet. Effectively the north range, together with the rooms in the north-west tower, had been converted into a reasonably large house with a large amount of storage space in the basement. It was approached by a grand entrance hall with a timber staircase inserted into what had been simply the lobby.

It would seem probable that the building inside the gatehouse, once possibly the living accommodation for the canons, was altered to provide additional rooms associated with the first floor of the north range. If this was the case then the gallery may well have continued across the south face (Fig. 7.3).

The Lobby

In their original state both the north-west tower and the adjoining lobby stood a whole storey higher than the north hall. To all intents and purposes, the west and north wall walks were at the same level as the first floors in the tower and vestibule. The lobby has probably been the scene of more changes and has suffered more loss of masonry than most rooms within the castle, making interpretation somewhat speculative. The middle part of the north wall survives, but both east and west ends have been lost. Part of the south wall – the north wall of the great hall – also survives, but again with considerable loss (Fig. 17.12). Only the footings of the east wall survive – sufficient to indicate the position of a doorway from the courtyard. The west wall collapsed in 1919 taking the western part of the north wall with it. A small 'buttress-like' block survives at the north-western corner; next to it is a 1m high piece of core work, apparently built in the 1920s as an early safety barrier.

The ground floor of the lobby is on two different levels. The eastern part is some 0.1m below the floor of the great hall and the adjoining part of the courtyard. The lower, western part is some 0.4m lower again, being on the same level as the ground floor in the vestibule to the north-west tower and the north hall. The fragmentary remains of the east wall, the steps leading down to the basement from the lobby, and the west wall buttress all take the same alignment as the north hall. The surviving fragments of the west wall (below the ground level of the lobby) and the south wall are aligned with the great hall and are therefore considered to have been built as part of the realignment associated with the construction of the great tower and new great hall (see Chapter 17).

The presence of the steps leading down to the basement, the need for a staircase to the first floor of the south-west tower and the alignment of the buttress and east wall all indicate that there was a stair tower of some description before the south and west walls were rebuilt.

The north wall contains the doorway leading into the ground floor of the north-west tower, and above it the east reveal of the first-floor doorway survives. The remainder of that doorway was lost during the 1919 collapse. Towards the eastern end of the north wall there is a line of small sockets for floor joists that are on a level with the doorway leading to the inserted first floor in the north hall.

The south wall contains the inserted doorway that provided an access to the great hall and above it a central opening that was probably associated with the great hall gallery (see Chapter 17). This opening is lower than the joist sockets on the north wall. At a higher level there is a sill and reveal of what appears to be a fireplace. On its left is a rather low trefoil-headed recess. It has been suggested that this first-floor room acted as a small private chapel. There is one solitary socket in the western part of the wall, approximately at the same level as the great hall gallery. The fragmentary remains of the east wall include the south reveal of the doorway from the courtyard and, directly above it, the chamfered reveal of a window opening.

The lobby must have had an almost total rebuild as part of the construction of the western great hall. The south and west walls are aligned with that building, leaving a slightly funnelled shape to the room. The original size and shape are unknown – the changes would almost certainly have involved new floors and a new roof to fit the different proportions. The change in floor levels may well date to that rebuilding work.

Whatever the method originally used, the problem was eventually resolved by converting the whole of the lobby into an entrance hall that incorporated a well-designed and reasonably palatial timber staircase. The various features in the surviving walls give some indication of the floor levels. In addition, engravings of this area show the arrangement of the windows (Fig. 14.1). It would seem that there was a very tall ground-floor single light with a smaller light above it, at first-floor level.

Thus, on entering the lobby from the courtyard, the doorway on the left led into the great hall, whilst the passage next to the south wall led down the three steps to the lower level and from there either directly into the ground floor of the north-west tower or down the stairs to the basement level. Straight ahead, and next to a vertical extension of the basement stair south wall, was the staircase rising upwards – placed centrally in the room. The stairs would have stopped at a half-landing in front of the long window in the west wall, where there were branches going to left and right. The left branch curved back to provide access to the great hall gallery, whilst the right-hand branch went up several more steps and curved back to a slightly higher landing, associated with the small joist holes, that led to the inserted doorway giving access to the new first floor in the north hall. From this landing, and curving back again in the centre of the building and above the first flight, the stairs rose once again to a second landing set against the west wall and illuminated by the smaller window. This was apparently at a different level to the original floor in this area, and to the south there must have been a doorway incorporating several steps leading down to the west wall walk and the leaded roof above the great hall. Access into the first floor of the north-west tower would also have been down several steps built into the thickness of the north wall. The joist holes indicate that the landing was at a higher level than the wall walk and the room in the north-west tower. It is quite likely that there was a further flight of stairs, following a similar course, that emerged onto the roof of the lobby and provided direct access to the roof of the north-west tower.

The New East Hall
The third major building on the eastern side of the courtyard was larger and more elaborate than both its predecessors, but very little remains and it is only by a close examination of the surrounding walls that an indication of its size and nature has been obtained.

The immediately obvious features that are associated with this building consist of two new doorways, roughly cut into the south face of the octagonal stair tower (Figs. 16.7 & 8). These openings, a high-level fireplace in the chapel wall, slight 'creasings' in the south and north walls and the associated joist sockets, together with a second set of stone footings running parallel with the earlier courtyard wall, represent the evidence for what is considered to be a galleried, three-storey building that replaced the single-storey building of the 14th century (Plate 20, p.197). The extension on the courtyard side, associated with the stair tower doorways, took the form of a series of galleries, running along the whole front of the range (Fig. 7.3).

The roof was much higher than that of the building it replaced and consisted of a standard gable over the main part of the range, with an almost flat roof over the wall walk and a similar roof over the front gallery. The flat roof over the wall walk was supported by a wall plate laid on the corbels that had been set in the parapet wall for the earlier pent roof. On the inside of the wall walk this roof, and the eastern half of the main gable roof would have been supported on a timber frame erected on the inside edge of the wall walk. This timber framework would also have supported the second floor which was some 1.8m above the level of the wall walk at the northern end (Plate 20, p.197). There are slight indications that the parapet was heightened and it would have been possible to access the flat roof as a high-level wall walk, accessed from the wall walk around the chapel tower by a short external flight of timber stairs.

The overall design of the building is somewhat difficult to determine, but the levels of the floors are given by the openings in the stair tower and by a series of inserted joist sockets in the east curtain wall at the same level. These have been considerably damaged, partly when the building was demolished and later when the deeper joist holes were filled as part of the conservation work in the 1920s, but sufficient remains to establish that the building probably had six bays. The front, single-storey stone wall of the earlier building was probably re-used as a support for the timber framing of the front wall of the first and second floors. In front of this wall would have been the galleries with accesses from the octagonal stair tower. It is assumed that the stone wall that formed the western side of the ground floor contained windows that provided borrowed light from the open gallery.

The ground floor of this three-storey building would have been some 4m high (allowing for joists) and 4.9m wide, with the lowest level of the gallery some 2.1m wide. There were several openings from the courtyard leading into the ground floor.

The first floor with its simple wooden west wall was wider than the ground floor at 5.5m (with a narrower gallery), but had a maximum headroom of only 2.5m (again allowing for joists). It would have been lit by windows in the west wall obtaining borrowed light from the first-floor gallery. The second floor was similar in most respects to the first floor apart from the headroom which was only 1.8m, if there was a flat ceiling. It is more likely that the chambers would have been open to the roof as shown in Plate 20, page 197. However, a considerable effort had been made at the northern end where a fireplace was inserted in the wall of the chapel (Fig. 13.8). The construction of this new building meant that the two windows that originally illuminated the wall passage leading from the first floor of the chapel to the eastern wall walk were blocked.

The relationship of this new three-storey building to the wall walk is of some interest. The first-floor level was about 1.1m below the wall walk at the north end (1.5m at the south end) whilst the second floor was 1.8m and 2.4m respectively above. To accommodate these floor levels the enclosed wall walk had a high ceiling at about 3.9m at the north end and, due to the steps in the wall walk, a full 4.3m next to the south-east tower. There was an access from the first-floor level of the east range up several wooden steps to the wall walk (and possibly a similar one down from the second floor) to a doorway set in the internal parapet wall next to the south-east tower. Here a draw-bar hole, rather high in the thickness of the tower wall, allowed the internal range to be bolted off from the wall walk. This may have been associated with an access to the 14th-century garderobe on the wall walk or more likely to the later, external ones (see below).

The reconstruction of the east range as a three-storey galleried building, reminiscent of the great galleried inns that were being built in many major towns, was the culmination of the change from defended castle to a sizeable private mansion complete with a large guest wing. Insufficient remains to establish the internal arrangements in any detail, but it is likely that the east hall continued to be separated from the area in front of the garderobe tower at ground floor level. This would have left a hall that was still some 17m long with a fireplace and at least two curtain wall windows apart from any in the western gallery wall. Above this the two floors must have been split into individual chambers. The available evidence indicates that the range was split into six bays, each about 3.4m wide, and it is suggested that each of these bays represents a separate chamber on both of the two upper floors. If this was the case then each of the twelve chambers would have been approximately 3.2m wide and 5.5m deep. With no means of direct illumination from the rear, the front, timber-framed wall of each chamber would have had a window and a door opening onto the gallery. Only one chamber, the northernmost one on the second floor, had a fireplace, but general heat would have been transmitted from the large fireplace in the ground-floor hall.

A Southern Extension to the East Range – A Question of Levels

It is now very difficult to establish the design of the southern end of the three-storey galleried building erected along the eastern side of the courtyard in the final phase of the development of the castle. The scars on the north wall of the south-east tower show that the gallery continued at least to this point (Fig. 16.7). The main west wall of the east range bends inwards as it approaches the south-east tower to allow a direct access from the ground-floor gallery to the steps leading to the first floor of the tower. The alignment of the front wall of the gallery is a little to the east of the east wall of the keep. The first and second floors of the gallery either came to an end on line with the north wall of the south-east tower or they continued further southwards, joining in some way with the complex levels between the keep and the south-east tower. Throughout most of the life of the castle efforts were made to ensure that there was a means of circulation at each level, and it is therefore suggested that the upper galleries of the

Fig. 18.3 The southern side of the castle from the south-west. The joist holes and the high sloping roof line of the eastern gallery are apparent on the keep

east range did indeed connect with the levels above the dungeon on the east and those south of the keep. This would also explain the indications of windows in the curtain wall at two distinct levels as shown in early engravings (Fig. 16.9).

It is all a question of levels. The first floor of the eastern gallery is about 2m over the paved surface above the dungeon. A flight of timber steps could have been positioned partly over the entry to the dungeon where the main front wall of the east hall veered to the east. The second floor of the gallery could have continued across the dungeon area leaving a headroom of almost 5m, assuming that there were no steps down. This upper gallery level would have been some 2.2m above the level of the southern wall walk.

However, the line of joist holes and the scar of a roof line on the external south wall of the keep evidently relate to a new room set above the one described in Chapter 16 (Figs. 11.7 & 18.3). Its floor was supported on a series of joists that ran from the holes cut into the keep wall to the curtain wall at wall-walk level, some 2.7m above the floor of the lower room. The roof of this room, as shown by the scar on the keep, sloped down very slightly to the east and would have extended out to the raised curtain wall parapet indicated in the early engraving (Fig. 16.9). Here, there were apparently two large and elaborate windows, built into the raised parapet, that would have provided ample light both for the stairs and for the room above. This room, between the keep and the heightened curtain wall, was some 10m long (for it extended above the kitchen ovens) but it was no more than 4m wide at a maximum, and had a surprisingly high ceiling. It could well have been partitioned into two chambers. Windows would have provided long views across the ditch towards Goodrich village. Because of the odd shape, there was not sufficient room to allow a separate passage through from the south-east tower to the great south-west tower – any such passage must have passed through the room(s). There is little to date these rooms that once filled the space between the keep and the heightened V-shaped curtain wall, but it seems likely that some parts, at least, are of 14th-century date and are associated with the covered south-east tower stairs and the room above the dungeon whilst others are probably later.

The difference between the level of the second floor of the gallery and this new boarded area on the south side of the keep was about 1.8m, and it is suggested that access was achieved by means of the spiral stair, built rather uncomfortably into the south-eastern corner of the keep (Fig. 11.7). It would have required nine steps, just sufficient to traverse three-quarters of a circle, to end up facing south at the gallery level.

To complete the design, the extended gallery would have needed a roof which, to perform well, would have had to be on a similar level to the east hall gallery roof and to the roof line indicated by the weathering on the south side of the keep. In addition this roof would have had to act as the 'bridge' that joined the keep to the roof of the south-east tower (Fig. 12.9), so it would have had to continue across the south-east tower stairs, presumably replacing the original sloping roof. This roof doubtless sloped slightly downwards, probably to the south, and would therefore have been supported on north / south joists. The 'bridge' from the upper floor of the keep to the south-east tower roof can thus be seen as a walkway across the southern extension of the roof of the gallery. The slight variations in level between the various roofs would have allowed for gentle pitches to take off rain water.

There is no direct proof that the gallery belonging to the east range connected with the various structures to the south and east of the keep as proposed above. However, any alternative would either have resulted in much 'dead' space, with insufficient headroom, or would have left the galleries without any southern communication.

Cleaner living – The Garderobe or Latrine Tower
The new eastern chambers and the rooms in the south-east tower needed sufficient latrines to satisfy the occupants as there were only two previously (see Chapter 16). This was achieved by building a new tower on the east side of the curtain wall close to the south-east tower (Fig. 11.1). The internal face of the curtain wall had already been brought forward so it was only necessary to create openings into the wall to lead into the inside of the garderobe tower (Fig. 12.2). As a result each of the three latrines was approached by a narrow passage, widening into the lavatory proper. Illumination was provided by small windows in the east face of the tower. The first floor of the east range was catered for by a further three latrines in the garderobe tower at the same level as the wall walk. Although there is now no trace of this floor, the outlet chutes are present within the thickness of the east wall of the garderobe tower. It is assumed that the latrines for this and the second floor were accommodated in a timber 'shed' set on top of the stone tower. At this point the curtain wall parapet was taken down to provide access to the latrines. The refuse went down the various chutes to a chamber in the ditch at the bottom of the tower where there is still an opening to allow it to be cleaned out (Fig. 11.1).

Extension in front of the gatehouse
At the eastern end of the gate passage the two high enclosing walls were extended for about 1m in front of the first-floor drawbridge room and thus a little way across the sides of the drawbridge pit. Only the southern wall survives to any height and, at the extreme eastern end, there is a springer for an additional outer archway (Fig. 18.4). It is of white stone and is much lower than the springers supporting the drawbridge room. Apart from this springer, the new front to the gatehouse has been almost entirely lost – only a few white ashlar stones high up on the left-hand side give a clue to its design. This type of stone was used throughout the castle in the 15th- and 16th-century alterations and so it may well be that the new front to the castle reflected the latest in architectural styles as befitted the importance of its owner. The springer was presumably associated with a ceremonial entrance archway with no defensive capability whatsoever.

Fig. 18.4 The southern side of the extended gatehouse showing the surviving springer for the arch

Indeed, it was positioned so far forward that the drawbridge would no longer have functioned and must therefore have been replaced with a solid bridge.

At some time after the permanent bridge had been installed, the area underneath the two arches was brought into use. Sockets indicate where timbers were set into the walls, and in the southern half arch a stone screen wall containing a doorway with a shouldered lintel was built. The resultant 'rooms' could well have been used for stabling, storage or the later pound (Fig. 15.13).

The Kitchen area

The area between the keep and the stairs leading up to the first floor in the great south-west tower was evidently the kitchen in the final phase of occupation of the castle and may well have been used for that purpose previously. There are no indications of any features that might be of an early period, although the footings of two north walls may indicate two separate periods of construction. The available evidence indicates that the kitchen was an irregularly-shaped building, some 7m wide and 8m deep. The west wall of the keep provided its east wall, the outer wall of the staircase serving the south-west tower formed the west wall, the whole being built against part of the elongated V-shaped section of the curtain wall. The north wall – the only one that had to be built to complete the room – only exists as footings. The entrance door was in the west corner of the north wall adjoining the doorway leading into the great hall. The present ground level within the kitchen is some 0.25m above the neighbouring courtyard level.

Much of the stretch of curtain wall in this area has been lost, but sufficient remains to establish that built into the thickness of the wall was a large fireplace flanked by two ovens (Plate 21, p.197). This did not seriously detract from the strength of the curtain wall, for in this area it was quite thick, partly due to the junction of the elongated 'V-shape' and the straight section of wall. Flanking the fireplace on each side are the remains of bread ovens. The 1.8m wide space between the south wall of the keep and the curtain wall was also utilised as part of the kitchen. An additional oven was inserted into this gap, presumably associated with a flue that went up the inside of the curtain wall.

The south-west corner of the kitchen contains the remains of a large stone tank or sink that provided the necessary washing facilities (Fig. 17.17). It included a drain that exited through the curtain wall. Behind the sink the end of a lead pipe, protruding slightly from the wall, is the only surviving trace of the piped water supply probably available in the castle in the late 16th century (see Chapter 7). There is also a cupboard built into the thickness of the west wall a short distance to the north of the sink.

The east wall of the kitchen has evidently suffered considerable modifications from the original design. There is a slight shelf between the buttresses and above this is a slightly inclined line of holes cut into the stonework of the keep. They are paired with a similarly sized set of holes that run horizontally, the gap between the pairs decreasing to the south. These small holes could have been associated either with a roof or, more likely, a ceiling to the kitchen (Figs. 11.2 & 5). There is no corroborative evidence from the fragments of the west wall, but it is suggested that the main supports came from the lost north wall and the curtain wall. If this level represents the roof then it would have been almost flat, sloping gently downwards to the south. A diagonal groove cut in the north buttress could indicate that this part of the roof sloped downwards, but this could represent a totally different period of construction. Because of its position between existing buildings, the room would almost certainly have been very dark. There could have been slit windows high up in the curtain wall above the ovens, but the main illumination must have come from the north, courtyard wall. This could have been of timber, allowing larger openings, but the amount of light that entered the room would have been restricted if, as has been suggested, a covered cloister or pentice continued across the front of the keep and kitchen (see Chapter 17).

If the rough opening at first-floor level in the west wall of the keep was indeed a doorway it is possible that there was another room above the kitchen. Alternatively it could have led onto the flat roof, but the levels seem to make this rather unlikely.

Formation of the North and West Outer Wards and their Walls

When it was first built the castle probably had steep slopes to the north and west. When defence became of less importance and there was pressure to expand the castle, it is suggested that the ground was built up on the west and north and held in place by a new encircling wall with its two corner turrets. The original contours of the ground can be appreciated to a certain extent outside this encircling wall, particularly at the north-western corner. There is no firm dating evidence for this work.

The outer walls run more or less parallel with the inner curtain walls and enclose the north and west wards. The north ward, which is almost level, but with a slight slope down to the west, varies in width from 9m to 12m, whilst the west ward, which slopes downwards slightly to the north, varies in width from 13m to 16m. The north ward is grass-covered; the west ward contains the remains of the stables.

The northern outer wall, some 1.4m thick, extends from the buttress associated with the north-west corner of the barbican to the north-west turret for a total distance of some 72m (Figs. 12.3 & 18.5). The first 18m is the only upstanding section of the wall; the remainder exists only as footings. There is little trace of the north face. The ground on the outside of the footings is some 2.5m below the average level in the north ward and falls off sharply to the north. The first 9m from the barbican buttress includes the remains of the 1.5m wide stairs that provided a direct access from the barbican to the north ward (Fig. 18.5). The total 'rise' from the north ward to the barbican is some 6m which, assuming steps of 0.2m high, would have required about 30 steps. Each step would thus have been about 0.3m deep. There was probably a thin wall or protective railing on the southern side of the stair.

Fig. 18.5 The northern outer ward showing, on the left, the remains of the stairs to the barbican

The foundations of a 0.7m wide stone wall crosses the north ward from the outer wall to the north-east corner of the gatehouse turret. Its function may have been associated with the use of the area underneath the drawbridge, or possibly for controlling stock when the ditch was used as a pound.

The masonry of the north-west turret survives to about 1m above the internal ground level, but because the ground falls off rapidly there is a considerable amount of masonry exposed externally. Unfortunately this cannot be properly examined (or maintained) as the present boundary fence prevents access to the whole of the curved part. From what can be seen, there is at least 6m of turret masonry exposed on the outside. The turret is not just the simple curved portion – the masonry extends to the east and south to form a gorge to the turret. The east and south extensions are built of well-coursed stone, but the courses are not as regular as those in the curved parts of the turret. All indications are that the turret was added to pre-existing walls. The internal faces are set at angles rather than following the external curve, suggesting a polygonal chamber with a maximum internal dimension of 4m. On the south side of the turret a rebate indicates a door position, whilst to the east there is a paved area and a garderobe pit. Within the turret proper there are slight indications of window openings. A low stone wall has been built across the gorge of the tower, probably in the 1920s for safety reasons. The turret and the area immediately outside the gorge were evidently roofed, creating a room some 4m square in front of the turret room. Apart from the general design, there is no indication that this turret was intended to have any defensive function and may have been associated with the probable garden in the north ward.

The west outer wall is 55m long. The ground level outside is from 1 to 2m lower, but the outer face is lost for much of its length. The upstanding section of wall close to the south-west turret is well-coursed. The use of a ladder with 11 rungs to scale the wall during the Civil War indicates that it could never have been very high. In addition, its thinness, the lack of any wall walk, and, indeed, the lack of any provision whatsoever for defenders to fire on any attackers, indicates that the wall was simply designed as a boundary and had no defensive function.

The south-west turret is slightly smaller than the north-west one (Fig. 18.6). The surviving part is solid apart from a garderobe pit and a hole for cleaning on the south-western side. It is evident that this turret had a purely utilitarian purpose probably associated with the stables.

A short stretch of outer curtain wall goes from the south-west turret eastwards towards the south-western corner of the great tower, but with a gap to the east. The wall is some 1.5m thick and includes the chamfer from around the turret. However, the

Fig. 18.6 The south-west turret

central section has no chamfer and it is evident that it once contained an entrance, presumably leading into the stables area, but is now quite well blocked. It is suggested that the eastern gap replaced the central opening, providing a new access to the stables area, but if so the ground levels must have been altered, for there is now quite a severe step over the wall footings.

The Stables

The remains of the stables occupy most of the west ward of the castle. They were burnt down during the Civil War (see Chapter 8) and only fragments of the cobbled surfaces and low stone walls survive. The remains were exposed and consolidated during the 1920s repair works. Although the cobbled surfaces are somewhat fragmentary, elements of the design still survive and sufficient of the stone walls remain to indicate the general shapes and sizes of the buildings (Fig. 18.7). There is no indication of their date of construction, but it is probable that they were built at slightly different dates late in the life of the castle.

The stables comprised at least two buildings – a small one to the south that apparently utilised the south and west outer curtain walls in its construction, and a northern building that was free-standing although the west wall was immediately adjacent to the west outer curtain wall. What appears to be a well-laid cobbled roadway some 2m wide led down the eastern side of the stables.

The northern building may well be the earlier structure – from north to south it is set centrally within the west ward and is so positioned that the blocked opening in the south outer curtain wall aligns centrally with it. Externally, the building was 8.5m wide and between 26 and 28m long, the southern wall having completely disappeared. The northern entrance led into a passage set between two small rooms which led into the main stable area. The side bays were quite narrow – only 2m wide on the west and about 3m on the east. It is assumed

Fig. 18.7 The remains of the main, northern stable building from above

Fig. 18.8 The lower part of the south-west tower showing the traces of a spiral staircase that once led up to the basement of the tower through a hole which was converted to a window during the 1920s repair work

that there was a southern entrance, to match the one at the north, providing easy access from the earlier opening in the south outer curtain wall. The area to the south of that opening was reasonably flat and there is a relatively gentle slope either up to the main castle entrance and the village or down to the river crossing at the Boat House. The stable would have been a half-timber structure, built on dwarf stone walls. It would have had a gabled roof, to allow for storage on an upper floor within the roof space.

The extension to the south is a rather odd-looking building that may well have had a timber wall on the east, whilst depending on the curtain walls on the west and south and on the south wall of the main stables to the north. In effect it would have consisted of a roof set on three existing walls with the access from the east. It was about 12m wide and 7.5m long. As part of the construction the opening in the south outer curtain wall was blocked and a new opening made further to the east. The two-bay building had a central 1m wide walkway with 2m wide bays on each side. There is a well-constructed drainage hole in the west curtain wall at ground level, and there are the remains of a tank or sink set into its south-western corner immediately adjacent to the corner turret.

There are several other structures between the stables and the main wall of the castle. An area surrounded by a low wall in the re-entrant between the north-west tower and the curtain wall that encloses an area some 4.5m long doubtless represents a lean-to shed. Further south was a more elaborate structure that allowed access into the basement of the great tower by means of a staircase built partly into the base of the tower and then, via a wooden spiral stair, to a passage and stair through the wall. This was blocked off and replaced by an arrow-slit during the 1920s work (Fig. 18.8).

Plate 15 A reconstruction drawing by Terry Ball of the gatehouse showing the operation of the drawbridge

Plate 16 A reconstruction drawing by Terry Ball showing the operation of the portcullis machinery

Plate 17 A reconstruction drawing by Terry Ball of the north range as it would have looked in the late 13th century

Plate 18 Reconstruction drawing by Terry Ball of the chapel

OPPOSITE:
Plate 21 Reconstruction drawing by Terry Ball of the kitchen looking southwards towards the curtain wall

Plate 19 Reconstruction drawing by Terry Ball of the 14th-century east hall

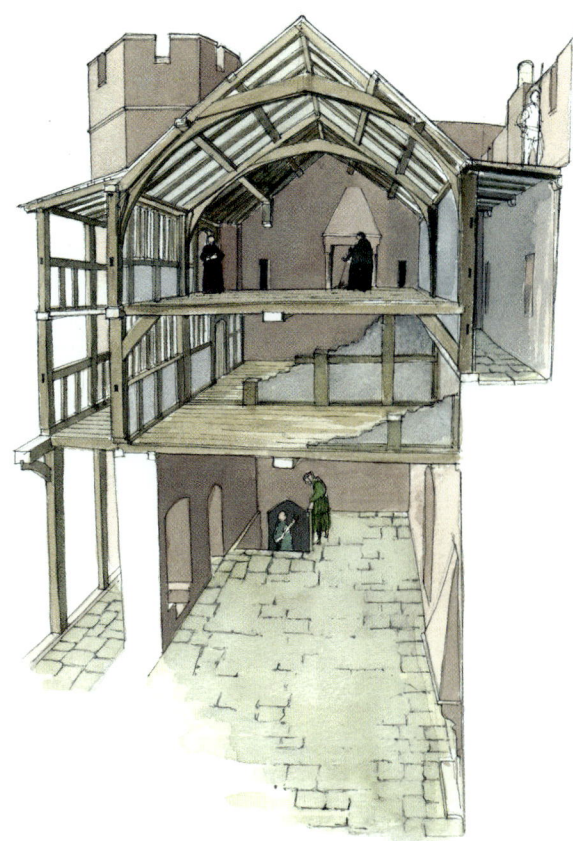

Plate 20 Reconstruction drawing by Terry Ball of the east range as it was re-built in the 16th century

Plate 22 A complete jug of a type manufactured in Hereford. This (fabric A7b) was most common type of pottery at Goodrich

Plate 23 A medieval table set on trestles. The tables would be set up and covered with a clean tablecloth every day. From the 13th-century Maciejowski Bible, leaf 16

Plate 24 A 'reckon-crook' from Goodrich and an illustration of one in use from the 13th-century Maciejowski Bible, leaf 20

198

Plate 25 A glazed medieval ridge tile from Goodrich. This tile was manufactured at Redcliffe, Bristol

Plate 26 A floor tile from Goodrich. These tiles were manufactured at Nash Hill in Wiltshire in the 13th century

Plate 27 The skillet found in the 19th century with a detail of the text on the handle

Plate 28 Ceiling plaster found in the basement of the North-west (Ladies') Tower

Plate 29 A Casket with the de Valence arms in the Victoria and Albert Museum which may have been used to store the countess's jewellery

Part Four

The Finds
& Life at the Castle

Chapters 19 – 20

south-west Herefordshire and Monmouthshire, but seems to have gone out of use before the de Valences held Goodrich. Inexplicably, considering the apparent random nature of its discovery, most of the pottery seems to have been manufactured during the time of William and Joan. 'As an assemblage, this collection appears to be consistent with material discarded after the rebuilding of the castle at the end of the 13th-century, with only a small quantity of material derived from earlier phases.'[26]

Thirty-eight percent of the sherds were from glazed jugs of the Hereford wares (Plate 22, p.198). These jugs may have been produced at a number of sites: there was a kiln at Weobley in north Herefordshire, and the presence of significant quantities of production waste at Hereford suggests another kiln in the southern suburbs of the medieval city.[27] Other pottery came from the Forest of Dean area (21%),[28] an apparently local, probably multi-sourced type of jug (18%),[29] and from the Malvern area (14%). All this pottery is likely to have been delivered to Goodrich directly from the kilns. The countess's accounts record pottery being bought in February and for Easter. There were a few sherds from production centres further away – Stamford in Lincolnshire and Kingston-upon-Thames – but the likelihood is that these were from tableware vessels purchased elsewhere which arrived with the rest of the baggage, to meet their end on a Goodrich floor.

Sherds of kitchen and tableware were not the only ceramic finds at Goodrich. The castle

Fig. 19.1 Floor tiles from Goodrich

roofs would have been formed of stone tiles, but the ridges were topped off with specially-made ridge tiles. These tiles are made from the same materials as the Hereford jugs and are likely to have come from the same kilns (Plate 25, p.199).[30]

The floors of the aristocracy were often tiled. At least one of the rooms at Goodrich had a tiled floor, possibly as early as the mid-13th century, although it may have been nearer the end of the century. This would have been a ground-floor room and the most likely candidate is the de Valences' now-lost great hall. Although ten of the tiles were found on the floor of the basement beneath the chapel, it is not likely that they were originally laid in what was probably a store-room. Forty-seven fragments of tile manufactured at a tilery at Nash Hill near Lacock in Wiltshire have been found at Goodrich (Fig. 19.1 & Plate 26, p.199).[31]

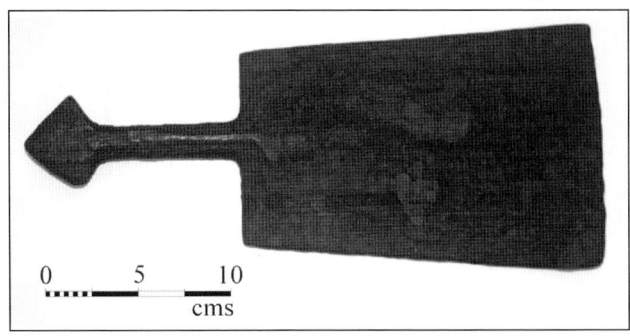

Fig. 19.2 A laundry bat from Goodrich

From the point of view of the servants, tiled floors had the advantage of being easy to sweep, (although the traditional rush floor covering was cleaned rarely, being refreshed with new rushes and occasionally strewn with herbs). Other surfaces would have been cleaned and washed, although the painted wall plaster which covered the walls of the better rooms would have had to have been treated carefully.

When the nobility had arisen, the servants would have emptied the chamber pots into the garderobes, they would have made the beds and, if necessary, changed the bedding and taken it to be washed. Although outer clothing was rarely laundered (spot cleaning was more common), underclothing was washed and the linen tablecloths and napkins used at meals needed constant laundering. In upper-class households tablecloths were expected to be gleaming white. Laundresses were proverbially hard-working, although their pay was not high. There may have been some rewards: Petronella, Eleanor de Montfort's laundress, was given a pair

Fig. 19.3 Using a laundry bat c.1327-1335:, from the Holkham Bible (British Library Add MS 47682 f 15v)

of shoes worth 12d for Easter and an additional one-off payment of 15d in May.[32] Although she could have expected help from other servants, the Countess of Pembroke's unnamed laundress (see Chapter 5) would have been very busy.

The washing was put into tubs of hot water and soap made of wood ash and lye (potassium hydroxide, also derived from wood ash) was used. The washing was agitated and beaten with wooden paddles before being taken out to dry (Figs. 19.2 & 3).

In the evening cressets (wick or rope set in oil in metal or ceramic cups) and candles would have been lit, but this was a daylight society and many members of the household would have retired early, the servants drawing the curtains of the beds before going to their own resting places, considerably less comfortable and private than those of their masters and mistresses.

20 THE DETRITUS OF WAR

by P.J. Pikes

In the 1920s the Office of Works began the clearance of Goodrich Castle (see Chapter 10). In November, pottery, leaded window frames and glass was found, and on the 15th of December the last of a 4ft 6ins depth of centuries-old rubble was removed from the basement of the Ladies' Tower (see Chapter 10). Beneath it, the workmen found material unseen since the tower collapsed following Birch's cannon fire in July 1646. Plaster mouldings, including a rosette (Plate 28, p.200), suggesting a degree of sophistication in the internal fittings, are likely to have been from an upper room that collapsed into the basement, as was glass still attached to its frame.[1] A few lumps of coal were presumably the remains of the previous winter's store. There were various tools – soldering irons, a knife, a scraper, and more excitingly, the remains of two swords (Fig. 20.1). In a west-facing window recess, half an iron cannonball was wedged. This had passed through the tower, having entered either through a window or perhaps through a hole knocked in the wall, and split on impact with the castle's stonework.[2]

By the mid-17th century Goodrich was an anachronism. Medieval castles had been vulnerable to pre-gunpowder artillery such as the ballista, but as long as the attacking force had nothing more powerful than pistols and muskets the castle would have been well able to withstand assault. Mining beneath the walls would offer the best hope of bringing them down and opening a gap through which a numerically superior force could enter. The standard response to mining was countermining – the digging of a mine by the defenders to intercept the mine of the besiegers. Attempts at mining and countermining were indeed carried out at Goodrich (see Chapter 8), but it was gunpowder artillery that ultimately decided the outcome.

First used by the Chinese in the 12th century, 'bombards' – guns designed to breach castle walls – had been used in the British Isles for two centuries by the time Birch laid siege to Goodrich. The bombard Mons Meg, now in Edinburgh Castle, was made for Philip the Good of Burgundy in about 1450 and given to James II of Scotland, who used artillery to great effect

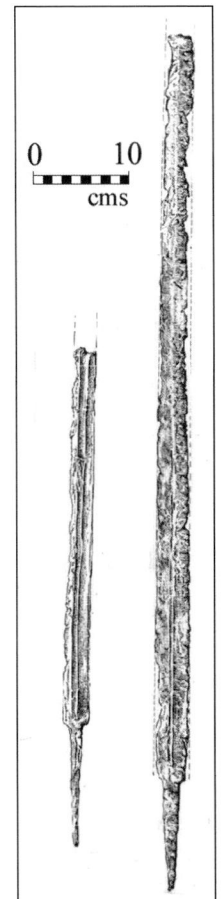

Fig. 20.1 Two swords found in the basement of the Ladies' Tower

against castles. His enthusiasm was ultimately fatal: a bombard named The Lion exploded as he stood near it at the siege of Roxburgh Castle in 1460.³

Fortifications had to adapt to the new warfare and by the 16th century castles were very different from their medieval predecessors. At Deal, Walmer, Southsea, and elsewhere Henry VIII built coastal castles, which were low-lying gun platforms with rounded stone turrets. Within a generation these had been superseded by earthen fortifications with pointed ravelins, made of earth to better absorb the impact of cannonballs. Not relying on medieval stone walls during the Civil War, earthen ramparts and ravelins had been built around many cities, as at Worcester, Oxford, Colchester and London.

Lingen seems to have made some effort to place earth defences around Goodrich, turf being taken from Richard Tyler's fields for that purpose (Chapter 8), but Goodrich's exposed and rock-built position made it vulnerable as soon as cannon could be brought within effective range. Out-works presumably existed, but were easily overrun such as the one at the Boat-House.

Fig. 20.2. A clutch of iron cannonballs at Goodrich

Birch's batteries played upon the castle walls. Much of the round-shot was stone; chiselling cannonballs was an important source of employment for masons, and stone cannonballs were recovered from the ditch in the 1920s. Round-shot of both iron and stone was directed at the castle in some quantity (Figs. 20.2 & 3). There was also incendiary shot – iron cannonballs with two spikes (Fig. 20.4) which were heated until red hot before being fired (the balls being carefully shielded from the powder in the gun). It was hoped that these would stick into woodwork and set it alight.

Even so, the guns which Birch originally had with him seem not to have been powerful enough. The names of different types of artillery pieces of the period are confusing and not standard, but the culverin was generally a long-barreled gun which fired a light shot.⁴ These were certainly at the siege, but something more was needed; in May Birch requested 'some battering cannon for Godrich, else I may sit long enough before it'. The guns he subsequently acquired were much more suitable to his purpose, their shot tearing holes in the castle walls.

Fig. 20.3 A stone cannonball found at Goodrich

But even behind the walls the defenders would not be safe. Birch resolved 'never to parley more; and

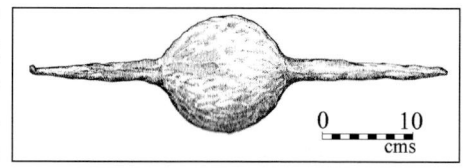

Fig. 20.4 Incendiary shot: heated red-hot these were intended to stick into timber and set it aflame

thereupon sent them in six grenadoes'. The word grenade meant what we would call a shell, that is a metal case filled with explosive which was ignited by a fuse. Small grenades would later be lobbed by hand – hand grenades – and soldiers trained in their use would be 'grenadiers'. Birch's grenadoes were fired from his new mortar, Roaring Meg (see Chapter 8).

Unlike cannonballs with their relatively flat trajectory, the grenadoes, fired high, plummeted down inside the castle walls. This was a weapon from which the defenders could not easily protect themselves and which caused great damage to the interior of the castle. Roaring Meg's shells are likely to have caused much fear. At the siege of Lathom House in Lancashire in 1644 it was reported that while the two young daughters of the Countess of Derby were not particularly frightened by the cannon-fire, even 'the stoutest souldiers had noe hearts for granadoes'.[5] At Goodrich 'the enemy was terified, much of the inner part of the castle ffallen down'.

Fig. 20.5 The bucket chain, found at the bottom of the well

One of these shells exploded on the head of the castle well, demolishing the winding gear and sending the bucket and chain (Fig. 20.5) crashing to the bottom of the shaft, together with pieces of the shell (Fig. 20.6). As the external water supply to the castle had been cut this meant that water had to be hand-drawn from Goodrich's deep well. Doing this in the open courtyard, with no certainty as to when the next grenado would fall, cannot have been a comfortable experience.

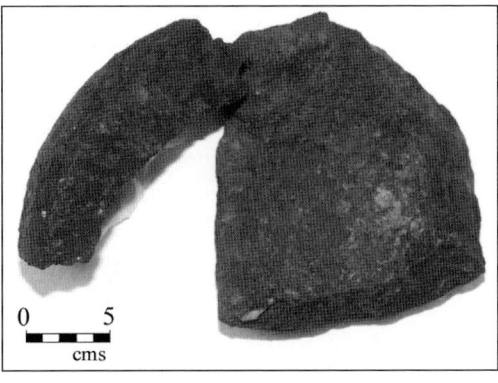

Fig. 20.6 Fragments of the mortar shell which exploded on the top of the well sending the bucket and chain to the bottom

Balls and fragments of shell may be evidence of the most dramatic aspect of the mid-16th-century events at Goodrich, but as the workmen continued to remove the rubble which lay two feet deep in the courtyard, and entirely filling and concealing the well, more and more tools and weapons were found.

That it was the Reverend Swift that seeded the ford with caltrops (see Chapter 8) may be no more than a legend, but caltrops were certainly found on the site. A caltrop is a device formed of four sharp spikes so arranged that, if tossed on the ground, one spike is always pointing upward. As such they were easily able to seriously inconvenience men and horses (particularly if placed in a ford where

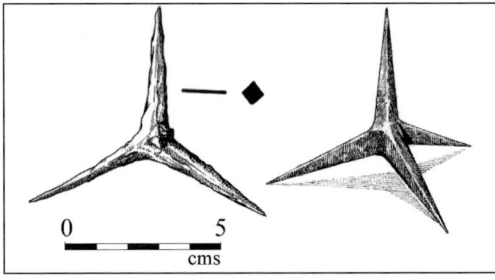

Fig. 20.7 Caltrops like this would disable advancing men and horses

they would not easily be seen). Caltrops were cheap and simple to make and could simply be strewn on the ground over which the enemy was expected to advance. Having their origins in antiquity, caltrops have survived, virtually unchanged, and are still used today (Fig. 20.7).

Throughout the clearance objects were continually being found – some wine glasses and broken clay pipes, a broken door-lock, bullets, harness fittings, spurs and coins. In general, little inference can be drawn from the positions in which these various objects were found, randomly distributed during the slighting of the castle in July 1656.

Lead bullets or musket balls were found in several places. The weapons of the defenders and attackers alike would mainly have been matchlock muskets (Fig. 20.8), although swords were far from obsolete. Matchlocks were fired by means of a burning wick, or slow match, on a curved lever or 'serpentine'. Pulling the lever (or later trigger) brought the match in contact with gunpowder in a pan on top of the musket. This, in turn, would ignite the main charge in the barrel and fire the ball.

Although an improvement on earlier firearms which needed to be lit by hand, leaving only one hand to direct the weapon, the matchlocks were cumbersome, weighing 6 or 7 kilos, and slow to load. The 'match' had to be lit before battle, and tended to go out in the rain. In set formations the musketeers were covered by pikemen, with pikes up to 18 feet long, to protect them from cavalry. Longbows may well have been more effective than these matchlocks, but archers were trained from boyhood: anyone could be trained in the use of a musket in a very short time, and the soldiers at Goodrich had mostly been civilians just a few years before.

Flintlocks were relatively new weapons, the first one being made for King Louis XIII sometime after 1610.[6] Officers may have possessed flintlock pistols (Fig. 20.9) and cavalrymen carried them in a holster. Swords too, such as those found in the Ladies' Tower basement, were in general use (Fig. 20.1).

Although 76 horses had been seized in Birch's raid on the stable early in the siege, there were still many left in the castle, but the losses were heavy. Spurs and horseshoes were among the most common of the objects recovered, being found throughout the ruins.

Less directly military were the various tools. Some, like the claw hammer (Fig. 20.10) and chisel (Fig. 20.11), are immediately recognizable and differ little from modern tools. A few are quite different – spades were wooden with iron 'shoes' forming the digging edge (Fig. 20.12). Such tools would have been used to construct the earthwork

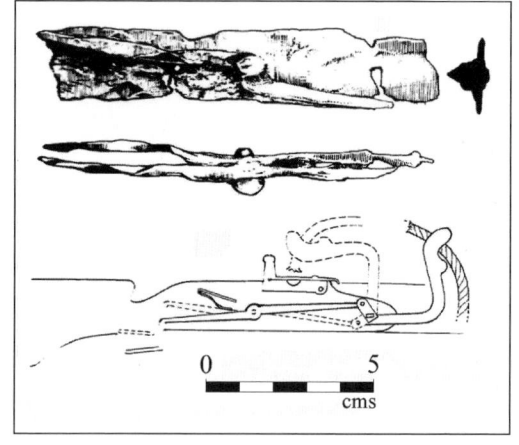

Fig. 20.8 The mechanism from a matchlock musket

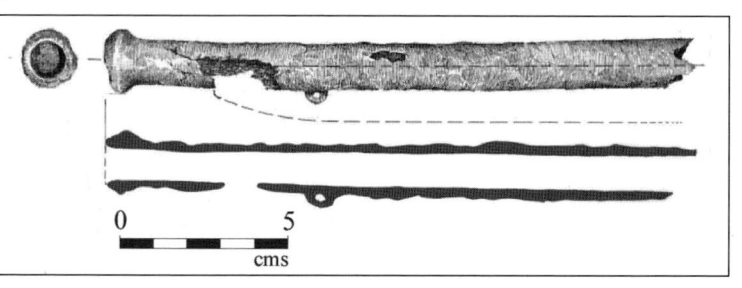

Fig. 20.9 The barrel of a flintlock pistol

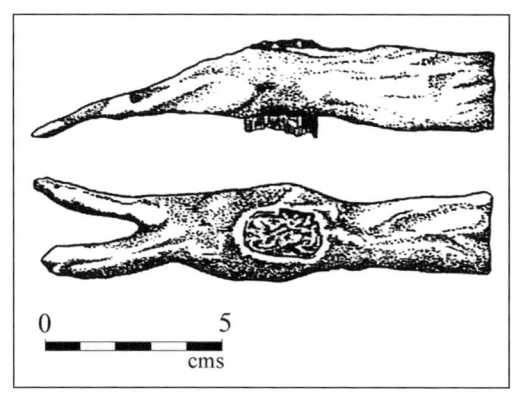

Fig. 20.10 This 17th-century hammer is very similar to modern hammers

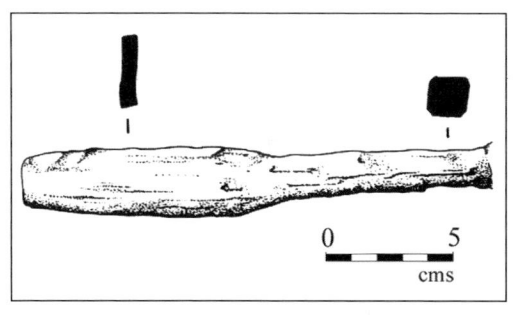

Fig. 20.11 A 17th-century chisel

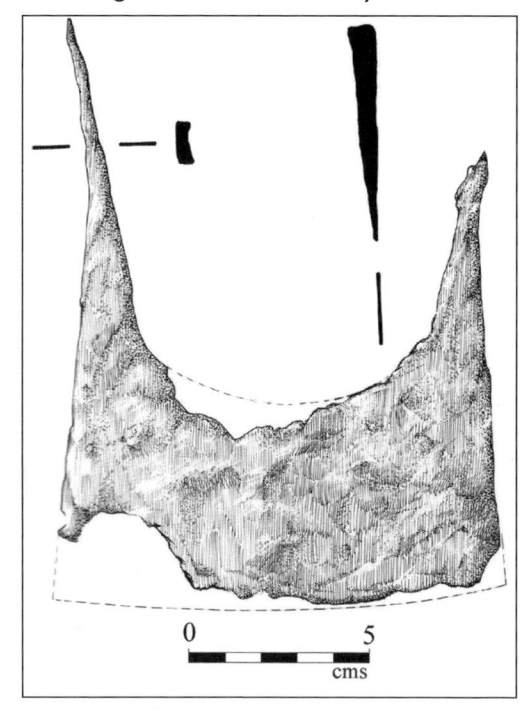

Fig. 20.12 The iron blade of a spade

defences built around the castle – such as those at the Boat House. They would have been little use in digging the rock-cut countermine in the Ladies' Tower.

The handcuffs are in a different category (Fig. 20.13). They are of a type in use until recently and clearly can have no other purpose than restraint of prisoners. There is no record of prisoners being released at the end of the siege and presumably these were used (if used at all) for individual people arrested by the authorities at some time before the siege when the castle was still the site of the local prison (see Chapter 7).

One of the requirements of the garrison would have been fresh bread. It is known that supplies were nowhere near exhausted when the castle fell and there was a plentiful supply of corn. Bread would have been baked regularly in the castle ovens and the peel that was found would have been used to put the unbaked dough into the oven and get the baked bread out (Fig. 20.14). Peels are usually made of wood, which doesn't get too hot for the baker to hold. This one is iron but it must have had a wooden handle.

For centuries all this material remained where it fell in 1646. Occasional probing would discover some artefacts, such as the skillet mentioned in Chapter 8 embossed with the slogan 'C. U. B. LOYAL TO HIS MAGISTEIE (Plate 27, p.199),

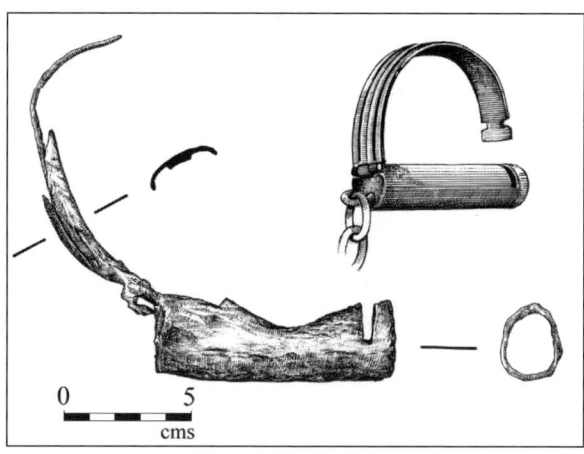

Fig. 20.13 These handcuffs were found in the dungeon

but mainly the visitors to the picturesque ruin dropped things. There are records in the Office of Works foreman's log to '2 knife clasps (modern)', '1 coin (copper) George III' and '2 copper coins George III'. Dropping things could be expected: a thorough exploration of the ruins must often have resulted in a stumble and would not have been without its dangers, although by and large these were as nothing compared to those faced by the 17th-century defenders.

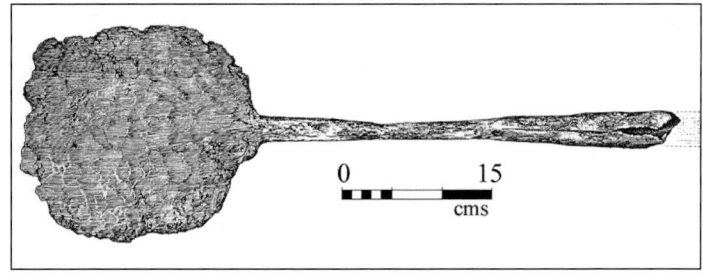

Fig. 20.14 This baker's 'peel', found in the kitchen, would originally have had a wooden handle

References & Endnotes

Abbreviations used

BL	British Library
BL Add Mss	British Library Additional Manuscripts
Bod. Lib.	Bodleian Library
Bod. Lib. Sel.	Bodleian Library Selden Papers
BRO	Bedford Record Office
Cal State Papers	Calendar of State Papers Domestic
Cam. Univ. Lib.	Cambridge University Library
CHAC	The early survey work is included in two A3 bound volumes in the Goodrich Castle archive. Vol. 1 includes survey and excavation work 1982–5; Vol. 2 includes work 1985–8. Individual Reports by the City of Hereford Archaeology Unit (HAS) started in 1988, the earliest being no. 26 – *The Display Panels*. Copies are in Hereford City Library
ChR	*Calendar of Charter Rolls*, PRO, 6 vols., 1903-27
ClR	*Calendar of Close Rolls*, PRO, 1900-32
DB	Domesday Book
DNB	Dictionary of National Biography
Duncumb	Duncumb, J. and continuators, *Collections Towards the History and Antiquities of the County of Hereford*, Vol.6, Wormelow Hundred, Upper Division (ed. Matthews, J.H., 2 parts, Hereford, 1912-13) and Lower Division (ed. Matthews, J.H., 2 parts, Hereford, 1913-15)
FR	*Calendar of Fine Rolls*, PRO, 1911-49
GEC	Cockayne, G.E., *The Complete Peerage*, ed. Gibbs, V. *et al.*, 14 vols., London, 1911-59
GRO	Gloucester Record Office
HAN	Herefordshire Archaeology News
HAS	Herefordshire Archaeological Series (HAS) by the City of Hereford Archaeology Unit later Archaeological Investigations Ltd
HHER	Herefordshire Historic Environment Record
HRO	Hereford Record Office
Ipm	*Calendar of Inquisitions Post Mortem*, PRO, 1898-in progress
King	King, E., *Monumenta Antiqua* (1804) Vol 3 pp.249 -260
Lam. Pal. Lib	Lambeth Palace Library
LL	*Liber Landavensis*
Meyrick	Lowe, R., *Sir Samuel Meyrick & Goodrich Court,* Logaston, 2003
NMR	National Monuments Record
PatR	*Calendar of Patent Rolls*, PRO, 1906-in progress
PR	*Pipe Roll*, by regnal year, as published by the Pipe Roll Society of London
PRO	Public Record Office, now the National Archives
RCAHMW	Royal Commission on Ancient and Historic Monuments Wales
RCHM	Royal Commission on Historic Monuments
SAM	Scheduled Ancient Monument
TWNFC	*Transactions of the Woolhope Naturalists Field Club, Herefordshire*

Introduction
1. 'A feasibility study and research design for a major publication', HAS 54, July 1989.
2. Baker, N., 'A Revised Project Design ... The Completion, Editing and Publication of Goodrich Castle, Herefordshire', February 2012.

Chapter 1
1. Barton, R.N.E., 'An interim report on the survey and excavations in the Wye Valley', *Proceedings of the University of Bristol Spelaeological Society*, 1993, 19. 3, 337-346
2. Herefordshire HER records 34710, 38473, 38497, 30157, 8355, 6245, 822
3. Ray, K., 'The Neolithic of the West Midlands: An Overview', West Midlands Regional Research Framework for Archaeology, Seminar 1
4. Cummings, V. & Whittle, A., *Places of Special Virtue: Megaliths in the Neolithic Landscapes of Wales*, Oxbow Books, 2004, 185 & 198
5. HHER record 824; Watkins, A., 'Excavations at the Queen Stone', *TWNFC*, 1926, 189-93; Shoesmith, R., *Alfred Watkins, A Herefordshire Man*, Logaston, 1990, 126-30
6. Children, G. & Nash, G., *Prehistoric Sites of Herefordshire*, Logaston, 1994, 61-2
7. RCAHMW NMR record 221159
8. Herefordshire HER record 30340
9. White, P., 'Herefordshire: From the Middle Bronze Age to the Later Iron Age', West Midlands Regional Research Framework for Archaeology, Seminar 2
10. Herefordshire SAM records 1016899, 1016900, 1016901
11. Herefordshire HER record 805
12. Taylor, E., 'Report on the Excavations of Huntsham Romano-British Villa and Iron Age Enclosures,' *TWNFC.,* 1995, 224-81
13. Stanford, *The Archaeology of the Welsh Marches,* Privately Published, 1991, 58-9
14. HAN 60, September 1993
15. Stanford, 1991, Fig 20, 58 shows hill forts with territories in relation to their enclosed area
16. Bull, H.G., 'Credenhill Camp ... and the Roman Stations and Towns in Herefordshire,' *TWNFC,* 1882, 236-59, esp. 258
17. Wright, T., *Wanderings of an Antiquary,* Nicholls, London, 1854, 14
18. Bridgewater, N.P., 'The Huntsham Romano-British Villa – First report', *TWNFC,* 1962, 179-91
19. Taylor, E., 'Report on the Excavation of the Huntsham Romano-British Villa and Iron Age Enclosure' *TWNFC,* 1995, 224-280 & 'Appended Note. A possible Roman Water Mill' *TWNFC,* 1995, 280-81
20. McCalmont, H.L.B., 'Roman coins, found at Bishopswood, near Ross', *TWNFC,* 1895-7, Additional notes at end of volume, 4-22
21. Dudley, D.R., 'The Herefordshire area in the Roman period' in *Herefordshire,* Gloucester, 1954, 120-129, esp. 127-8
22. Bull, H.G., 1882, 236-59, esp. 258; Jack, G.H., 'Roman Roads ...' *TWNFC,* 1909, 107
23. Dudley, 1954, 127
24. Margary, I.D., *Roman Roads in Britain,* 1967, 323-4, route 60a; Shoesmith, *Excavations at Chepstow, 1973-1974,* Cambrian Archaeological Monographs No. 4, 1991, 156-60
25. Margary, 529
26. Jack, G.H., 'Roman Road between Monmouth and Gloucester', *TWNFC,* 1908, 105; Lamont, A.H., 'Fords and Ferries on the Wye', *TWNFC,* 1921-23, 73-94
27. Bridgewater, N.P., 'Ancient Buried Roads in South Herefordshire, Part 1', *TWNFC,* 1959, 218-227; Also a short note by the same author in *TWNFC,* 1956, 186-7
28. see note 28
29. See Coplestone-Crow, B., *Herefordshire Place-Names,* 2nd ed., Logaston Press, 2009, for the origins of its name and its possible extent
30. *LL*,72. Professor Wendy Davies, formerly of University College London, has trenchant views on this document, which she regards as a foundation tradition rather than a genuine charter: *The Llandaff Charters*, Aberystwyth, 1979, 92-3
31. *LL*, 164-5,230-1
32. I am grateful to Richard Morgan of Glamorgan Archives for advice on this placename
33. *LL*,72. For the probable boundaries of Garthbenni, see Watkins, M.P., 'LannCustenhinnGarthbenni', *TWNFC,* 1964-7,196-202
34. Davies, W., *An Early Welsh Microcosm*, London, 1978, 157; White, R., *Britannia Prima, Britain's Last Roman Province*, Stroud, 2007, 206
35. *LL*,72
36. *LL*,237
37. *Annales Cambriae*, ed. WilliamsabIthel, J., Rolls Series, 1860, 9; see also Jones, T., ed. & trans., *Brut y Tywysogyon: Peniarth MS 20 version,* Cardiff, 1952, 2 and note on 131
38. *LL*,175-6 (with its doublet at 186-7), 178, 184-5
39. *Annales Cambriae*, 10; *Brut y Tywysogyon*, 2
40. Swanton, M. (ed.& trans.), *The Anglo-Saxon Chronicle*, London, 1996, 98-9
41. Davies, 154-5
42. *DB*, f.181
43. *LL*,276
44. Barrow, J. (ed.), *English Episcopal Acta VII: Hereford 1079-1234*, Oxford, British Academy, 1993, No.47
45. *DB*, f.181

Chapter 2
1. Coplestone-Crow, B., *Herefordshire Place-Names*, Logaston, 2009, 216
2. *RCHM, I*, 78–9
3. HAN, 39, Jan 1981, 13-16
4. *RCHM, I*, 73–4; Brooks, A. & Pevsner N., *Buildings of England – Herefordshire*, 2012, 251-2
5. Meyrick
6. Twamley, L.A., *Autumn Ramble by the Wye*, London, 1838, 107-15
7. Hutchinson, T., 'Wordsworth and Goodrich Castle', *TWNFC*, 1901, 206
8. Meller, H., 'The Architectural History of Goodrich Court' *TWNFC*, 1977, 175-85
9. Anon, *Felsted in Herefordshire*, privately published, n.d.
10. Lowe, 125 & Fig. 67
11. Lowe, 200-201
12. Nash, C., *Goodrich Court Guide*, 1867, 31-2
13. Lowe, 201-3 & Figs. 106, 107
14. *RCHM, I*, 80
15. Pers. Inf. from R. Lowe
16. *RCHM, I*, 80; Lowe, 111 & Fig. 55
17. *RCHM, I.*, 80 & Pl. 105

Chapter 3
1. Mawer, A., Stenton, F.M. & Houghton, F.T.S., *The Place-Names of Worcestershire*, English Place-Names Society, 1927, 148
2. An Aelfric Mapson, who may have been a relative, had held land at Droitwich in Worcestershire in the time of Edward the Confessor: *DB*, f.176b
3. *DB*, f.181
4. Watkins, M.P., 'The Lordship of Monmouth and the Herefordshire-Monmouthshire Border', *TWNFC*, 1962, 67-76
5. *LL*, 277-8; *DB*, f.180b
6. PRO, E326/11722 in a hand of *c*.1100, but part of which has become illegible, and E210/4437 a copy made in the 16th century when more of it was legible. I am indebted to Mr Alasdair Hawkyard MA FRHistS for transcriptions of these deeds
7. Marchegay, P. (ed.), *Chartes Anciennes du Prieuré de Monmouth en Angleterre*, Les Roches-Baritaud, 1879, no.6
8. Davis, R.H.C. (ed.) *et al.*, *Regesta Regum Anglo-Normannorum*, 3 vols., Oxford, 1913-68, ii, nos.547-8
9. *LL*, 37, 93
10. Morey, A. & Brooke C.N.L. (eds.), *The Letters and Charters of Gilbert Foliot*, Cambridge, 1967, No.13
11. Orderic Vitalis (ed. & trans. Chibnall, M.), *The Ecclesiastical History*, 6 vols., Oxford, 1969-80, vi, 520-1
12. GEC, x, 349
13. Marchegay, *Chartes Anciennes...*, No.9; Wood, J.G., *The Lordship, Castle and Town of Chepstow, Otherwise Striguil*, Newport, 1910, 45-51
14. King, E. & Potter, K.R. (ed. & trans.), William of Malmesbury: *Historia Novella, The Contemporary History*, Oxford, 1998, 36
15. *PR 23 Henry II*, 56
16. *PR 32 Henry II*, 31
17. *PR 33 Henry II*, 133
18. EH report on burials
19. CHAC Vol.2 & HAS 30
20. Dickinson, J.C. & Ricketts, P.T., 'The Anglo-Norman Chronicle of Wigmore Abbey', *TWNFC*, 1969, 430-1
21. *An Inventory of the Historical Monuments in the County of Northamptonshire, Volume 2: Archaeological sites in Central Northamptonshire*, London, 1979, 40-2
22. Shoesmith, R., *Excavations at Castle Green, Hereford*, CBA Research Report 36, 1980, 57-9
23. Murphy, K. & Crane, P., 'Burials at Narberth Castle, Pembrokeshire', *Archaeology in Wales*, 42, 2002, 73-7; Ludlow, N. & Jamieson, T., 'Narberth Castle', *ante*, 43, 2003, 143
24. Marchegay, *Chartes Anciennes...*, No.18
25. RCHM Herefordshire, I, 1931, 73

Chapter 4
1. *Rotuli Chartarum*, Record Commission, 1837, 124
2. *Liber Feodum: The Book of Fees*, 3 vols., London, 1920-31, 99
3. scutage – a payment made in lieu of military service
4. *Rotuli Litterarum Clausarum*, 2 vols., Record Commission, 1835-6, i,4b: *PR 13 John*, 175
5. Conway Davies, J. (ed.), *Cartae Antiquae Rolls 11-20*, Pipe Roll Society, 1957, 165-6
6. Carpenter, D.A., *The Minority of Henry III*, London, 1990, 43
7. Meyer P. (ed.), *Histoire de Guillaume le Marechal*, 2 vols., Paris, 1891-4, ll.15352 to 15372. On line 15355 the name of the earl's besieged castle, which lay only 12 miles from Gloucester according to the author, is given in the corrupt form *ge dus*. The editor (ii, 390) makes the very reasonable amendment to *godris* or Goodrich (which is 16 miles from Gloucester)
8. *Rotuli Litterarum Clausarum 1204-27*, 2 vols., Record Commission, 1833-44, i,314; *PatR 1216-25*, 79
9. *Curia Regis Rolls*, PRO, 1922, x, 260
10. *PatR 1364-7*, 274 (an exemplification made in 1364 of the partition of the lands of Walter Marshal in 1246); PRO C134/83
11. *PatR 1364-7*, 275

12. *Ipm*, vi, No.518
13. *ClR 1227-31*, 539
14. *ClR 1227-31*, 528; Cazel, F.A. (ed.), *Roll of Divers Accounts; Accounts of Escheats; Wardrobe Receipt Roll: reign of Henry III,* Pipe Roll Society, London, 1982, 66
15. *ClR 1231-4*, 331
16. *Ibid*, 336. See also Walker, R.F., 'The Supporters of Richard Marshal, Earl of Pembroke, in the Rebellion of 1233-1234', *Welsh History Review,* **17**, 1994, 41-65
17. *PatR 1232-47*, 52
18. *PatR 1232-47*, 468
19. *ClR 1237-42*, 365; *Liber Feodum: The Book of Fees,* 1273
20. *PatR 1364-7*, 274-5
21. PatR1232-47, 505-6; ClR 1247-51, 20

Chapter 5
1. *ClR 1259-66, 329*
2. *PatR 1258-66*, 150
3. Lewis, F.R., 'William de Valence (*c.*1230-1296)', *Aberystwyth Studies,* **14**, 1936, 69-92; *Oxford Dictionary of National Biography, 2004, s.n.*
4. *ClR 1251-3*, 354
5. *ClR 1259-61*, 420; *ClR 1261-74*, 74
6. *ClR 1264-8*, 189; *ClR 1272-9*, 208, 398
7. *Ibid*, 26, 171; Robert Cockerel was provost or constable of Goodrich Castle and 'a dependant of that noble man William de Valance' in 1284; Capes, W.W. (ed.) *Registrum Ricardi de Swinfield, Episcopi Herefordensis,* Canterbury and York Society, 1909, 61-2
8. *ClR 1288-96*, 244, 286
9. Ridgeway, H., 'William de Valence and his *Familiares'*, *Bulletin of the Institute of Historical Research,* **65**, 1992, 242-3 and note 19; Maddicott, J.R., *Simon de Montfort,* Cambridge, 1994, 55; Morris, M., *The Bigod Earls of Norfolk in the 13th Century,* Woodbridge, 2005, 40-1
10. Denholm-Young N., *Seignieurial Administration in England,* Oxford, 1937, 23
11. Duncumb, Lower Division, Part 14
12. *Rotuli Hundredorum,* 2 vols., Record Commission, 1812-7, i,186b; *PatR 1281-92,* 43-4
13. *Placita de Quo Warranto,* Record Commission, 1818, 272-3; *ClR 1288-96*, 241
14. Morris, J.E., *The Welsh Wars of Edward I,* Oxford, 1901, 146; *Aberystwyth Studies,* 14, 1936, 74-5
15. *Calendar of Various Chancery Rolls 1277-1326,* London, 1912, 314.-
16. *Ipm*, iii, No.362; PRO C133/76 No.2
17. 'Miracles of St. Thomas Cantilupe' in *Acta Sanctorum Octobris,* tomus 1, Antwerp, 1765, 684
18. Colvin, H.M. (ed.), *The History of the King's Works,* vol.1, London, 1963, 231 note 3
19. *ClR 1288-96*, 490; *ClR 1296-1302*, 3; PRO E101/505/25-26; *PatR 1292-1301*, 289
20. PRO E101/505/26, consisting of 32 unnumbered membranes
21. *Getelynde* was the name of a 'gate' through Offa's Dyke at Symonds Yat: Copleston-Crow, B., *Herefordshire Place-Names,* Logaston, 2009, 106
22. Capes, W,W. (ed.), *Registrum Ricardi de Swinfield, Episcopi Herefordensis,* 537
23. PRO C134/4 No.1
24. *PatR 1364-7*, 274-5; *Ipms*, iii, No.362 & v, No.56. There was a similar decline in the value of the county of Wexford under William's stewardship
25. Phillips, J.R.S., *Aymer de Valence, Earl of Pembroke 1307-2: Baronial Politics in the Reign of Edward II*,Oxford, 1972
26. Bannister, A.T. (ed.), *Registrum Ade de Orleton, Episcopi Herefordensis,* Canterbury and York Society, 1908, 122-3
27. PRO C134/83
28. *FR 1319-27*, 338; Phillips, *Aymer de Valence ...,* 244-5
29. Rees, W. (ed.), *Calendar of Ancient Petitions Relating to Wales,* Cardiff, 1975, No.8132
30. PRO SC2/18/41
31. See *PatR 1334-8*, 234-5, which says they gained the castle 'in the time when queen Isabella and the king landed in the realm'
32. Baddeley, W.St.C., *A Cotswold Manor: Painswick,* Gloucester, 1907, 92
33. *PatR 1334-8*, 234-5

Chapter 6
1. *PatR 1334-8*, 234-5
2. *PatR 1338-40*, 107
3. Goodall, J., *The English Castle,* New Haven and London, 2011, 249
4. Harvey, J.H.,'Side-lights on Kenilworth Castle', *The Archaeological Journal,* **101**, 1944, 91-107
5. *Calendar of Papal Registers: Papal Letters 1198-304*, Stationery Office, 1893, 46, 53
6. Potter, K.R. & Davis, R.H.C. (ed. & trans.) *Gesta Stephani,* Oxford, 1976, 108-11
7. Thompson, E.M.(ed.) *Adæ Murimuth Continuatio Chronicarum,* Rolls Series, 1889, 128-9
8. *Calendar of Papal Registers: Papal Letters 1342-62*, PRO, 1893, 69
9. Shropshire County Library Deed 138
10. *Calendar of Papal Registers: Papal Petitions 1342-1419*, PRO 1896, 16
11. *ChR 1341-1417*, 51; *ClR 1346-9*, 213; *PatR 1345-8*, 134
12. *PatR 1345-8*, 220; Parry, J.H. (ed.), *Registrum Johannis de Trilleck, Episcopi Herefordensis,* Canterbury and York Society, 1912, 88-9; *Calendar of Papal Registers: Papal Petitions*

1342-1419, 336
13. *PatR 1348-50*, 193-4
14. *Ipm*, x, No.326; Duncumb, Upper Division, Part 1, 21
15. PRO E149/39 No.9 (ii)
16. *Ipm*, xiii, No.213
17. *PatR 1358-61*, 132
18. *Ipm*, xvi, No.468; Duncumb, 22-3
19. *PatR 1396-9*, 88, 116, 145; *ClR 1396-9*, 462
20. *PatR 1396-9*, 28; *ClR 1396-9*, 264
21. Griffiths, R.A., *The Principality of Wales in the Later Middle Ages: The Structure and Personnel of Government: I. South Wales 1277-1536*, Cardiff, 1972, 139
22. *ClR 1396-9*, 506
23. *FR 1399-1405*, 17-18
24. *Ibid*, 161-2
25. Hingeston, F.C., (ed.), *Royal and Historical Letters During the Reign of Henry the Fourth*, 2 vols., Rolls Series, 1860, i, No.62
26. *ClR 1402-5*, 111
27. *Ibid*, 98
28. *Proceedings and Ordinances of the Privy Council of England,* 7 vols., Record Commission, 1834-7, i, 223-5, dated 10 June
29. Devon, F., (ed.), *Issues of the Exchequer from Henry III to Henry VII*, 302; *PatR 1405-8*, London, 1836, 113; Wylie, J.H., *History of England under Henry the Fourth*, London, 1884, ii, 412
30. *PatR 1405-8*, 50; Parry, J.H., (ed.), *Registrum Roberti Mascall, Episcopi Herefordensis,* Canterbury and York Society, 1917, 20-1
31. *ClR 1405-9*, 202
32. *Ipm*, xx, Nos.112-3; Duncumb, Lower Division, Part 1, 23-4
33. Devon, (ed.), *Issues of the Exchequer from Henry III to Henry VII*, 357
34. *Calendarium Inquisitionem Post Mortem,* 4 vols., Record Commission, 1806-28, iv, 59: 9 Henry V, No.44
35. *PatR 1422-9*, 261
36. *GEC*, xi, 699; Cosgrove, A., (ed.), *A New History of Ireland: Medieval Ireland 1169-1534*, Oxford, 1987, 536, 543-4, 571; Otway-Ruthven, A.J., *A History of Medieval Ireland*, London & New York, 1968, 356
37. Harleian ms. No 6726, fo. 54
38. The French had originally demanded a large ransom for Talbot. But in August 1431 Talbot's father-in-law, Richard, Earl of Warwick, captured Talbot'sown captor, Jean Poton de Xaintrailles, one of the chief lieutenants of Joan of Arc. Negotiations for the exchange of the two were completed early in 1433, but Talbot was worth more than de Xaintrailles and so still had to pay money (Pollard, A.J., 'The Family of Talbot, Lords of Talbot and Earls of Shrewsbury in the Fifteenth Century', unpublished dissertation for the degree of Doctor of Philosophy submitted to the University of Bristol, 1968, 326)
39. A badly damaged petition of 1442 in the National Archives, SC 8/182/9099
40. Talbot's legend tended to exaggerate his skill and downplay his ruthlessness, but he certainly inspired the English and gained the admiration of his enemies. (Pollard, 1968, 208-213)
41. Pollard, A.J., 'Talbot, John, first earl of Shrewsbury and first earl of Waterford (*c*.1387–1453)', DNB, Oxford University Press, 2004; online edn, Oct 2008 [http://www.oxforddnb.com/view/article/26932, accessed 1 Oct 2013]
42. Talbot, H., *The English Achilles: an account of the life and campaigns of John Talbot, Ist Earl of Shrewsbury (1383-1453)*, London, 1981, 183-6
43. *PatR 1461-7*, 30, 99, 114, 339
44. *Ibid*, 166-7
45. *Ibid*, 411
46. PRO SC/1122/12
47. *PatR 1477-85*, 414
48. DNB
49. DNB
50. Justice in Eyre – circuit judge, Oxford English Dictionary
51. Some authorities say 1541
52. BL Add Mss 11042 f. 94
53. DNB
54. HRO G38/1/14, 12
55. HRO G38/1/21, m4
56. HRO G38/1/1, m3v
57. DNB
58. Lam. Pal. Lib. Ms.3206 f393
59. BL Add.Mss 11042 ff.103, 104
60. Durant D.N., *Bess of Hardwick*, Littlehampton, 1977, 55
61. Durant D.N., 57
62. Brayley, E.W. & Britton, J., *Description of the County of Herefordshire*, 525
63. *Ibid*, 79
64. *Ibid*, 87, 103
65. Taken from calendar: Duncumb 82; Tweed, H.W., *Wilton Castle*,1884, 30; Lam. Pal. Lib. Ms 197 f. 189; 3206 f. 803
66. Meyrick, 78
67. Girouard,M., *Robert Smythson and the Elizabethan Country House*, New York, 1967, 113
68. HRO AW 87
69. Lam. Pal. Lib. Ms. 3206 f. 903
70. Durant, 108, 109
71. HRO G38/1/17 (15), 19(9)
72. Lam. Pal. Lib. 3206 f. 933; HRO G38/1/15, 17(m1) 20, O68/1/23; BL Add Mss 11042 f.69, Durant 112

Chapter 7

1. Shoesmith R., *The Pubs of Hereford City*, Logaston, 2004, 196-200; Lam. Pal. Lib. Ms 3199, f. 293;BL Add Mss f. 44
2. Lam. Pal Lib. Ms 3200, f.170; Lam. Pal. Lib. Ms 707, f.205
3. HMC vol., De L'Isle and Dudley Papers, II, 397
4. Lam. Pal. Lib. Ms. 704 f. 139, 705 f.150; 703, f.167
5. It may be that the stables were extended over part of the garden during the Civil War occupation by Sir Henry Lingen
6. Lam. Pal. Lib. Ms. 703 f.167, 702 f. 160; HRO G38/1/35
7. Lambeth Palace Lib. Ms. 703 f.167; Sheffield City Lib. Bacon Frank Mss 2/220, 222
8. BL Add. Mss 11042, f.118. William Scudamore, was, no doubt, a younger son of the Scudamores of Ballingham, perhaps the William who was born in 1603, the son of Sir William Scudamore, who was High Sheriff under Charles I, but the relationship has not been established.
9. GRO D1086/E147; Duncomb p. 93, quoting Pat. Rot. 16 Jas I.
10. Bod. Lib. Selden Supra 113 ff.2, 3
11. HRO K2/II/6, 8, 11, 20, 21, 24; G38/1/46-49
12. Bod. Lib. Selden Supra 113 29v; HRO G 38/1/56; HRO R90 Hopton 3-8
13. Bod. Lib. Selden Supra 113 f.13
14. Bod. Lib. Selden Supra 113
15. Bod. Lib. Selden Supra 113 f.65. All the indications are that this Benjamin Hale is one and the same as Benjamin Hare
16. Bod. Lib. Selden Supra 113 ff.6,14, 22; 125 f.20; Bod. Lib. Selden Supra 113 f69
17. HRO 068/1/35
18. Hughes, P., 'Buildings and the Building Trade in Worcester, 1540-1660', unpub. Ph.D Thesis, Birmingham University 1990, 334. During the 1630s in Worcestershire, the going rate for sawing was 22d per 100 feet
19. pers.comm. Richard Morriss
20. Selden Supra 113 f.13
21. *Ibid*
22. Selden Supra 113 f.12, 22
23. *Ibid*
24. HRO Goodrich Parish reg; HRO O68/1/21; PRO Prob 11. 312 136
25. Bedfordshire RO L26/1022

Chapter 8

1. The general historical background to this chapter is taken largely from: Webb, T.W. (ed.), *Memorials of the Civil War ... as it affected Herefordshire*, Two Vols., London, 1879 & reprint 2002, Golden Valley Publications; Roe & Webb, T.W. (ed.), *Military Memoir of Colonel John Birch,* London, 1873 & reprint, 2004, Golden Valley Publications; Meyrick, S.R., 'History of Goodrich Castle' (ms. Hereford City Library, PC F960)
2. *Mercurius Rusticus,* 1685, 82
3. Shoesmith, R., *The Civil War in Hereford*, Logaston, 1995
4. Webb assumed that the castle to which the Royalists fled was Wilton Castle, but Meyrick's account indicates that Goodrich Castle is meant. Meyrick, 89; quoted from Corbet's 'Military Government of Gloucestershire', 97
5. HRO O68/1/38
6. Furniture was relatively cheap. Although, in 1654, the bed in the best chamber belonging to William Moreton at Little Moreton Hall in Cheshire, was valued at a pricey £8, the total value of goods in the chamber came to £10 6s 10d. The goods in one other chamber and two parlours added up to £12 1s 10d. Richard Tyler's own probate inventory, taken in 1663, when the castle had been slighted, valued the property in his bedchamber at £9 7s 2d, and his silver at £6. Also pers.comm. Roz Lowe
7. Webb, I, 354; II, 410
8. Webb, II, 277. It should be noted that this document, like many sources known to Rev J. Webb in the mid-19 century, can no longer be traced
9. Cal. State Papers Domestic 1648/9, 1053
10. PRO Committee for Advance of Money – Index, 1187
11. Corbet, J*., An Historical Relation of the Military Government ...,*Tewkesbury, c.1850, 97 (an abridged version of the story is in Rushworth, J., *Historical Collections*, 1691, 3rd Part, Vol II, 743
12. Meyrick, 89 and note
13. HRO O68/1/38
14. Webb, II, 119. Caltrops were four-spiked iron balls or four joined spikes laid in the river to lame cavalry horses
15. Sir Barnabas Scudamore quoted from Webb, II, 219. See also Shoesmith, 82-109
16. Hill, M., *A True and Impartial Account of the Plunderings, Losses and Sufferings of the County of Hereford ...*, 1645
17. Rushworth*,* 4th part, Vol I, 1701, 123; Webb, II, 391-398
18. Corbet, 127
19. Shoesmith, 136
20. Roe, 31-33; Vicars, *Burning Bush*, 396; Cam. Univ. Lib. Sel. 4. 7. 1001, *Perfect Diurnall*, March 16th 1645/6
21. Roe, 31/2; Roe; *Perfect Diurnall*
22. Roe, 31/2
23. Roe, 226

24. Meyrick, 90
25. Webb, II, 268; Cal. State Papers Domestic Chas., I, 1645–7, 394
26. Meyrick, 91; *Perfect Occurrences* June 1st 1646
27. Heath, C., *The Excursion down the Wye ...*, 1799, 64 & reprint, General Books, 2012; Bonner, T., *Perspective Itinerary*, 1798, 29; Webb, II, 279
28. A long range medium to heavy cannon
29. *Perfect Diurnall*, 1229
30. Meyrick, 91: *Perfect Occurrences* June 1st 1646; State Papers Domestic 1645-7, 440
31. *Ibid.*
32. Meyrick, 93; Webb,II, 414; *Perfect Diurnal*
33. Meyrick, 94; *Perfect Occurrences,* 15th July
34. Taylor, E., 'The Seventeenth century iron forge at Carey Mill', *TWNFC*, 1986, 450-468. I am grateful to both Elizabeth Taylor and Roz Lowe for discussion of this matter
35. Watkins, A., 'Roaring Meg', *TWNFC*, 1919, 172-4
36. Meyrick, 94; *Perfect Occurrences* 15th July
37. Meyrick, 94; *Perfect Occurrences* 15th July
38. Meyrick, 94; *Perfect Occurrences* 31st July
39. Roe, 36
40. Roe, 36
41. Meyrick, 93; *Perfect Occurrences* 26th June
42. Meyrick, 95; *Perfect Occurrences* 31st July
43. Roe, 36
44. Webb, II, App., 417: *Perfect Diurnall*, 1265
45. Letter attached to Meyrick after 95; Webb, II, 280
46. Webb, II, 280, 417; Roe, 196; Meyrick, 96; *Perfect Occurrences* August 7th 1646
47. The skillet is in the Hereford museum collection
48. Roe, 37; Webb, II, 417; Meyrick, 95, 96; *Perfect Occurrences* 31st July, August 7th 1646
49. Webb, II, 415, 416, Roe, 36; Cam Un.Lib Sel 4. 7. 1265; *Perfect Diurnall* June 22nd 1646
50. Meyrick, 98 quoting *Perfect Occurences*; HRO O68/1/38; O68/11/43, 44
51. Bod. L. Sel. 4.8. 1506 *Diurnall*: Webb, J., II, 280
52. House of Lords; PRO SP 28, 299
53. DNB, Elizabeth Grey, Countess of Kent
54. Brit Lib.Harleian MS No 6726 fo. 54
55. Bonner, 28, VIII
56. Heath, C., 65
57. Bonner, 28; King, *Monumenta*, 1804, 255
58. Cal. State Papers Domestic 1649-50 Vol. I 151
59. Cal. State Papers 1649-50 Vol. II 225
60. Cal. State Papers 1654 18/67 Item no. 57
61. PRO L21/76/2
62. HRO O68/1/43,44
63. B.L. Harl. Mss. 6726, f.119
64. GRO D33/359; PRO PROB 11 312/136; pers. comm. Roz Lowe

Chapter 9
1. HRO G38/11/13
2. HRO G38/1/40 f. 5
3. HRO G38/1/57 f. 21
4. e.g. HRO G38/1/15 f.8; G38/1/31 f.11
5. HRO G38/1/40 viii. It should be noted that earlier references to this lane do not mention the prison
6. HRO O68/1/37
7. HRO O68/II/49
8. HRO O68/II/24
9. HRO O68/II/49
10. HRO 068/1/45,46; BRO L24/391
11. BRO L24/391
12. Stockinger, V.R., *The Rivers Wye and Lugg Navigation,* Logaston, 1996, 83-108; BRO L24/394
13. BRO L26/8
14. HRO AW87
15. HRO AK 94
16. HRO G38/1/122; O68/III/19
17. HRO G38/1/122
18. HRO G38/1/122
19. HRO O68/1/26
20. BRO CRT 190/45/31
21. BRO CRT 190/45/31
22. HRO 068/II/33
23. HRO G38/II/1b/4
24. Fosbroke, T.D, *The Wye Tour*, 1818, introduction
25. Gilpin, W., *Observations on the River Wye, 1770*, 1782
26. Hon. John Byng *Diaries* 1787, vol 1, 264
27. Heath, Charles, *Excursion down the Wye*, 1828
28. Kissack, K.,*The River Wye*, Terence Dalton Ltd., 1978, 74
29. Stockinger
30. Twamley, L.A., *Autumn Ramble by the Wye,* London, 1838, 113-115
31. Timmins, H.T., *Nooks and Corners of Herefordshire*, London, 1892 & reprint Lapridge Hereford, 1992
32. G.C.G., *Camping on the Wye,* Logaston, 2003
33. 'Ross, the Wye and Symonds Yat Meeting', *TWNFC,* 1870, 31-86, esp. 33-38
34. *TWNFC,* 1870, 33
35. 'Fourth Field Meeting', *TWNFC,* 1901, 200-206
36. Seaton, D.,'History of Goodrich', *TWNFC,* 1901, 211-224, but much of this was deemed inaccurate by James G. Wood in his article 'Notes on the Early History of Goodrich Castle' see below
37. 'Third Field Meeting', *TWNFC,* 1917, 197-200; Wood, J.G., 'Notes on the Early History of Goodrich Castle', *TWNFC,* 1917, 261-267

Chapter 10
1. Most of the documents at the PRO are referenced under Works/14/1061 AA 96239/3 and Works 14/1062 AA 96239/2
2. PRO Works 14/319 AA 96239/3A
3. PRO Works 30/31 2057/2058
4. In preparation for the RCHM volume *An Inventory of the Historic Monuments in Herefordshire – Volume 1 – South-west,* 1931 (Goodrich Castle, 74-78)
5. Bristol and Gloucester Antiquarian Society, 1931, liii, 3
6. Photogrammetric survey, Institute of Advanced Architectural Studies, York
7. CHAC Vols. 1 & 2
8. *ibid*
9. HAS 73. *Survey Work in the Keep,* 1990
10. HAS 94, *The Great Hall,* 1990; HAS 100, *Lost timbers of the Great Hall, north and east ranges,* 1991
11. See note 7
12. HAS 30. *Excavation for a supply of Electricity to the Castle,* 1988
13. Shoesmith, R., *Watching brief on the excavation of a trench for a new telephone duct,* 1998
14. HAS 639, *North Range, Solar Arch, Historic Building Recording Additional Record,* 2004; Has 805, Solar Arch Pier Capital and Remedial Works, 2008
15. Shoesmith, R., *The Barbican: Archaeological Resource Assessment,* 2002; Shoesmith, R., *The Barbican; Removal of the Shop and Ticket Kiosk,* 2008

Chapter 11
1. Waugh, R., *Guide to Goodrich Castle,* Monmouth, 1878, 4
2. RCHM, I, 1931, 61-2 and update in *TWNFC,* 2012, 143-4
3. Shoesmith, R. & Johnson, A., *Ludlow Castle, Its History and Buildings,* Logaston, 2000, 125
4. Lamont, A.H., 'Fords and Ferries of the Wye', *TWNFC,* 1921, 73-94, esp. 93
5. Thurlby, M., *The Herefordshire School of Romanesque Sculpture,* 2nd ed., Logaston, 1999, 133-4
6. Curnow, P.E. & Thompson, M.W., 'Excavations at Richard's Castle, Herefordshire, 1962-1964', *J. Brit. Archaeol.Ass.,* 3 ser., **32**, 1969, 105-27
7. Turner, R. & Johnson, A., (eds.), *Chepstow Castle, Its History and Buildings,* Logaston, 2006, 63-71
8. Thurlby, *op. cit.*
9. Bonner, T., *Perspective Itinerary ... of Ten Views of Goodrich Castle,* London, 1799; King, E., *Munumenta Antiqua or Observations on Ancient Castles,* Volume 3, London, 1804, 249-260, esp. 252
10. Knight, J.K., *The Three Castles, Grosmont Castle, Skenfrith Castle, White Castle,* Cadw Guide, nd.; Radford, C.A.R., *White Castle,* HMSO, London, 1962
11. Renn, D., 'The Norman Military Works', *Ludlow Castle,* 125-38
12. Renn, D. & Shoesmith, R.,'The Outer Bailey', *Ludlow Castle,* 191-4
13. Jope, E.M., & Threlfall, R.J., 'The twelfth-century castle at Ascot Doilly, Oxfordshire, its history and excavation', *Antiq J.,* **39**, 1959, 219-239
14. Brewster, T.C.M., 'Tote Copse Castle, Aldingbourne, Sussex', *Sussex Archaeol. Collect.,* **107**, 1969, 141-79
15. Renn, D., 'The Keep at Wareham Castle', *Medieval Archaeology,* **4**, 1960, 56-68
16. Craster, O.E., *Skenfrith Castle, Monmouthshire,* London, 1967
17. Thompson, M.W., *The Rise of the Castle,* Cambridge, 1991, 65-6
18. Thompson, 1991, 65
19. pers.comm. B. Copleston-Crow
20. Renn, D., *Norman Castles in Britain,* London, 1968, 342-3 & Pl. XLVII

Chapter 12
1. Seaton, Rev Preb, *The History and description of Goodrich Castle,* Hereford, 1903
2. Fosbrooke Rev. T.D., *The Wye Tour or Gilpin on the Wye ...,* Ross, 1818
3. CHAC Vol.2

Chapter 15
1. RCHM, I, 78
2. Thompson, M.W., *The Rise of the Castle,* Cambridge University Press, 1991, 102
3. Keynon, J.R., *Medieval Fortifications, Leicester,* 1990, 78-82

Chapter 16
1. Ancient Monuments Laboratory Report 22/97
2. King, E., *Munimenta Antiqua ...,* Vol. III, London, 1804, 249-60, esp. 250
3. King, 252

Chapter 17
1. Seaton, D., *The History and Description of Goodrich Castle,* Hereford, 1903, 8
2. Thompson, *Rise,* 113
3. CHAC Vol.2

Chapter 19
1. Labarge, Margaret Wade, *A Baronial Household of the Thirteenth Century,* Eyre and Spottiswoode, 1965

2. A roll of the household expenses of Richard de Swinfield, Bishop of Hereford, during part of the years 1289 and 1290. Camden Society, 1985
3. Phillips, J.R.S., 'Valence, Aymer de, eleventh [sic] earl of Pembroke (d.1324)', Oxford Dictionary of National Biography, Oxford University Press, 2004; online edn, Jan 2008 [http://www.oxforddnb.com/view/article/942, accessed 1 Sept 2013]
4. pers.comm. Bruce Coplestone-Crow
5. Stone, D.J., 'The Consumption of Field Crops in Late Medieval England', Chapter 2 in Woolgar C.M., D. Serjeantson, & T. Waldron *Food in Medieval England: Diet and Nutrition* (Kindle Location 1). Kindle Edition. OUP 2006
6. The symbols £, s and d were in use for English currency (pounds, shillings and pence) within living memory. 'd' is the symbol for the *denarius*, a 4th-century Roman coin. Twelve *denarii* were equal to 1 gold *solidus* and 240 *denarii* should weigh 1lb (Latin *libra*, French *livre*) of silver. £, s and d were reintroduced to the Holy Roman Empire by Charlemagne and adopted throughout Europe. The Latin *libra pondo*, 'a pound weight', became in German a *pfund* and in English, a pound, but retained the 'L' symbol – '£'. At this time the wages of tradesmen could be counted in pennies: a thatcher would have earned about 2d per day, a carpenter 3d. Tradesmen would not be counted among the poor. Typically a chicken would cost about 1½ to 2d – on 21st January 1297 the Countess paid 19½d for 12 pullets (young hens)
7. The spelling has varied over time: potage, pottage, porrige, porridge; largely interchangeable until very recently. On Monday 25th February 1661 Samuel Pepys 'did eat some nettle porrige ...'
8. Middle English potache; potege: Middle French potage; potaige – food cooked in a pot (1240) OED
9. Genesis 25, 34 'w'yaáqov nätan l'ësäw lechem ûn'ziyd ádäshiym waYokhal waYësh'T' waYäqäm waYëlakh' waYivez ësäu et-haB'khoräh š' in Hebrew. In modern translations 'pottage' has been dropped and New International Version UK has 'Then Jacob gave Esau some bread and some lentil stew'
10. Bread was hugely important in the West throughout most of history; it provided up to 46% of the calories of Westminster monks in about 1500. Harvey, Barbara, *Living and Dying in England 1100-1540: The Monastic Experience*, 1993, 57 cited in Stone, D.J., 'The Consumption of Field Crops in Late Medieval England'
11. For hadde ye potage and payn ynogh, and peny ale to drynke, And a mees thermyd of o maner kynde, Ye hadde right ynogh ye religiouse – and so youre rule me tolde. *Piers Plowman* 15.316-317
12. Woolgar, C.M., *Group Diets in Late Medieval England*, Chapter 13, 2006
13. Davis, Edward H. and John T. Morgan, 'Collards in North Carolina' in *Southeatsren Geographer*, Volume 45, Number 1, May 2005, 67-82
14. Harvey, J.H., *Vegetables in the Middle Ages, Garden History*, 12 (2), 1984, 89-99
15. Dyer, C.C., 'Gardens and Garden Produce in the Later Middle Ages', Chapter 2 in Woolgar, Serjeantson and Waldron, 2006
16. Woolgar, Chapter 5
17. *Ibid.*
18. Chaucer's Franklin broke his fast with bread dipped in wine 'Well lov'd he in the morn a sop in wine'.
19. Brears, Peter, *Cooking & Dining in Medieval England*, Prospect, 2012, 216
20. 'At meate [at meals] was she well y-taught withal; She let no morsel from her lippes fall, Nor wet her fingers in her sauce deep. Well could she carry a morsel, and well keep, that no droppe ne fell upon her breast. In courtesy was set full much her lest [pleasure] Her over-lippe wiped she so clean, That in her cup there was no farthing [speck of grease] seen, when she drunken had her draught; Full seemely after her meat she raught [reached]'
21. Bishop Robert Grosseteste wrote these rules for his friend, Countess Margaret of Lincoln, probably shortly after the death of her husband, John de Lacy, in 1240. They are concerned with the way that nobles should manage their estate and their people. The 21st rule says 'Command that your knights, and chaplains, and servants in office, and your gentlemen, with a good humour and hearty cheer and ready service receive and honour, within your presence and without, all those in every place whom they perceive by your words or your manners to be especially dear to you, and to whom you would have special honour shown, for in doing so can they particularly show that they wish what you wish. And as far as possible for sickness or fatigue, constrain yourself to eat in the hall before your people, for this shall bring great benefit and honour to you.' http://www.penultimateharn.com/history/grosseteste.html accessed 14th July 2013

22. Grosseteste's 23rd rule
23. 'His bread, his ale, was alway after one [presed on the guest];
    A better envined [having a good store of wine] man was nowhere none;
    Withoute bake-meat never was his house,
    Of fish and flesh, and that so plenteous,
    It snowed in his house of meat and drink,
    Of alle dainties that men coulde think.
    After the sundry seasons of the year,
    So changed he his meat and his soupere.
    Full many a fat partridge had he in mew [cage],
    And many a bream, and many a luce [pike] in stew [fish-pond]
    Woe was his cook, but if [unless] his sauce were Poignant and sharp, and ready all his gear.
    His table dormant in his hall alway
    Stood ready cover'd all the longe day.'
24. Swinfield, *Roll of the Household Expenses of Richard de Swinfield, Bishop of Hereford during part of the years 1289 and 1290*, edited by John Webb, Camden Society, 1854, 60
25. A8 is the designation of this pottery in The Hereford Pottery Type Series, a reference collection of dated and categorised pottery. Archaeologists use it to help to date and understand their sites. The original Hereford fabric series was based on the late Alan Vince's PhD thesis 'The Medieval Ceramic Industry of the Severn Valley' University of Southampton, 1984. Summaries of the series are given in *Hereford City Excavations Volume 3*, Shoesmith, 1985, and *Hereford City Excavations Volume 4*, Thomas and Boucher, 2002
26. Vince, MS
27. Dale Rouse, pers.comm.
28. Fabric A8
29. Fabric G7
30. Fabric A7b
31. Vince, Archive Report on the Ceramic Material from Goodrich Castle, 1995
32. Labarge, 1965, 68

Chapter 20
1. More plaster was found outside the tower when that area was cleared in 1923
2. The position of all the finds was recorded at the time in a log kept by the foreman
3. Borthwick, Alan R., 'James II (1430-1460)', Oxford Dictionary of National Biography, Oxford University Press, 2004; online edn, Jan 2010 [http://www.oxforddnb.com/view/article/14588, accessed 6 May 2013]
4. Henry, Chris *English Civil War Artillery, 1642-52*, Osprey, 2005
5. Knight, Jeremy, *Civil War & Restoration in Monmouthsire,* Logaston Press, 2005
6. Kinard, Jeff, *Pistols: An Illustrated History of Their Impact*, Weapons & Warfare, 2004

Index

Anarchy, The 26-27
ap Gruffudd, Rhys 29
ap Llywelyn, Madog 39
Archenfield 11
   Hundred of 46
archives 86
Ariconium 11

Barry, Lord John of 41
Benet, John 51
Berkeley, Thomas of 41
Berthwyn, Bishop 11
Bess of Hardwick 54
Birch, Col John 75, 77-82, 212
Blore, Edward 16, 17
Bonner, George 66
   Thomas 82, 90, 91
Bosanquet, Louisa 95, 96, 98
Boulsdon, Robert of 36
Bronze Age 6-7
Broughton, Col 74
Buck, Samuel and Nathaniel 83
Buckley, Richard 74
Burnel, Edward 40
Busser, messenger of Joan de Valence 40, 42
Byng, Hon. John 89

Cassie, Capt. 73
Cavendish family 54
   Bess 54
   Henry 54
   Mary 54, 66
Cely, John 40
Chepstow Castle 27, 28
Civil War 71-84, 211-216
   artillery 211, 212-213
Clare family 22, 24, 27-29
   Gilbert V 41
Claxton, Mr 69
Cockerel, Robert 37

Comyn, John 43
   Elizabeth 43, 44
Constantine, King 11
   Saint 12
Corbett, John 73
Croft, Richard 51
Crump, John 38
Cyfeiliog, Bishop 11

de Bohun, Humphrey 37
de Braybeof, Sir Thomas 41
de Broase, Reginald 34
de Chanceaux, Emery 36
de Charney, Geoffrey 46
de Grandison, Matilda 41
de La Boussac, Wihanoc 24, 25-26
de la Roche, Sir Thomas 41
de Molis, Nicholas 36
de Montfort, Simon 37
de Mountchesney family 22
   John 36
   William 40
de Mucegros, Cecilia 41
de St Amand, Emery 36
de Valence family 22, 24
   Aymer 35, 39, 41, 43, 203
   Beatrice 40, 203
   Elizabeth 43, 44
   Joan, Countess of Pembroke 36, 39-43, 203-210
      household 40-43, 203-210
      jewellery casket 200
   William 34-35, 36, 37-39, 203
Despencers 43
Drake, William 70
Drew, Anthony 74
Duck, Thomas 69
Dyfrig, Bishop 11

Edward II 43
Ergyng 11
Eva, dau. of Dermot MacMurrough 29, 61

FtizBaderon, William 24, 25-26
FitzGilbert, Gilbert 27-28
FitzOsbern, William 25
Flanesford Priory *see* Goodrich
Fletcher, Thomas 86
fords 10
Fosbroke, T.D. 89
Frontinus, Sextus Julius 8

Gallus, Aulus 8
Garthbenni 10-12
   Church of 11, 29-32
Gatelyn, Walter 40
Geology 3-5, 113
   Old Red Sandstone 3-5
Gilpin, William 89
Glyndwr, Owain 47-48
Goodrich
   Castle (archeological finds) 98
      caltrops 213
      ceiling plaster 200
      floor tile 198, 208-209
      handcuffs 214, 215
      pottery 199, 207-208
      skillet 198, 216
      reckon-crook 199
      ridge tiles 198, 208-209
   Castle (attacks upon)
      de Braose, Reginald 34
      Llewelyn Fawr 34
      Henry III 36
      Owain Glyndwr 47-48
      Civil War 71-84, 211-216
         artillery 211, 212-213
            Roaring Meg 78-79, 213
   Castle barony 35
   Castle (building of)
      church on site of 29-32
      first earthwork castle 31, 105-107
      Narberth, similarities with 31, 32
      first stone castle 26, 106-116
      Edwardian castle 37-38, 106, 117-154
      14th-century alterations 155-164
      15th-century alterations 179-181
      16th-century alterations 55
      17th-century repairs 67-70
      slighting 81-82, 83
      as ruin 85-88
      as tourist attraction 88-94, 100
      Scheduling as Ancient Monument 95
      collapse 1919 95, 96
      in government care 95
   Castle (buildings)
      barbican 101, 102, 147-154
         drawbridge & ditch 150, 151
      buttery 171, 177, 206
      chapel 45, 102, 131, 135-140, 155-157, 196
         stained glass 62, 63, 102
      curtain walls 106-108, 115, 118-119, 129-130, 161, 166-167
      ditch 117-118
      dungeon 111, 161-163, 214
      east range 146, 159-161, 183-187
      entrance, early 108
      gaol 46, 56, 85
      gardens 39, 43, 54, 65, 205
      garderobe tower 187
      gatehouse 102, 131, 132-136, 139-140, 157-159, 193, 194
         extension to 187-188
         drawbridge 132, 133, 134, 153, 193
         portcullis 133, 134, 194
      great hall 98, 168-173
         lobby 173, 182-183
      keep 26, 64, 99, 101, 108-116, 141
         geology of 113-114, 164
      kitchen 177, 188-189, 197
      motte 108-109, 115-116, 164
      north range 143-145, 179-181, 195
         postern 144, 145
      north-east tower 131, 132-136
      north-west (ladies') tower 127-129
      outer wards 189-192
      pantry 171, 177, 206
      pentices 173-174

plan 57
  pound 54, 85, 190
  south-east (prison) tower 101, 120-27
    carvings in 126-127
  south-west (great) tower 98, 99, 100,
    101-102, 129-30, 174-78, 192
  stables 77, 191-192
  water supply 55, 77, 98
    well 77-78, 99, 115, 213
  western range 165-74
Castle (college of secular canons) 45, 155
Castle (life at 1296-97) 40-43, 203-210
  ale 204
  bread ovens 204, 215, 216
  cider 204
  garderobes 209
  cutlery 207
  daily routine 206-210
  fish 205
    herring 205
    lamprey 206, 207
    salmon 206, 207
  Lent 205
  meals 206
  laundry 209-210
  meat 205, 206-207
  potherbs 204
  pottage 204
  sleeping arrangements 207
  utensils 207
Castle (ownership)
  Godric Mapson 25
  Crown 25, 27, 29, 33, 36, 39, 43, 51
  William FitzBaderon 25-26
  Baderon of Monmouth 26-27
  Gilbert FitzGilbert 27-28
  Marshal family 33-35
  de Valence family 36-44
  Talbot family 44-49
  Shrewsbury, Earls of (Talbot family)
    49-56, 65-66
  Kent, Earls of 66-88
  Griffin, Admiral Thomas 88

  Bosanquet, Louisa 95, 96, 98
  government care 95-102
Castle Farm 85
Court 16-18, 85
Estate
  fishing & weirs 65, 86
  management of 52-53, 56, 65-68, 85
  part of March or Hundred 34-35, 38
ferry 11, 26, 53, 60, 86, 89, 90
  Boat House 75, 77, 86, 89, 90
Flanesford Priory 14-16, 45-46, 48, 60,
  67, 68, 74, 84, 85, 87
  dissolution 52
ford 10, 53, 86
Geddes 19, 74
Gilpin, William 88, 89
Kerne Bridge 13
lock-up 85-86
market, grant of 34
New House 20
Old Court House 19
parish 13
Priory Farm 87
St Giles's Church 16
village 13-20
Y Crwys 18-19, 86
Ye Hostelrie 19
Grey, Thomas, Lord Ferrers 51
  Sir William 55
Grey family, Earls of Kent 66, 68, 71, 73,
  81, 84, 88
  Henry 66
Grubb, Anthony 74
Gwillims, Rudhall 74
Gwillym, Thomas 66
Gye, John 50

Hale, Benjamin 66
Hall, Benedict 74
  Robert 54
Hare, Benjamin 69
Hastings, John of 41
Hawise, dau. of Godric Mapson 24, 25, 26
Heath, Charles 84, 89

Henry II 28-29, 33
Henry III 34, 36, 37, 38
Henry IV 47, 127
Herbert, William, Earl of Pembroke 51
   Lord 65
Hereford, battle at 760 11
   siege of 1645 75-75
Herefordshire School of Romanesque
   Sculpture 64, 106
Hevant, Thomas 54
Hill, Miles 74
Hopwood, Nichola 102
Hulla 12, 25

Inabwy, Bishop 11
Inkpen, John of 41
Iron Age 7-8, 105
iron-working 8-9, 34, 53, 65, 66, 78, 86
Isham, Mr 69

John, King 34

Kent, Earls of *see* Grey family
Kerry, John 65
   Thomas 65
King Arthur's Cave 6
King, Edward 91
Kyrle, Capt. Thomas 71-72

Lawrence, Edward, surveyor 86-87
Lestrange, John 47
Lingen, Sir Henry 72-78
Llanwern 35
Llewelyn Fawr 34
Llewelyn, Christopher 84
Lucas, thomas 86
Ludford, Capt. Clement 74

MacMurrough, Donat, imprisonment of 49
Mapson, Godric 12, 22, 24, 25, 105
Marshal family 22, 24, 35-36
   William I 33-35
Marshall, George 95

Mary, Queen of Scots, imprisonment of 53, 54
Massey, Col Edward 73, 74
Mesolithic 6
Meyrick, Lt Col 17
   Sir Samuel 16, 18, 19, 55, 77, 80
Moffat, George 17
   Harold 17, 18
Monmouth, John of 36
Monmouth Priory 26
Moore, George 66
Moreton Valence 37, 41, 42

Narberth Castle, similarities to Goodrich 31, 32
Neolithic 6
Nether Gwent 28
Neville, Maud 49
   Thomas, Lord Furnival 47, 48
Nicolls, John 54
Nudd, Bishop 11

Orleton, Bishop Adam of 43
Owen, Frank, MP 98

Palaeolithic 6
Pembroke, Joan Countess of
   see de Valence
Pencoed, battle at, 722 11
Powell, Sir Edward 74
   Joseph 86
Purfrey, William 66, 67

Richard I 33
Roaring Meg 78-79, 213
Roman period 8-10

Scudamore, John 47, 49, 65
   William 66
Seaton, Prebendary 94
Selden, John 67, 71, 81, 84
Shrewsbury family (*see also* under Talbot) 23, 24, 49-56

Silures 8
Stamford, Earl of 71, 72
Stephen, King 26-27
Strongbow, Richard 28-29, 61
    Gilbert, son of 29
    Isabel, dau. of 33
Sutton, John of 43
Swift, Revd Thomas 20, 71-72, 74
Symonds, Richard 41, 42

Talbot family 22, 24, 44
    Angharad (wife of Richard 4th Lord) 47, 48
    Angharad (dau of Gilbert 5th Lord) 50
    Elizabeth (née de Valence) 45-47
    Elizabeth 66
    Francis (5th Earl of Shrews.) 52
    Francis (son of 6th Earl of Shrews.) 53, 56
    George (4th Earl of Shrews.) 51-52
    George (6th Earl of Shrews.) 53-56
    Gilbert (3rd Lord) 47
    Gilbert (5th Lord) 47-49
    Gilbert (7th Earl of Shrews.) 54, 55, 56, 65
    John (6th Lord, 1st Earl of Shrews.) 49-51
    John (2nd Earl of Shrews.) 51
    John (3rd Earl of Shrews.) 51
    John of Grafton 65
    Mary 54, 66
    Richard (2nd Lord) 44, 45-47
    Richard (4th Lord) 47

Taylor, Capt. Silas 82, 84, 172
Tewdos 12
Thomas, William 49
Tibberton, Matthew of 41
Timmins, H.T. 92, 93
Trafford, Dorothy 18, 98
Trewen 34
Twamley, Louisa Anne 16, 92
Tyler, Richard 19, 67, 68, 69-70, 71, 73, 81, 82, 84
Tyrchan, Bishop 11

Ufelfwy, Bishop 11

Waller, Sir William 72-73
Walters, Aymer 40
Waterton, Hugh 47
Welsh Bicknor, church 12
Wendogeda, John of 40
Wenland, Eustace 65
Westbury-on-Severn 46
Wigfall, Godfrey 56
William II 25
Williams, Richard 51
Wilton Castle 55
Woolhope Naturalists' Field Club 94, 95
Wordsworth, William 16, 17
Wormelow 46
Wye Tour 88-91

Other Titles from Logaston Press

The Herefordshire School of Romanesque Sculpture
by Malcolm Thurlby

Paperback (with flaps), 320 pages, 400 colour photographs. Price: £17.50

This book, first published in 1999, has been much enlarged and extended, is printed in colour and includes a history of the Anarchy in Herefordshire by Bruce Coplestone-Crow. This vibrant collection of work was carved between *circa* 1134 and 1155 by a group of sculptors who, it would seem, had received their initial training at Hereford Cathedral. This book explores their work, considering the careers of the two main sculptors, the role of the patrons, the sources of inspiration, the coming together of the work of the sculptor with that of the metalworker and the illuminator and painter, and the intended meaning behind some of the imagery. The sculptors were working on or near the front line between the opposing factions supporting Stephen or Matilda: strange as it may seem, the patrons of the work were also warlords.

Castles & Moated Sites of Herefordshire
by Ron Shoesmith

Paperback, 320 pages, over 130 black& white illustrations. Price: £10

First published in 1996, now much updated and expanded, this book is in two parts. The first gives an overview of the early history of the county and explains how castles came to be built, and why they were built in the places they were. The gradual development from a myriad of mottes and baileys with or without stone defences to fewer larger 'castles' is traced, along with the plethora of defensible 'moated sites'. The second part of the book is a gazetteer, arranged in alphabetical order of parishes, with information given for all the sites in each parish.

Royalist, but ... Herefordshire in the English Civil War, 1640-51
by David Ross

Paperback, 208 pages, 45 b/w illustrations. Price: £12.95

On the eve of the Civil War in 1642, Herefordshire's leading families were all, to a greater or lesser extent, for the King – with the one notable exception of the Harleys at Brampton Bryan. As a result, Herefordshire was seen as a recruiting ground by Royalist military commanders, and as rather backward by some on the Parliamentary side. But once war had broken out with all its consequences, the majority were seen to be rather lukewarm in their support for the King. David Ross has a deep knowledge of this period which he uses with skill to craft a vivid picture of Herefordshire's inhabitants in these years of turmoil.

Herefordshire's River Trade; Craft & Cargo on the Wye & Lugg
by Heather Hurley

Paperback, 208 pages, 190 illustrations over half in colour. Price: £12.95

The story of the trade on the rivers Wye and Lugg in Herefordshire has never been told in its entirety – until now. It covers the type of craft used, the cargoes carried, the families of boat owners, the masters and crew of the boats, accidents on the water, the development of wharves, the hiring of bowhauliers and the advent of the horse towing path. Perhaps most surprising is the extent of boat building along the banks of the Herefordshire Wye, with craft ranging from small ferries to barges and even steam-powered vessels. The book also covers the transporting of timber to the Naval dockyards, the need to reduce the price of coal in Hereford, the trade in cider, wine and spirits, and the requirement of lime for agricultural and building purposes. There are also hints of the lifestyles of some of those living near the Wye, indicated by the goods that were ordered and transported by boat.